A Young Sailor at War

A Young Sailor at War

The World War II Letters of William R. Catton Jr.

EDITED BY

Theodore Catton

THE KENT STATE UNIVERSITY PRESS
Kent, Ohio

ISBN 978-1-60635-393-6
Manufactured in the United States of America

Cataloging information for this title is available at the Library of Congress.

24 23 22 21 20 5 4 3 2 1

Contents

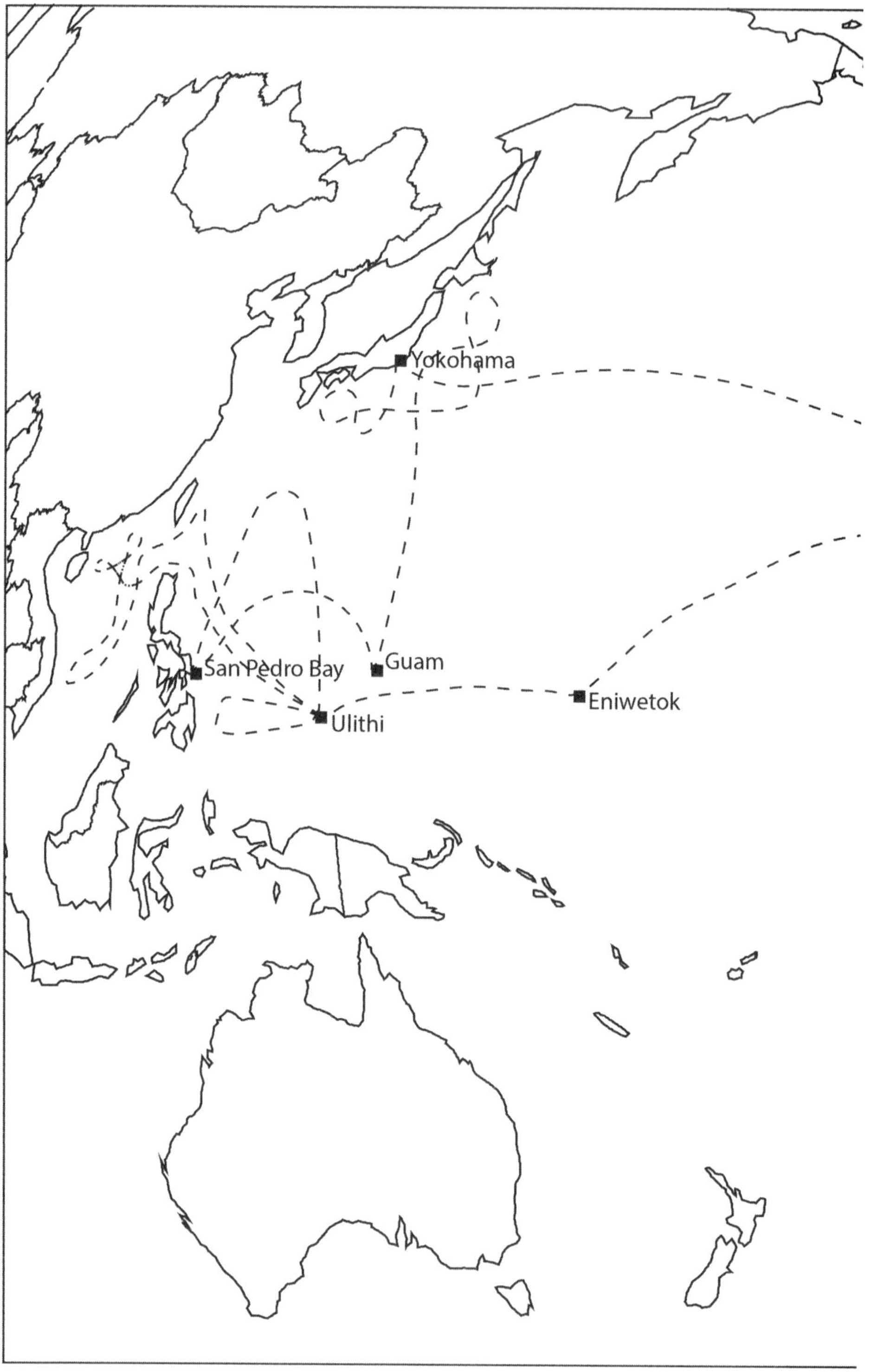
Yokohama
San Pedro Bay
Guam
Eniwetok
Ulithi

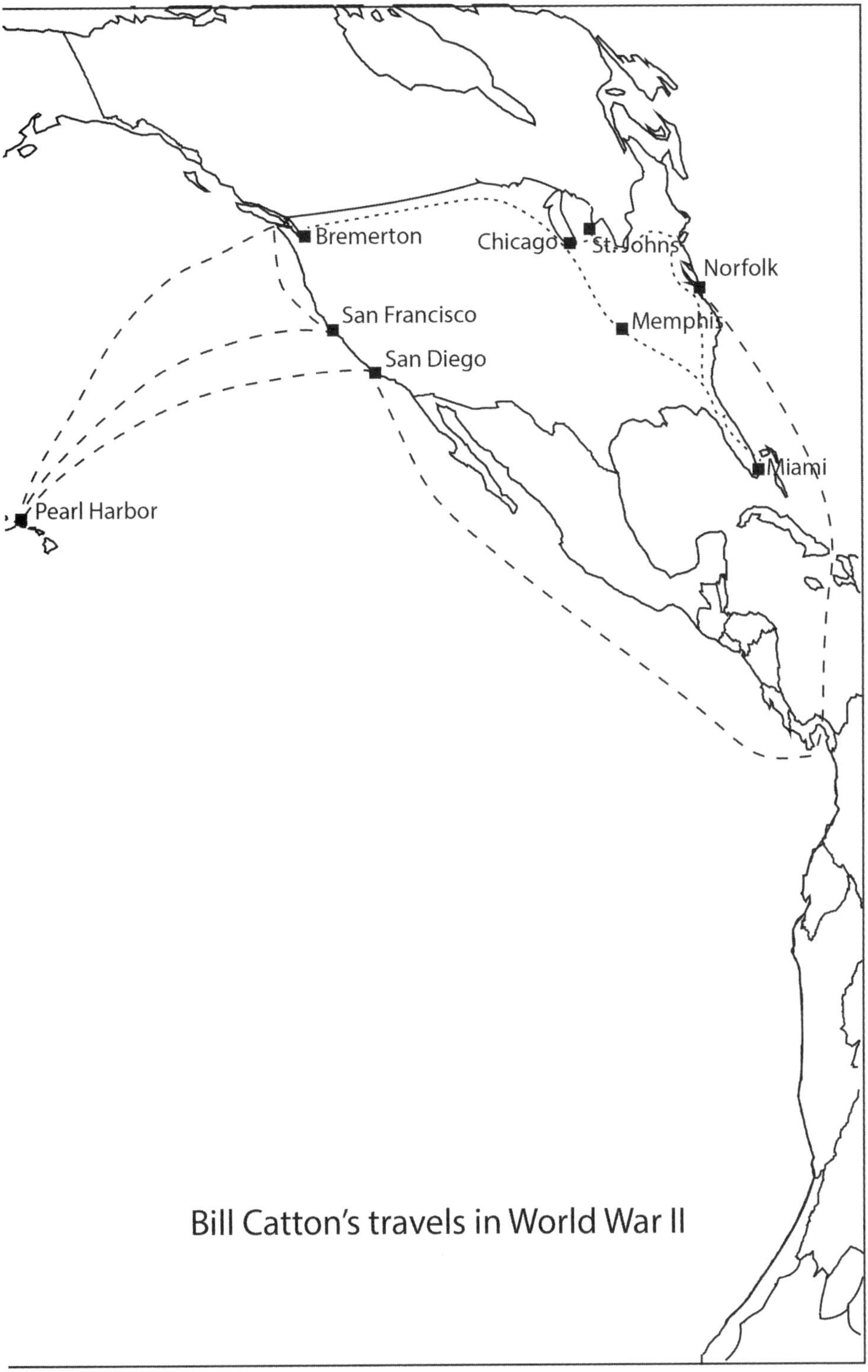

Bill Catton's travels in World War II

Preface

Sixteen million Americans served in the military in World War II, and nearly all of them wrote letters home. A typical soldier wrote six missives a week, according to a survey conducted in 1944. All told, US military personnel in World War II wrote several *billion* personal letters to family and friends back home. Everyone recognized how important personal mail could be for keeping up soldiers' and sailors' morale. The armed services and the US Postal Service made titanic efforts to facilitate letter writing and ensure timely delivery of personal mail. Popular culture reinforced the importance of such correspondence through its many portrayals of writing and receiving letters from loved ones. Under these favorable conditions the volume of letters burgeoned through the course of the war, exceeding what had occurred in all previous wars. Indeed, the letter-writing performance by the World War II generation will likely never be repeated, long-distance communications afterward having evolved toward other forms of media, from long-distance telephone and audio cassette to email, Skype, and social media.

To read these World War II letters now, seventy-five years from when they were penned, is to catch an over-the-shoulder view of an individual's reporting of events practically as they occurred. Writing letters to the people back home was, in part, an act of bearing witness: one strove to describe the unfamiliar circumstances as clearly and accurately as possible. A letter from overseas was like a postcard conveying the sentiment of "miss you" or "wish you were here," with descriptive prose standing in for the postcard picture. Military censorship prevented a letter writer from reporting facts about a ship's location or an army unit's movements, but the censorship rules did not stop the correspondent from conveying all kinds of other information about the war experience.

One of the attractions of World War II letters for readers today is that they were written not for us but for someone else. We come to them as onlookers, taking the writer unaware. Personal letters have an authenticity, an immediacy, an assumption of privacy that brings the modern reader close to the historical time and place (and people) in a way that no other account does.

The value of World War II correspondence has long been recognized. As early as 1948, the Indiana War History Commission collected some 3,500 letters written by Indiana men and women during the war and published a selection of them, *Letters from Fighting Hoosiers.* That work, edited by Howard H. Peckham and Shirley A. Snyder, was published anew in 2016 as *Letters from the Greatest Generation: Writing Home in World War II* (Bloomington: Indiana University Press, 2016). Historians Judy Barrett Litoff and David C. Smith have edited several books featuring World War II letters. In the 1980s Litoff and Smith initiated a project to collect correspondence written by women during World War II, which netted some 30,000 items. Selected letters from that haul are featured in their book *We're in This War, Too: World War II Letters from American Women in Uniform* (New York: Oxford University Press, 1994).

The present collection of letters, which tells the wartime story of my father, William R. "Bill" Catton Jr., joins a large literature of other collected letters, diaries, and memoirs from the World War II era. My father volunteered for the US Navy in January 1943 and served in the Pacific onboard the aircraft carrier USS *Ticonderoga* (CV-14) from August 1944 through the end of the war. After his discharge from the service, he became a professor of sociology. His sociological mind was already at play, however, when he was a young sailor. He was a keen observer and often reported conversations in dialogue form. He held strong opinions about the meaning of the war and the future international world order. Though I am not a World War II history specialist, I am a practicing historian with an abiding interest in the subject. I have edited this collection in the firm belief that my dad's letters will make an outstanding contribution to the literature based on the high quality of the writing; the intellectual precociousness, idealism, and wholesomeness of the writer; and the collection's completeness for conveying the story of one very young serviceman's growth to manhood.

The collection contains more than 400 letters written between the time of Bill's enlistment in January 1943 and his discharge from the navy in July 1946. About 228 letters are included here, selected for their intrinsic quality as well as their ability to connect with one another to form a complete, cogent narrative.

Most of these letters are reproduced in their entirety. In my editorial judgment it was important to present most of them whole so that readers would have access to the full gamut of information that was passed between Bill and his folks. In those few cases where a sentence or paragraph was omitted, the omission is shown with ellipsis points. I did make an exception to this rule by "silently" striking numerous "P.S." one-liners from the end of his letters.

Bill's youthful misspellings and idiosyncratic capitalization and punctuation are mostly preserved as they occur in the original document. Misspellings resulting from a handwritten typo, such as "than" instead of "that," have been corrected to improve readability. Misspelled words that Bill sometimes got right, such as "recieve" instead of "receive," or "revielle" instead of "reveille," have also been corrected to improve readability. Where he underlined a word for emphasis, the underline is rendered in italics. Bill was inconsistent in how he wrote the titles of books, underlining some titles and putting quotation marks around others. He was consistent in placing quotation marks around the titles of newspapers, but sometimes he put them in the wrong place (for example, New York "Times"). For consistency and readability, all titles of newspapers and books as well as the names of ships are in correct form and set in italics. Since he always put movie titles in quotation marks rather than underlining them, his incorrect punctuation is left unchanged.

Bill was inconsistent in how he wrote dates, sometimes putting the month before the day and sometimes the other way around. All letter dates are now rendered in a consistent style of day-month-year, but all dates mentioned within the body of letters are left unchanged. Bill was also inconsistent in how he wrote the hour of the day, sometimes using military time and sometimes not. All these renderings, too, are left unchanged.

He mostly wrote the numbers one through ten as numerals. For consistency and readability, the numbers one through ten are spelled out as words (except where they appear as an hour of the day, dollar amount, or percentage value). His frequent use of the shorthand "thru" is changed to "through."

The young sailor made a frequent pattern of dropping the pronoun at the start of a sentence, as in "Had a swell time on liberty." While the dropped initial pronoun may be conventional and easily overlooked in a handwritten letter, it tends to be a distraction when the text is rendered in type. Therefore, the missing pronoun has been supplied in most such cases.

Bill absorbed from his surroundings the word "Japs" for Japanese. Now generally considered a racial slur, the word became ubiquitous during World War II as it was used routinely in public discourse, official statements, and all kinds of media, from newspapers to movies to popular songs. Although he used the term freely in his letters, it is evident from the context that he did not intend a racial slur.

The primary sources used in editing and presenting Bill Catton's letters were, first, his military service record, held by the National Personnel Records Center, and second, the USS *Ticonderoga*'s deck log, war diary, and action reports at the National Archives in College Park, Maryland. Full citations for the National Archives documents can be found in the footnotes.

Perspective on my dad's World War II experiences in and around the family home in Michigan came from conversations with my aunt, Ruth Catton. Ruth, who was thirteen years old when Bill went into the navy, has clear firsthand memories of the family's wartime experiences. She also shared with me her trove of family photographs from the 1930s and early 1940s.

For other helpful insights on what my dad was like as a young man, I benefited from conversations with my mother, Nancy Catton. Although my mom did not meet my dad until two years after the war, she heard a few more stories than me and she has a lot of insight from their sixty-five years of marriage.

Fairly late in life, Bill was inspired to write a short reminiscence of his navy experience. A short history of the USS *Ticonderoga* had been published by the Navy Department in *Dictionary of American Fighting Naval Ships* in 1980; it now appears online at several websites. One Veteran's Day, probably in 1996, my brother Steve sent that history to our dad. Bill then annotated the ship's history with his own recollections of his experiences aboard ship. On 2 April 1997 my dad emailed the annotated history to my brothers and me. While that is how his reminiscence originated, the piece was subsequently printed in *Local Heroes: Olympia Veterans Remember World War II,* edited by Garnest H. Turner (Lacey, WA: Turner Type and Design, 2013). A few passages from Bill's original version are quoted at length in the footnotes. I made the editorial decision to maintain a separation between his youthful letters penned during the war and his mature reflections on the same events written more than fifty years later. But the reader may find a comparison of the two distinct narrative voices fascinating and colorful. The two forms of reportage can be read in tandem by turning back to the footnotes. Excerpts from the reminiscence may be found in the footnotes to the letters of 2 August 1944 (assignment to *Ticonderoga*), 5 September 1944 (Panama Canal), 17 September 1944 (San Diego), 26 September 1944 (Honolulu), 5 October 1944 (assignment to master-at-arms force), 26 October 1944 (Eniwetok), 5 November 1944 (Philippine Sea), 24 December 1944 (Ulithi), and 10 April 1945 (Bremerton).

The outstanding secondary source for placing *Ticonderoga* in context with the larger naval operations is Samuel Eliot Morison, *History of the United States Naval Operations in World War II,* vol. 13, *The Liberation of the Philippines: Luzon, Mindanao, the Visayas, 1944–1945,* and vol. 14, *Victory in the Pacific, 1945* (Boston: Little, Brown, 1959, 1960). Two good books specifically about the significance of aircraft carriers in World War II are Clark G. Reynolds, *The Fast Carriers: The Forging of an Air Navy* (New York: McGraw-Hill Book, 1968), and James H. Belote and William M. Belote, *Titans of the Seas: The Development and Operations of Japanese and American Carrier Task Forces during World War II* (New York: Harper and Row, 1975.)

For background on two significant events in Bill Catton's story, I turned to Bob Drury and Thomas Clavin, *Halsey's Typhoon: The True Story of a Fighting Admiral, an Epic Storm, and an Untold Rescue* (New York: Atlantic Monthly Press, 2007), and Raymond Lamont-Brown, *Kamikaze: Japan's Suicide Samurai* (London: Cassell, 2000).

On the wider Pacific War, I relied most on Ronald H. Spector, *Eagle against the Sun: The American War with Japan* (New York: Free Press, 1985), and John W. Dower, *War without Mercy: Race and Power in the Pacific War* (New York: Pantheon Books, 1986). For the military history of World War II, my main references were John Keegan, *The Second World War* (New York: Viking, 1989); Gerhard L. Weinberg, *A World at Arms: A Global History of World War II* (Cambridge: Cambridge University Press, 1994); and B. H. Liddell Hart, *History of the Second World War* (New York: G. P. Putnam's Sons, 1970).

There is now a huge literature on the American home front during World War II. The sources I found most helpful were David M. Kennedy, *Freedom from Fear: The American People in Depression and War, 1929–1945* (New York: Oxford University Press, 2005); John Morton Blum, *V Was for Victory: Politics and American Culture during World War II* (New York: Harcourt Brace Jovanovich, 1976); Richard R. Lingeman, *Don't You Know There's a War On?: The American Home Front, 1941–1945* (New York: G. P. Putnam's Sons, 1970); and Geoffrey Perrett, *Days of Sadness, Years of Triumph: The American People, 1939–1945* (New York: Coward, McCann, and Geoghegan, 1973). Several more specialized works about the home front are cited in the footnotes. On Franklin D. Roosevelt and American politics, I relied most on Kennedy's *Freedom from Fear* as well as James McGregor Burns, *Roosevelt: The Soldier of Freedom* (New York: Harcourt Brace Jovanovich, 1970).

The best sources on personal mail in World War II are Judy Barrett Litoff and David C. Smith, "'I Wish That I Could Hide inside This Letter': World War II Correspondence," *Prologue* 24, no. 2 (Summer 1992): 103–14; and Litoff and Smith, "'Will He Get My Letter?': Popular Portrayals of Mail and Morale during World War II," *Journal of Popular Culture* 23, no.4 (Spring 1990): 21–44.

Among the World War II memoirs, diaries, and collected letters that I read or consulted for background and comparison with Bill's experience, three stood out in relation to Bill's collection. *Miss You: The World War II Letters of Barbara Wooddall Taylor and Charles E. Taylor*, edited by Judy Barrett Litoff and David C. Smith (Athens: University of Georgia Press, 1990), is remarkable in its delivery of an intimate and reciprocal correspondence of a couple, one reporting from the home front and the other from the war front. I also found a pair of memoirs by US seamen compelling in their honesty and fascinating in their similarities and differences to Bill Catton's story. Louis R. Harlan, *All at Sea: Coming of Age in World War II* (Urbana: University of Illinois Press, 1996), is the mature memoir of a man who, like Bill, was an intellectual in the making when he served in the war but who had a few years on my father and struggled with his duties as a junior officer. The other, E. J. Jernigan, *Tin Can Man* (Arlington, VA: Vandamere, 1993), is an appealing narrative about the grittier side of navy life as experienced by an ordinary sailor who served in both the Atlantic and the Pacific.

It has been a great privilege to edit my father's World War II letters into a book. I have family and a few key professionals to thank for that. I am grateful to my mother, Nancy Catton, for allowing me to take it on and to everyone in the family—especially my mom, my Aunt Ruth, and my brothers, Steve, Philip, and Jon—for allowing the letters to go forth to publication. Said one, "Labor of love deserves to succeed." I humbly acknowledge that the work is more Dad's than mine and represents a joint effort, one might say.

My wife, Diane, was encouraging and endlessly patient with me even when my effort bordered on obsession. She was a good listener as I read the letters aloud to her. I am so glad she knew my dad in later life.

Researching the archival records of the US Navy for this work was truly a case of searching for a needle in a haystack. I could not have done it without the help of three navy-records specialists at the National Archives in College Park, Maryland: Nate Patch, Jacob Haywood, and Alicia Henneberry.

I am grateful to Will Underwood, acquiring editor at Kent State University Press, for seeing the potential of this work and carrying it forward. I also want to thank two anonymous readers for the press. One of them subsequently shed her anonymity and generously aided the project through two further readings and sets of comments. It was a pleasure to work with Judy Barrett Litoff in this way.

Getting to know the young Bill Catton through his World War II letters home was a revelation to me. I had not known how determined he was to get into combat or how sophisticated he was in his thinking about the war and the peace. And yet the young man in the letters was totally recognizable to me too. His qualities of character, his humor, his sentimentality—these were all keenly familiar traits. Editing his letters was a little like having more precious time with my dad. Now it ends. I salute his memory.

Introduction

Bill Catton served in World War II in the Pacific as a young seaman onboard the aircraft carrier USS *Ticonderoga*. Just shy of sixteen years old when the United States entered the war, he was eager to do his part, and so he volunteered for the navy on his seventeenth birthday in January 1943. After going through basic training at Great Lakes Naval Training Center in the spring of 1943, he received specialized training in airplane mechanics at the Navy Pier, Chicago, and further training in air gunnery at the Naval Air Gunners School, Hollywood, Florida. He worked on refitting fighter planes at Norfolk Naval Air Station, Virginia, before joining the crew of *Ticonderoga* in August 1944. While onboard the "Big T," he was involved in actions in the western Pacific during the last year of the war with Japan.

My father, who died in 2015, was modest about his military service all his life. Like so many veterans of World War II, he averred that he merely did what he had to do. Upon returning home, his sea stories mostly went untold, his Purple Heart medal and stripes went into a box of mementos never to be shown, while his letters from the war—carefully saved by his mother—went unread and unremarked upon. We in his family knew that he had been awarded the Purple Heart for a wound in the arm received during a devastating kamikaze attack on his ship. We knew that, after the surrender of Japan, he was seriously injured in a loading accident that put him in a stateside navy hospital for six months. Those were the basic facts of my father's military service known to me as a boy. I proudly recited those facts to my friends, but I never pried my father for more. He shared with us a few other stories about his years in the navy, but those stock stories were in the vein of humorous anecdotes, nothing heroic, thrilling, or very suitable to repeat to my friends. So the outline of my father's World War II story jelled around the bare facts of his service aboard an aircraft carrier and the two times he got hurt.

But on one occasion many years ago, I got a singularly intimate glimpse into my dad's experience. It was the summer of 1982, and I was between my junior and senior years of college taking a cross-country trip with my parents. When we reached the Atlantic coast at Charleston, South Carolina, we found that the USS *Yorktown* (CV-10) had been recently decommissioned and turned into a floating aircraft-carrier museum in the harbor. My dad explained to me that the ship was an *Essex*-class aircraft carrier, meaning it was very similar to his ship, *Ticonderoga.* As *Ticonderoga* had been decommissioned and sold for scrap metal after the Vietnam War, our tour of its sister ship *Yorktown* would be the closest we would ever come to going aboard his vessel. So while my mom went on a walking tour of stately historic homes along the harbor front, my dad and I went aboard the *Yorktown* for a look around.

I was twenty-two years old that summer, already a shade older than my father was at the end of his World War II service. It was humbling to consider how different his coming-into-manhood experience was from my own to that point. Even now, I find it staggering to think that he had learned how to rebuild an aircraft engine and fire a .50-caliber machine gun before he was eighteen, then had made two voyages across the Pacific and saw a year of combat before he was twenty. It is a cliché that war ages young men quickly. Yet it was hard for me to see any evidence of that premature rush into manhood in my dad—a mild-mannered college professor whom I always knew as a good-natured, self-assured, clean-living family man, not to say my own loving parent.

Onboard the *Yorktown* that day in 1982, he gave me a personal tour of *Ticonderoga*'s sister ship. As we paced out the flattop's vast length, he pointed out the modifications to the flight deck that were made after World War II to accommodate jet warplanes. We went below to the hangar deck, where he showed me the cavernous space in which he had worked at the head of a plane-handling crew. We walked back to the ship's stern, or what he called the fantail, the place where he had gone to relax and think, write letters home, breathe fresh air (for the air inside the hangar deck could get quite stale), and watch the sea. Down below the hangar deck, he found the place in the crew quarters where he had bunked. Then we came to a spot on the vessel that triggered sharp memories of the kamikaze attack on his ship.

On 21 January 1945 *Ticonderoga* was a hundred miles off the island of Formosa (now called Taiwan) conducting air strikes against enemy airbases. Japanese suicide planes came diving out of the sun and clouds, having eluded the ship's radar detection by trailing a group of US planes back to the carrier. When the ship's crew sighted the incoming kamikazes, my dad was below deck with his plane handlers. He heard the sudden dub-dub-dub of the antiaircraft guns and then the siren for General Quarters (GQ). Instinctively, he started to run toward his battle station. But then he checked himself, turned on his heels, and ran the other way when he remembered at the last moment that he had hung his helmet and flak jacket in a handier spot where he had been working that morning. That was lucky for him: seconds later the area around his battle station exploded in a white ball of fire and a hail of shrapnel, leaving a hundred men dead and dying.

A swarm of kamikazes dove on the *Ticonderoga* and other nearby ships in that attack. The one that made the explosion hit the flight deck near the forward elevator. The aircraft had crashed through the wooden deck, and its bomb exploded inside the hangar compartment. Several planes parked there blew up or caught fire.

A metal fragment from the explosion hit my dad just below the left shoulder. In all the excitement the piece of shrapnel felt to him like just a friendly punch in the arm, but he saw blood spreading on his shirtsleeve and realized he was wounded. A hospital corpsman saw his bloody sleeve and sat him down to treat the wound, then told him to take cover. He went aft and found shelter in a narrow bay between steel beams, joining a wounded officer whom he recognized as one of the pilots in his air group.

While he and the pilot huddled there out of the way of the medics and firefighting teams, more stationary airplanes burst into flames, and oily smoke billowed through the gaping hole torn in the flight deck. The ship listed hard to port, and it seemed it might be sinking. In fact, the skipper of the ship, Capt. Dixie Kiefer, had ordered portside magazines and other compartments to be flooded, putting the ship on a 10-degree list so that burning oil would pour out through the hangar deck's panel doors and burning airplanes and flammable debris could be rolled or skidded to the edge of the deck and dumped overboard. The captain's brilliant, desperate, original maneuver to tip the whole giant flattop like a dustpan and slide the raging fire into the sea saved the ship from destruction.

A second wave of kamikazes saw the smoke and dove on the burning carrier. Antiaircraft gunners shot down three planes, but a fourth one got through the barrage and struck the starboard side of the ship's island, erupting into another fireball. The second kamikaze strike on the *Ticonderoga* killed many more crewmembers and badly wounded Captain Kiefer, who nevertheless stayed on the bridge through the rest of the ordeal. The attack commenced at a few minutes past noon, with the resulting fires at last brought under control about two hours later.[1]

After the attack, the *Ticonderoga* remained in the area until sundown while her marines searched the surrounding waters for survivors, then headed east for safety. A memorial service was held on the fantail for the ship's 144 dead, whose remains were buried at sea. On 24 January the stricken *Ticonderoga* made port at the US fleet's base at Ulithi Atoll. There, its air group was transferred to another carrier, and the badly wounded crewmembers were taken aboard a hospital ship. My dad was on deck when Captain Kiefer was taken off the ship on a stretcher. He recalled the popular commander saying to the sailors as he was leaving his ship, "Remember! You're still Dixie's kids!"[2] After four days at Ulithi, the *Ticonderoga* set out for the US mainland to undergo extensive repairs.

Now, what I remember my dad sharing with me about his experience has to do with what occurred *after* the attack. During the cleanup, fragments of the Japanese aircraft were collected and laid out on the hangar deck for navy intelligence officers to examine. Nearly every scrap was tagged with the name of the man who had picked it up in the hope that the item would be returned to him as a souvenir.[3] My dad recalled that the ship's new commander had other ideas about these scraps. After the *Ticonderoga* cleared port for the long homeward voyage, some of the items from the airplane's cockpit were culled from the collection and put on display below decks for the seamen to inspect. A few pieces must have reflected the fact that the pilot had been on a suicide mission. The purpose of the display, as my dad recounted, was to show the shaken crew that the kamikaze airman, so terrifying in the abstract, was just an ordinary human being.

It was the memory of that display that so struck my dad as we stood below decks on the *Yorktown* that day, nearly four decades on from the war. He recalled the surprise he had had as a young man when he went to examine those recovered items. There was one artifact in the display—a photograph or some other memento, perhaps, if such an item could have survived the inferno—that suddenly made him see the Japanese pilot as a person not so different from himself, with similar attachments to family, home, and country. It made him think that under different circumstances their roles could have been reversed. The realization shook him. Recalling it nearly forty years later, he said that a profound feeling of empathy for the dead man had welled up inside him in that moment.

Now many years after that tour of the *Yorktown,* I have no doubt that my dad had an epiphany from that episode in 1945, when he was a young seaman just past his nineteenth birthday. An enemy plane carrying a 250-kilogram bomb had deliberately crashed into his ship, killing scores of US servicemen, including two men from his own plane-handling crew, and in that charred hole of death he had discovered a comforting ember of shared humanity with the enemy. That ember would glow inside him the rest of his life. After the war it fueled his irrepressible desire to talk to strangers, to step outside his own skin, to understand the point of view of the Other, and to challenge the cultural paradigm. In no small part it made him the man he was. After he was gone, I found he had assembled a modest half-shelf of books about the Pacific War amid his vast personal library of academic tomes. Two titles in that little collection jumped out at me: *The Divine Wind: Japan's Kamikaze Force in World War II,* by Rikihei Inoguchi (1959), and *Kamikaze: Japan's Suicide Samurai,* by Raymond Lamont-Brown (1997).

Next to my laptop as I write this, I have a stack of photocopied documents ordered from the National Personnel Records Center: Bill Catton's military service record.[4] It adds up to 114 pages exclusive of his separate medical record. The many official forms are the dry bones of a seaman's enlistment, training, transfers, promotions, benefits, awards, and discharge. On one document, "Consent, Declaration, and Oath of Parent or Guardian, in the enlistment of a minor under twenty-one years of age," is Bill's father's signature. Evidently, father and son had gone to the recruiting station together on Bill's seventeenth birthday, 15 January 1943. On that day he entered the US Naval Reserve as an apprentice seaman for a four-year hitch, which would have ended on 14 January 1947 had the war gone on longer. Ultimately, he was discharged six months before that date.

Concerning the kamikaze attack on the *Ticonderoga,* the dry service record offers only a citation for the Purple Heart awarded to William Robert Catton Jr., aviation boatswain mate, second class, US Naval Reserve, "for wounds received in action against an organized enemy of the United States on 21 January 1945 in the vicinity of Formosa Island."

Bill Catton entered basic training on 24 February 1943 at the US Naval Training Station, Great Lakes, just north of Chicago. Three months later he qualified for duty as an aviation machine gunner and proceeded to a twenty-one-week course of instruction at the Naval Air Technical Training Center, Navy Pier, in downtown Chicago. He graduated from the training school seventh in a class of 120 with the rank of aviation machinist's mate, 3rd class (AMM3/c). On 20 November he transferred to the Naval Air Technical Training Center, Memphis, Tennessee, for two weeks of instruction in radar. On 4 December he transferred to the Naval Air Gunners School, Hollywood, Florida, for further training to become an aviation gunner. On 15 January 1944—his eighteenth birthday—he transferred to US Naval Air Station, Miami, Florida. There, he expected to train in the air as well as on the gun range, then enter upon naval airman's duty as a gunner. But then his navy career took an unexpected turn.

Four days after the transfer, on 19 January, his service record states that he was dropped from aircrew training "for failure to meet physical standard set for Air-crewmen." His medical record indicates that he received a doctor's examination two days after reporting to Miami and was diagnosed with tachycardia, a faster-than-normal heart rate, which disqualified him for air service. His service and medical records notwithstanding, Bill's letters home indicate that he continued training in the air for three more weeks. He made several "hops" as he eagerly anticipated assignment to an air unit, being not yet informed of the medical disqualification. When at last in early February he was informed of the navy's decision to deny him air service and to reassign him to an aircraft-maintenance crew instead, it came as a bitter disappointment.[5]

On 9 February, according to his service records, he transferred to Carrier Aircraft Service Unit 21 at Norfolk Naval Air Station, Virginia, where he was stationed for the next six months. He worked in a kitchen, then was assigned to a crew of aircraft mechanics to perform maintenance on navy fighter planes and torpedo bombers at Fentress Field, south of Norfolk.

He volunteered to join the crew of the USS *Ticonderoga* on 31 July. *Ticonderoga* was the tenth *Essex*-class aircraft carrier launched by the navy. It was commissioned on 8 May 1944 and completed its shakedown voyage to the West Indies in July. The "Big T," as it became known, sailed for the Pacific theater in late August, passing through the Panama Canal and making stops in San Diego and Pearl Harbor in September and October. The carrier arrived at Ulithi Atoll on 29 October, where it joined Task Force 38. On 5 November kamikazes attacked the aircraft carriers *Ticonderoga* and *Lexington,* scoring one hit on the latter; it was Bill's first experience in combat. Over the ensuing two months, the Big T saw nearly continuous action in the campaign to liberate the Philippine Islands. In January 1945 it moved into the South China Sea to launch air attacks on Japanese forces of occupation on Formosa and on mainland Southeast Asia.

After sustaining damage in the kamikaze attack of 21 January 1945 and undergoing lengthy repairs in drydock in Bremerton, Washington, *Ticonderoga* set out on its second Pacific voyage in April 1945. Reentering the combat zone in the western Pacific, it launched one air attack after another aimed at demolishing Japan's airbases and few remaining warships in preparation for the invasion of Japan. A four-by-six-inch sheet of paper in Bill Catton's service record lists the actions that he saw through the end of the war. It reads:

PARTCIPATED IN THE FOLLOWING CARRIER
TASK FORCE OPERATIONS AGAINST THE ENEMY WHILE SERVING
ON BOARD THE U. S. S. TICONDEROGA.

17 May 1945.
Taroa Island, Maloalap Atoll, Marshall Islands.
28–29–30–31 May 1945.
Okinawa, Ryukus Islands.
2–3 June 1945.
Kokobu and Ronchi Airfields, Kyushu, Japan.
4–6–7 June 1945.
Okinawa, Ryukus Islands.
8 June 1945.
Kanoya Airfield, Kyushu, Japan.
9–10 June 1945.
Minami Daito Jima.
10 June 1945.
Kita Daito Jima.
24–25 July 1945.
Hiroshima Bay, Honshu, Shikoku, Naval Base Kure.
28 July 1945.
Airfields and Shipping, Kure.
30 July 1945.
Tokyo Area, Honshu.
9–10 August 1945.
Northern Honshu, Ominato and Amori Areas.
13 August 1945.
Tokyo Area.

D. J. CORCORAN,
Lieutenant, USNR,
By direction.

Following Japan's surrender, the *Ticonderoga* stood offshore of Japan's home islands and sent reconnaissance aircraft in search of prisoner-of-war camps so that medics and supplies could be rushed to the POWs there. On 6 September the ship entered Tokyo Bay. On 15 September Bill joined a shore party on a tour of the bombed-out city of Yokohama. On 20 September the ship embarked for the US mainland with a few thousand returning troops aboard.

From his time in boot camp through the end of the war, Bill Catton wrote more than five hundred letters home.[6] Some were just brief notes or postcards; most, however, contained several paragraphs of reportage or musings written in lively and precise prose. He averaged three to four letters a week; while his output varied, it never lapsed for more than a couple of weeks at a time. He wrote the most letters to his mother but also wrote many to his father, who was also in the US Navy from May 1943 through the end of the war. Bill wrote occasional missives to his teenage sister and kid brother as well as to his grandparents, aunts, and uncles. The young sailor wrote more and more letters to his high school sweetheart as time passed, especially after their relationship deepened during his third and fourth home leaves. He also kept up a correspondence with several high school buddies as those young men entered the armed services and scattered to training camps and battle fronts around the globe. He exchanged letters with a few navy comrades. Precociously, he wrote one letter to US senator Arthur Vandenberg concerning the United Nations charter, and a few more letters to other public figures.

Bill used letter writing as a form of journal keeping, approaching his years in the US Navy with a wide-eyed sense of adventure and a self-conscious pride in being a witness to history. Once, while home on leave, he read through a batch of his saved letters. Inspired by the example of Ernie Pyle, whose Pulitzer Prize–winning journalism captured the perspective of the regular GI, he found that his writing style had a similar quality to Pyle's columns. With characteristic hubris, he thought that his writings, too, made a worthy record of a certain little piece of the great human story of his time. In a missive to his father, he suggested that the whole collection, with his father's letters also, could someday be edited into a book. "The two contrasting points of view of the war, yours and mine, would really just about cover the whole Navy," he exulted, only half-jokingly.[7]

Letter writing helped him cope with homesickness too. The minutes and hours spent in writing to his loved ones acted as a balm for his soul when he longed for home. Writing home elicited feelings of nostalgia and stirred up crisp memories of family interaction. "A year ago," he wrote in a characteristic passage, "I was spending my leave at the cottage with you folks at Crystal Lake. I wish I could be repeating it now: swimming in the lake with Butch, sleeping on the sleeping porch, going to Manistee in the evenings, even helping up at Uncle Dayton's."[8]

Receiving letters from home was vital to servicemen's morale, and so it was for Bill's. He craved mail and anxiously awaited mail call, the more so after he put to sea. No military service could be more isolating than serving on a ship in the vast Pacific Ocean. Mail deliveries were less frequent for men at sea, despite the US Postal Service's and US Navy's strong efforts to keep letters and packages flowing for the sake of the men's morale. When the bugle call for mail sounded, the men literally dropped whatever they were doing and ran to get their deliveries. A new sailor once mistook the excitement for a call to General Quarters and asked what was up. "Mail call," Bill explained to him, "the best music ever written!"[9]

Generally, he fared well with the incoming mail. His mother and father were almost as prolific letter writers as he was. His strong family support from home did not go unnoticed by his fellow seamen. At times, he felt a little sheepish about it. "I really got more than my share of the mail last night," he wrote to his mom one time. "I'm not kicking, of course, but it was tough to watch the few who didn't get any mail look at me with envy each time my name was called. A mail call that doesn't bear fruit is worse than no mail call at all."[10]

Outgoing mail was censored, screened for militarily sensitive information in case the correspondence fell into enemy hands. Servicemen were not allowed to write anything about military operations. For seamen, that meant they could not disclose where their ship was located, where it had been, or where it was going. After the *Ticonderoga* first entered the combat zone in the western Pacific, Bill had to stifle the urge to inform the people at home that he was finally engaging the enemy. "There is much I wish I could write about but can't," he informed his mom on 7 November 1944, two days after the carrier launched its first airstrike. Ten days later he closed another letter with the remark: "I wish I could write more about life and adventures out here. My 'sea stories' will have to wait, though. One guy had a letter rejected today with the following inscription on the envelope: 'Too much dope, dope.'"[11] All mail was censored before it left the ship. If servicemen slipped up and wrote a piece of information that was disallowed, the censor would black it out with ink or cut it out with a razorblade.

The censorship notwithstanding, Bill filled his letters with observations and vignettes of navy life. Much was permissible to write about. He described interesting ports of call without actually naming the place. He narrated incidents aboard the carrier. As soon as the censorship was lifted at the end of hostilities, he wrote retrospectively about places and experiences that previously had been forbidden information.

Bill's mother carefully saved all the letters he sent home or sent to his father in the navy, stowing them away in boxes. The collection was still in her care when she died. Bill's younger sister—Aunt Ruth to me—moved into Grandma Catton's house and eventually mailed the boxes of letters to my dad. He saved the boxes of letters, packing them each time he moved, but never reread the correspondence, it seems. A few months after he died, I asked my mom if I could see them. I was surprised to find they had not been read in many years, probably not since the war. Each was folded up and stashed in its original stamped envelope. V-mails—one-page handwritten letters that were microfilmed for shipment, then printed onto photographic paper and delivered as miniature facsimiles smaller than a postcard—were folded and tucked into their miniature envelopes. The V-mails, letter-size envelopes, and postcards were tied in bundles with white string. As I untied them one by one, I had the feeling I was untying my grandmother's bow knots from the mid-1940s.

When I arranged all the letters in chronological order and began to read each one, I soon recognized their historical value. I was struck by the quality of the writing, the power of observation in the writer, and the appealing narrative voice of a young man so eager to fight for a righteous cause. The World War II letters of Bill Catton add up to a rich firsthand account of one seaman's experiences through more than a year of training at various naval bases in the United States followed by two voyages to the western Pacific on a fleet aircraft carrier.

I would note three outstanding themes in the collection. The first is the abundance of interesting detail contained in the letters. Bill had a roving eye for recording human experience. Reporting on his attendance at a Bears-Packers football game in Chicago, he observed that there were a great many men in military uniform standing in the overcapacity crowd, and still the gatekeepers were letting more servicemen into the stadium free of charge. With wry humor, he wrote that it occurred to him "that just outside the gate would have been an ideal spot for a recruiting officer to situate himself."[12] He used his liberties to go off base and explore, often thumbing his way out of the city. The letters written from base while he was stationed in Chicago, Miami, and Norfolk are a tableau of the home front in places thrumming with support for the war effort.

In his observations about the navy and the enlisted man's lot, one finds the mind of a future sociologist at play. For example, there is one entire letter devoted to observations on the nature of navy "scuttlebutt." Why was it that enlisted men were so prone to spreading rumors? Bill's theory: in a hierarchical organization, the enlisted man at the bottom of the chain of command craved to know what was next in store for him. In the absence of authoritative information, speculation ran rampant. One rumor that went around the ship held that American newspapers had mistakenly reported that *Ticonderoga* was sunk by the Japanese. Seamen who were gulled by this story were frantic to tell their folks back home that they were okay. The way that rumors aboard ship mutated and escalated reminded Bill of the game of "telephone" that he and his mother, father, sister, and brother had played when they were seated around the dinner table at home.[13]

The second theme of note in the letters is the process of maturation. There is evidence of a gradual transformation from the seventeen-year-old high school graduate who went off to boot camp in February 1943 into the twenty-year-old navy man who returned home in 1946. The collection provides an opportunity to view the maturing influence of naval service on one very young enlisted man.

Bill wrote to his parents from boot camp almost daily. Those initial letters give a sense of the eager, earnest, precocious youth he was when he joined up. They not only exhibit his outsized ego but also, in more subtle ways, reveal his inexperience and vulnerability. How he enjoyed receiving packages of cookies from home! How he liked the navy's ice cream sundaes! And, to read a bit between the lines, how he missed his mother's tenderness each time the navy gave him another dreaded vaccine shot in the arm. (Those shots—what an ironic foreshadowing of the "punch in the arm" he received from a piece of shrapnel in the kamikaze attack!)

The short, teasing missives to his younger sister, Ruth, and his incessant, ribbing asides to his mother reveal the progress of his maturation over the three-year period. His role in the family changed during the war. An older brother, John, had died of spinal meningitis when Billy was just three years old, leaving the family missing its firstborn child. When he went off to war, Bill left another big void in the family. Naturally, his mother dreaded the thought of losing her son and tried to talk him out of pursuing the more dangerous lines of combat service. As he matured in the role of big brother, he also came to honor his mother's feelings about him and to wear the mantle of oldest son at last.

Bill's man-to-man letters to his father about navy life display his growth from a raw recruit into a respected petty officer. One short period in his time aboard ship deserves highlighting here. In October 1944 he was assigned master-at-arms in the ship's mess. Bill confided to his father that the law-enforcement role was uncomfortable, but he took the job to avoid being transferred off the ship in Hawaii.[14] Being a master-at-arms put him in authority over much older men than he, and it gave Bill a different perspective on navy discipline. It also prepared him for the role of heading a crew of ten men when, to his relief, he returned to his former outfit on the hangar deck six weeks later.

The third theme that runs through the collection is Bill's strong bonds to family. The thing to consider is how his closeness to family shaped his experience in the war, providing him a profound base of emotional support. Certainly, he was not exceptional among World War II servicemen in enjoying strong family support from home, but the rich flow of letters, books, newspapers, and care packages that came to him from home was not typical, either. One thing that made his experience truly rare—and gives the collection added interest—is the fact that Bill's minister-father entered the service right behind him as a navy chaplain. Father and son formed a tight bond over their shared naval experience. Their correspondence is studded with queries about one another's well-being, some of which are couched in humor (more ribbing, a family pastime), while others are direct. In one arresting passage his father gently inquires if being a minister's son was a burden to him socially among his peers. I believe my dad, who was an atheist by the time I knew him, may have already begun to have doubts about religion by this stage in his life (although it is hard to see it in the letters he wrote to his religious-minded parents), but his faith was not the point of this query from his father. Rather, the point was to acknowledge that Bill's upbringing in a tight, churchgoing family had given him certain traits that made him peculiar—even priggish—in the rough society of sailors. I do not know if Bill ever gave his father a direct answer to his question—if he did, the letter did not survive—but I am confident of what his answer would have been: I never heard him express one iota of regret about having been a preacher's kid.

The family discussed world affairs in the home constantly. The parents generally approved of FDR's internationalist foreign policy, though they were not among the president's ardent supporters. In the elections of 1932, 1936, and 1940, Bill's father had cast his ballot for Socialist Party candidate Norman Thomas. His mother's votes were not a matter of record in the family, but she certainly distanced herself politically from her arch-Republican parents, both Roosevelt haters. Bill, as an inquisitive teenager in the early 1940s, picked up the political views expressed in the home, listened to the radio broadcasts that were frequently the center of attention, and acquired strong opinions about America's place in the world even before he was out of high school. By 1943, his core beliefs were that the United States must uphold the Anglo-American alliance to defeat fascism and that isolationists in Congress must be opposed so they would not stand in the way of a new international order after the war.

Bill entered the war brandishing high-minded ideals about what he was fighting for and why he had a moral duty to get into it, as he said, "all the way." He was fortunate that his mother and father made him talk these ideas through with them and that they continued to support his thinking about the war by sending him books and opinion pieces through the mail. His idealism never wavered.

Bill Catton was born in Minneapolis, Minnesota, on 15 January 1926 to Helen Willard and William Robert Catton. His parents belonged to that generation who came into adulthood around the time of World War I and whose own childhoods, astonishingly, reached back into the pre-automobile age. There is a photo of Bill's mother as a young teenager on the family's farm in northern Michigan taking a wagonload of produce to market. She is standing behind her family's horse Dolly, which was said to have been ridden by her father during the Spanish-American War (1898).

Helen Willard was the oldest of four children. Her father was a medical doctor with a private practice in Oak Park, Illinois. When she was a teenager, the Willards acquired a summer residence in Benzonia, Michigan, a village up north where the family could escape Chicago's sultry summer heat.[15] Helen graduated from high school during World War I and went off to Mount Holyoke College in Massachusetts. Lonely there, she soon transferred to Oberlin College in Ohio, where a few of her friends from Benzonia were enrolled—including a special someone, William Robert Catton.

Bill's father, William Robert Catton Sr. ("Robert"—he always went by his middle name), grew up in Benzonia, where his father was principal of a tiny preparatory school, Benzonia Academy.[16] Graduating from that institution in 1912, Robert worked for a year and then went to Oberlin College, graduating in June 1917 shortly after the United States entered World War I. As with many of his classmates, the degree was awarded in absentia following his enlistment in the military in April of that year. Robert served two years in the US Navy, trained as a pilot, and flew dirigibles. After the war he went to Chicago Theological Seminary and graduated with a bachelor of divinity. Helen and Robert were married in 1922. They had four children: John (born in 1925; died in 1928), William Robert Catton Jr. (born in 1926), Ruth (born in 1929), and Edward (born in 1935).

Robert Catton became a Congregationalist minister. The family lived in several locations in the upper Midwest and Colorado as he moved from ministry to ministry during the Great Depression. In September 1936, when Bill was ten, the family moved to Manistee, Michigan, a town of about 8,000 on the shore of Lake Michigan. Manistee was just thirty miles south of Benzonia, where both sets of Bill's grandparents by then resided.

Bill entered Manistee High School (eighth grade) one year later and completed his freshman, sophomore, and junior years and the first half of his senior year there. In January 1942 the family moved to St. Johns, Michigan, about 130 miles from Manistee. Bill took a few required courses at the high school in St. Johns and returned to Manistee to graduate with the class of 1942 in June.

Bill had a pleasant time in high school and made many friends. His classmates voted him "brightest" and "most likely to succeed" at the end of his sophomore and junior years. His best friend, Tom Stege, was voted best "arguer" at the end of their sophomore year, but Bill was able to claim that title for himself the next year while Tom was named "class wit" instead. Bill's girlfriend, Jane Hanson, was voted "best natured."[17]

His extracurricular activities in high school included football and photography. His high school football career was decidedly modest. A year young for his grade and small for his age besides, Bill did not pack much weight on the football field. He practiced with the team but seldom got to play in the games. Bill also joined the camera club, became an avid photographer, and found an afterschool job at a photo studio.

On Sunday, 7 December 1941, at around one in the afternoon, Bill got together with his friends for a casual game of football. Unknown to the group of high school seniors, the Japanese were right at that hour making their air raid on Pearl Harbor five time zones to the west. After the game ended, the boys drifted away to their separate houses to do their Sunday chores, still unaware of the bombing attack that had just devastated the US fleet in Hawaii. Bill parted with his friends and sauntered home to an empty house; his family had gone to St. Johns that day for his father to preach a sermon as part of his candidacy for the ministry there. So Bill, eating his dinner alone without the radio on that evening, remained unaware of the day's momentous events. His meal completed, he went to the Pilgrim Fellowship at the church. Stege arrived at the church shortly after him and immediately blurted out the news: Pearl Harbor attacked! At first Bill thought his best friend was pulling his leg, but others at the meeting confirmed that it was true. After the service he and Stege went downtown to the office of the *Manistee News Advocate* to get the first extras as they came out.[18]

The following summer, after graduation from high school, Bill joined Stege and several other members of the class of 1942 for a summer session at Central Michigan College in Mount Pleasant, Michigan. In the college dormitory the boys talked about signing up with the armed forces.[19] The minimum age for joining the US Army or Navy was seventeen, provided the enlistee had the permission of a parent or guardian. Most of the boys had passed their seventeenth birthdays by then; Bill's was not until the following January. At the end of the summer, Bill informed his parents that he wanted to sign up as soon as he turned seventeen, five months hence.[20]

To occupy his time through the fall, Bill found a job with a photo studio in Detroit. He moved into an apartment at 878 Blaine in the city and went to work at Redman's Personality Portraits. He worked in the darkroom developing portrait photos, sometimes working until eleven at night. On weekends he rode the train up to St. Johns to visit his folks or hitchhiked over to Ann Arbor to visit friends who had enrolled at the University of Michigan. Among those at the university was Jane Hanson, his high school girlfriend. One weekend he took her to the movie *Pride of the Yankees.* On another weekend they attended church together.[21]

Bill went on his own to a showing of *Mrs. Miniver,* a Hollywood picture about an English middle-class family steeling itself to fight Hitler's Germany. He had already seen this popular movie earlier that year at a theater in Mount Pleasant, but he was eager to see it again on a big screen in the grand Fisher Theater in downtown Detroit. He found the story deeply affecting. Fond of going to picture shows in general, he would go see *Mrs. Miniver* five more times in the next two years. He no doubt identified with the character of young Vin, a pilot in the Royal Air Force (RAF). In the film's final shot, the camera points skyward out of a bombed-out church as RAF fighter planes fly over in "V" formation. That fall Bill adopted Britain's signature "V-for-Victory" as a signoff in his letters home.[22]

Sometime while he was living in Detroit, Bill wrote a letter to his mom explaining his reasons why he had to sign up for the navy come January and beseeching her to give her blessing.[23] It was among the first of his letters that she saved:

> Dear Mom,
>
> I have been trying to think, as you asked me to do, of what I would do if you kept me out of the Navy. I can't. The only thing that occurs to me is either to go to U. of M. or try for Annapolis. But I don't want to do either of them as an alternative to immediate enlistment. I just can't see myself not enlisting.
>
> Besides wanting to win the war, I have another reason for wanting to get in. You remember I said in the car Sunday that I thought before Dec. 7 that we should be in the war. That if we admitted it was our war and we wanted the Nazis beaten we should get into it all the way. Of course we had our lend lease business and we were economically in it but we stayed home and let the British and the Chinese and the Russians do the fighting and dying.
>
> Well, it's the same way with me. This is my war just as much as it's David's or Paul's or Jack Brennan's. I want to be all the way in it then. It's not just a matter of where and how I can accomplish the most. I want to be in action against the enemy.
>
> You said you folks wouldn't think any less of me if I changed my mind about January. You seem to have the wrong idea entirely. I'm not enlisting to make a hero of myself, or even just to save face. Of course I want people to respect me, but my reputation would be secure if I went to Annapolis. The trouble is, so would I be secure. It's a matter of conscience. After the war I don't ever want to feel that I wasn't as much exposed to the risks as anyone else. You can say what you like about "Soldiers of Production" and "defense on the home front" and all that but, no matter how much a civilian war worker is *accomplishing* towards victory he's not *giving* as much as a soldier. If I were in England it might be different.

There it is true that "This is the People's war!" as in "Mrs. Miniver." But here the war affects us only economically and socially but not physically.

In high school, I could have gotten into the games free, even would have travelled to all the out of town games, by being student manager. I would have been accomplishing more for the team than I did by being in uniform. I wasn't a star, so I got no glory. I would have won a letter as a manager, too. But—I wouldn't have been playing football.

It's the same in this war. I don't want to work. I want to fight. And I see no reason why I shouldn't.

I still can't make myself believe you will keep me out of the Navy.

Yours truly,

Bill

Helen's letter of reply has not survived, but she evidently gave him her blessing. When his seventeenth birthday came, Bill immediately went to the naval recruiting station to enlist in the naval reserve. There was a kerfuffle over his flat feet. He was kept in suspense until the recruiting station determined whether to take him anyway or give him a second medical examination. While awaiting the decision, he paced around the house in bare feet with a marble clenched in his toes to improve his chances of passing the exam. At last the matter was resolved. On 23 February 1943 his father drove him to Detroit to sign up.

At the recruiting station Bill filled out a slew of forms. He was fingerprinted and submitted to a second medical examination. (His height measured five feet, nine and a half inches—he would grow a half-inch taller while in the navy. He weighed 145½ pounds. His blood pressure and heart rates before and after exercise all measured in the normal range.) After the medical exam there was a long wait while a handful of other recruits were processed after him, then the whole lot took part in a small swearing-in ceremony. Bill and the other young recruits stood together and recited the navy's oath of allegiance. With his induction complete, he was issued his first transfer: he was to ship out next morning for the Great Lakes Naval Training Station in north Chicago for basic training.

He was in.

CHAPTER 1

Naval Training Station, Great Lakes, Illinois

Dear Pop, 28 February 1943

Things are *starting* to move around here now. On Friday, we were given another physical exam. My feet are O.K. apparently. We were then issued our uniforms and transferred from receiving station to permanent barracks.

The chief in charge of our company is a southerner with a very interesting accent. We got our bunks made up and stowed and our stuff in our sea-bags and he gave us a lecture on saluting, keeping the barracks clean, how to stand watch, etc.

Saturday morning, we had to be ready for inspection by some officer. Our bunks had to be just so. Sea-bags had to be properly strung and hung from the jack stays. The decks and windows were spotless, all waste baskets empty, papers picked up from the grounds around the building.

About 11 o'clock the officers came around and we came to attention. They looked the place over and told the Chief it was very good for a new bunch. It looked good to me for *anybody.*

Yesterday afternoon we got our haircuts. On some of the guys it was a marked change. On me they just trimmed up the back and sides and left the top as is. When we came in all the fellows already here yelled at us, "Barber Bait," and "You'll be sorry!" Now we can be the ones to yell when new guys show up. Some fun.

This morning we all went to church. (Required.) The whole place goes in three shifts. We went in the middle shift, 9:30. It was very interesting. There must have been a couple thousand in the congregation. The choir is made up of seamen and is one of the ones which sing on the radio. They're pretty good too. The chaplain wasn't bad at all. He had a very good voice for the bad speaker system.

As I understand it, we have the rest of the day off. I think I'll get some sleep this afternoon as I was up most of the night before last on watch. It wasn't much fun as there were no fires and nobody tried to break in or out. All I did was stand around and stay awake. I had to salute the chief when he came in once and say, "Front door guard, Co. 262, reporting, sir." That was all. At 3:30 I woke up the guy who followed me and he relieved me as soon as he was dressed. I turned in again at 4:00 and was up at 5:00! Ho-hum!

We start getting our shots tomorrow. We get I think six or seven shots and a vaccination. That takes two or three weeks. During that time, we are in quarantine and can't have visitors. They say the sore arms aren't bad except for pulling off jumpers. If the shots are no worse than the needle they took blood out with, then they'll be a *cinch.* Several guys fainted when they took blood samples, though. I would say it was a matter of psychology.[1]

Have my clothes arrived yet? Please have the "M" sweater cleaned and have Mom put it away in moth balls. I think I may be able to wear it still after the war.

The food here is reasonably good tasting and comes in very pleasant quantities. I tried coffee the first day and have not taken any since. It was sickening. Ruth would enjoy our meals. We have beans every day, even sometimes for breakfast.[2] . . .

Please send me that little column on the front page of the *[Detroit] Free Press* which summarizes the news. Send three or four days at a time. We have a radio here but it's turned on jazz music most of the time.

Bill

Dear Mom, 3 March 1943

I just got the section of the *New York Times* Dad sent. I haven't yet had much time to read it. What's going on in the world, anyway? Our radio here is busted, and I haven't heard any news since Sunday.

I got a letter from Grandma Catton with an enclosed newspaper clipping. I'm sending the whole thing on. The clipping expresses somewhat the same thoughts I had last week.[3]

As I was being sworn in, all the things which had led me to that ran through my mind. I was filled with determination and felt "Let's get going."

We did some drilling today out on the field. It was pretty cold, but I didn't mind as we kept moving. I'll be glad when we get good and snappy at marching. Then it ought to be really a lot of fun.

They announced today that we would graduate about May 12th. At that time we get 9 days leave. In the meantime we get no weekend liberties. It used to be 5 days at the end *with* a couple weekends. But I'd say it was a fair exchange.

We got all cleaned up in our barracks today, decks, bunks, racks, bulkheads, windows, everything spotless and then the officers didn't come to our dorm. Both our chief and the one upstairs said it would have won high praises. Fooey.

Tell Ruth we had beans for breakfast today. Also, she better get in practice if her pies are going to satisfy me when I come home. They have *excellant* pastries here. Write soon—Bill

Dear Mom, 4 March 1943

The candy and gum came this morning. Also, your letter with the enclosed letter from Uncle Tubby.[4] I am enclosing a postcard which I got from him this morning.[5] Thanks for the candy. We can get it (sometimes) here at the canteen but the variety is small.

As to the rouge on my undershirt: I hadn't thought how suspicious that might look. But to begin with it isn't rouge, it's mercurochrome. At Detroit, they painted numbers on our chests when we got examined. When we put our clothes back on it rubbed off onto them. I'll bet you were surprised when you saw it!

I stood watch again this morning—from 8 to 12 A.M. Several officers came through and I had to salute them but otherwise it was uneventful.

It's fairly cold here, with a reasonable wind. The barracks are warm but your face gets cold when drilling.

We are to drill some more this afternoon and then I think we get swimming tests. Luckily, we haven't had any shots yet or swimming would be *work*.

Mail seems to take about a day and a half to get here from St. Johns. How long does it take to get there?

We are in "detention" till Mar. 19. After that we can see visitors on Saturdays and Sundays 1 to 6 P.M. They are required to write for visitors passes ten days in advance. I don't suppose this means anything to you but we are supposed to write it to our folks.

I must write Uncle Tubby now so—
Oh river.[6] Bill

Dear Mom, 5 March 1943

We got our first shots today. We got one typhoid and one tetanus shot in the left arm and a vaccination in the right arm. So far, my arm is not sore. It's a little stiff when I raise it. They told us to keep moving them, so I'm taking time out between lines. One of the shots I actually didn't feel—even the pinprick. The guy said, "Move on." and I said, "What for?"

We had our swimming tests yesterday. The pool was 50 yards long and we were supposed to swim the length of it. We all swam bare tail. I made it easily. It was the most effortless swim I've ever had. The water temp was 74°.

We are allowed to swim from 1:00 to 5:00 on Saturdays and Sundays. I think I'll go over there tomorrow.

Some of us went to a movie they had here last night. It was "Lucky Jordan" with Alan Ladd. Pretty good. There was also a Popeye cartoon, a sports-reel, and a newsreel. It was shown in the drill-hall and the first ones to get in formation were the ones who got to go to it.

Well, I'm going to stop now and work on my arm.
Yours truly, Bill

Dear Mom, 6 March 1943

After I wrote you yesterday about our shots, the reaction came on a little stronger. Some of the guys got real sick. One fellow fainted, one vomited, and several got chills. However, I got off fairly easy. My hands turned blue for a while, but otherwise I was O.K. In the afternoon when we were cleaning up I felt very lazy but I don't know whether to attribute it to the shots or to me.

We had inspection this morning and were put down as very good. Chief says our salutes are excellent and also our positions "at attention." I went swimming again this afternoon. My arm is feeling swell so I thought I'd go while I could. The water was swell. I did some diving off a 10 ft. springboard, swam the length of the pool several times and did between 60 and 70 feet under water.

There is an Andy Hardy movie on tonight and I believe I'll go.

The St. Johns paper came today and looked good to me. I also heard that my name and address had appeared in the Manistee *News Advocate.*

I ate the last Milky Way today. We were told not to eat too many sweets just before our shots. I'm just starting on the gum.

We get our *Bluejacket's Manuals* next week.[7] There is a desk-copy here in the barracks and I've been looking it over. It's a lot different than Dad's.
Yours truly, Bill

Dear Mom, 7 March 1943

I got your letter, written Saturday morning, today. We get one mail delivery on Sunday. I also got Butch's card and letter. He said, "Dad carried the ashes out today. He misses you." Clever Butch.[8]

I haven't heard from Jane or Stege or any of the other classmates yet. I have sent my address to all and sundry, though.

Our whole company is in one big room in the barracks here. It is an even 100 fellows. I have a lower bunk. The guy above me is a fellow from Kentucky, Carl Burnette. About half the fellows are from Ky. and most of the rest from Mich. There is a constant North-South feud.

We get up at 5:30, clean the barracks, go to breakfast, clean the barracks, drill or something, clean the barracks till 11:30. Then we can write, read, etc. till 12:30 when we go to lunch. Then we clean the barracks, march, or exercise or some other thing, clean the barracks, and get off at 4:30. Our time is our own till 5:30 chow, and again till about 8:30, when we clean the barracks before taps at 9:30.

On inspection days (Saturday) we spend most of our time cleaning the barracks. Sundays, we clean them once in the morning, go to church and have the rest of the day off till 8 or 8:30 when we clean the barracks. "We joined the Navy to see the world. And what did we see? We saw the dustpan and the broom!"

I went to another movie last night. "Andy Hardy's Double Life." It was reasonably good. There I met a guy from Cadillac who knew Laurent La Mond, and Herb Holland, who were at Mt. Pleasant this summer. Also, Joe Rumbel from M.H.S. is in his Company. I may get to see him this afternoon.

Naturally you didn't see the *Chicago Tribune* today,[9] but if you can get a copy there's a big illustrated article in one picture-section about Great Lakes [Naval Training Station].[10]

'Bye Now, Bill

Dear Mom, 8 March 1943

This morning we got up at 4:45 and went to the drill hall at 5:45. We had a session of calisthenics which really were nice and rigorous. It took me back to the first days of my senior year at M.H.S. when [Coach] Holzaepfel gave us our workouts.[11]

Later in the morning we went to a "visual education" movie which showed how to tie several useful knots. They looked easy in the picture. We get a crack at them in a few days.

This afternoon we had a lecture from Chaplain McCormick (a protestant) on religion's place in the Navy. He was very interesting. He is a lieut. j.g. [lieutenant junior grade].

Then we had a "musical" session singing some Navy songs. We are to practice them in our barracks and get the time perfect so we can sing while marching instead of having the C.O. [commanding officer] say "left, right, left."

Tonight, I went over to the canteen and had a strawberry sundae and a chocolate sundae. Those and the exercises, working together should put some weight on me, like they used to in football.

I stand watch tonight from 8:00 to 12:00, so I'll get about five hours of sleep. That isn't as bad as the 12:00 to 4:00 A.M. one that I had last week. We rotate in alphabetical order and it doesn't come out even, so we have a different watch each time.

'Bye now. Write soon. Bill

Dear Dad, 9 March 1943

This Navy is beginning to get a little less housewifish and somewhat more nautical now. Yesterday we had a movie on knots and today we had a session of learning to tie several of them. Overhand, figure eight, square, bowline, fisherman's bend, clove hitch, double half hitch, ditto with a loop, etc. Some fun. Then we had some practice laying lines on the deck. Flemishing, faking down, loose coil down. More fun.

This afternoon we got our first pay, "the flying five." First, we made out pay receipts. Then we went over to the canteen and lined up. We exchanged the receipt for a five-dollar bill. *Two steps* farther on we handed this in. Another two steps and we were given a two-dollar bill. Then we got a package of small stores; razor, razor blades, soap, tooth paste, and brush, etc., and the *Bluejacket's Manual.* I never saw so many two dollar bills in my life!

Boy do we eat here! My last slice of meat loaf didn't go down quite as easily as the first four tonight. We were the last company into the mess hall so we got all the left overs. I haven't had any coffee since the first day here. I prefer water.

I got a letter from Grandma Catton today. She says she's afraid you're going to be very disappointed if you don't get your appointment as Chaplain. If you get in, try to get to Great Lakes. I think you'd like preaching to a Congregation of *several thousand.*

Bill

Dear Dad, 10 March 1943

. . . We got our *Bluejacket's Manuals* yesterday and by tomorrow we are supposed to know the semaphore alphabet! I hope we stay busy like that as it will help pass the time and anyway that's what we're here for, to learn all that stuff.

We all saw a movie this morning on life in the Navy. It was produced for the Navy Dept. by The March of Time. It was very interesting and contained some scenes recently familiar! It's fun to realize I'm at last a part of it all. . . .

I got a letter from Jane today. She says they are reading *A Time for Greatness* for English at U. of M. and have to write a paper on it. It looks as though the schools were keeping pace with the needs of the time. Could be that Slosson and Bingay will be at it again soon, too?[12] . . .

I gave a buck to the Red Cross the other day here. We don't get anything for it, not even buttons, *yet.* But I'm in the Navy and there is still a war going on.

Oh river, Bill

Dear Mom, 13 March 1943

This morning we had weekly personnel inspection. Our company won the "rooster" for the week. That means we have averaged best on barracks inspection during the week and on this morning inspection. We have a two-foot square wood plaque with a silhouette of a rooster on it which hangs by the door of the barracks. It just means extra work for the next two months in order to keep it. Otherwise we lose face. However, they say it's very unusual, though, for a company to win in the first week of Rooster Competition.

It has turned nice and warm here the last two days and the snow is melting rapidly. In a few days it will be dry, and we will be drilling without our coats and rubbers. I like to drill when the ground is dry but when it's icy or mushy it is hard to be snappy.

We had double typhoid shots yesterday. My arm is slightly sore but nothing else is wrong with me from it. I felt this shot a little as it was going in but it wasn't bad. I think the needle was dull.

Detention ends next Friday for this company. That only means we can see visitors and can leave Camp Green Bay. But we still don't get outside the station. However, it's less than two months now till we graduate, so that isn't bad.

We had a class in hand-to-hand combat (Jap style)[13] the other day and one in gunnery the day after. It makes the war much less distant.

I got out of guard duty this time around from having been on battalion fire patrol on Thursday.

The lowest 25 percent of the company in the "strength test" we had last week have two extra hours of marching this afternoon. I'm not in that bunch, as my score was above average by a good margin. Also, a large share of the boys are taking swim-tests this afternoon. Those who didn't take them last time or didn't pass them. The rest of us have to stay in the barracks till 1630 (4:30 P.M.) but have the time to ourselves. After that I think I'll go over to the canteen for a sundae. They really have swell ones there.

I tried to get you a Navy pin but they are temporarily out of them at the canteen. They are going to have some swell ones in next week, though.

I'm sending you a book of stamps, seeing as how I get my own postage free.

Write and tell Butch and Puddle Mush to write, too. How does Shrimpy look in his helmet and goggles?[14]

Yours truly, Bill

Dear Dad, 15 March 1943

I read your "unsent" letter with interest and think you should have sent it. I didn't read the pamphlet till afterwards. The encircled part made me very mad. It sounds as though the writer disapproves of guys like me being in service. He definitely does not understand my point of view. He says further on that it's a matter of pride with the American boys; that they want to do some of the fighting, too. Why and how he considers this wrong, I don't understand.

I wonder if he would rather have me in college accomplishing nothing toward victory or where I am and where I'm headed for, fighting his war. *At least* he should be consistent enough to say that College boys should help to supply *civilian* manpower. . . .

Did you read "America's New Mood" in the March *Reader's Digest?* It is interesting, encouraging, and gratifying *if true.* But I notice today that B. K. Wheeler says (concerning peace commitments) "We should wait till we see what Russia is going to do."[15] What makes him think Russia is any more desirous than we of taking the lead? Anyway, if we are to *distrust* Russia, by all means *we* should take the lead while the taking is in our favor.

Personally, I think the majority of Americans, even the majority of internationalists are on the wrong track entirely. They are all looking for an organization to *settle* disputes between nations rather than one to *prevent* them. How much more valuable are the shots I'm getting now than any amount of medicine later! . . .

Not much more to report from here so—

Toodle oo, Bill

Dear Mom, 18 March 1943

The old saying, "Never put off until tomorrow what you can do today," certainly applies in the Navy. We have really been busy this week.

We've done quite a bit of drilling now that the ground is dry. We've had exercise with arms. We had our service school tests. We've had assignments from the *Bluejacket's Manual.* We've been really working to keep the "rooster," too.

Today we got two more shots. I'm getting an attitude of recklessness toward them now. I have a feeling of amusement when we go to the hospital for them.

Tonight, I ate a bigger meal than I've ever had before in my life I believe. Our company was the last in line so we got all the excess food. I had a serving of potatoes big enough to satisfy you four at home with the swellest gravy just running over it. I had a slice of meat loaf and a big serving of lima beans. Also, a full bowl of pea soup. I had a big helping of cabbage salad, bread and butter, milk and an apple. Then to top it all off I had some raspberry jello to the quantity of a full casserole (small one) at home. I was one of the last two to leave the chow-hall. When Dad goes to pay up his bet (on who would be first to enlist) he'll have a real man-sized appetite to contend with.

I have to start sweeping up now and then turn in as we have a session of "road work" (running) to do tomorrow.

Write, Bill

Dear Mom, 23 March 1943

Today was a swell day and we got in considerable marching. This morning we were out on the drill field and we took off our coats for physical exercises. It sure felt swell to be so unhampered. Then with them still off we did some marching and got pretty snappy.

Then we had some semaphore practice. Mr. Delk, the company commander, led us through the alphabet twice. Then he asked for volunteer leaders from the ranks. Naturally, nobody spoke up. Someone nominated a guy by the name of Allen. He went through it and then fell back in. Then the chief picked out me for the job. After I went through it without a slip he said those who couldn't do it would get five demerits. Ten demerits (which are acquired by misconduct in any form, style, or manner) means two hours exercise with arms. So far, I haven't gotten any. One guy got 20 today for carving his initials in a bench.

This afternoon we had the rest of our service school tests. They were on arithmetic, English (grammar) and spelling. I had no trouble with them and got a kick out of some of the questions. We haven't yet committed ourselves to what service school we'd like. They don't ask us that till our qualifications are tabulated.

Today we had an opportunity to transfer to the regular Navy if we wanted too. For most of them it would mean a six-year stretch. For a seventeen-year-old it's till he's 21. I didn't do it as I figured much could happen between now and then. If I should wish to stay in the Navy after the war, there will be opportunities to do so.

While we were drilling this afternoon six Navy fighter planes were flying overhead in formation very low. They were beautiful. It made me fighting mad to think that the only reason I was on the ground looking up at them was because of my age. Arbitrary limitations are necessary because of the scale of the whole business but they do cause inconveniences.

We get our ten dollars tomorrow, which is O.K. by me. I am down to about 75 cents now. I had another good strawberry-marshmallow ice cream sundae tonight.

The cookies came today and were promptly devoured. I gave the mailing case to "Red," the company mailman to mail back next time he goes to the main post office. . . .

Bill

Dear Pop, 25 March 1943

. . . This morning we started learning the international flag code. The chief has a deck of cards with the flags printed on them. He holds one up, we identify it, and tell what it means. I know the whole alphabet and some of the numbers. It doesn't take long to learn them with the cards.

We have a process of association of ideas which is very interesting. For instance; "D" or "Dog" implies a mad dog, which is a thing to stay away from. Therefore, the flag D means "Stand clear; I am maneuvering with difficulty."

I just now took time out to engage in an argument with three or four other guys. Subject: was England fighting *our* war for two years and so what? I stood alone on the side that she was and that Americans are the snootiest people in the world. One guy took a middle point that it was our war but it was to our advantage to let Britain fight it. Two other guys said it was not our war until we were attacked. One argument was that those who were doing the fighting were not British but Canadians and Australians. I mentioned the little episode called the Battle of Britain. I said, anyway, that even if their statement were true it is not a credit to us but rather to the Dominions who have a sense of allegiance transcending lack of political ties. I mentioned further the fact that Britain had an alliance with us against Japan before Japan attacked us, whereas we completely washed our hands of the British-German affair until Germany declared war against us. It was interesting while it lasted.[16]

Thanks for sending me Churchill's speech.[17] I read it a few lines at a time all day yesterday. I should like to have heard it as some of it sounds as though it could really be orated beautifully.

I got a letter from Uncle Tubby today. He said to tell you he had heard reliably that they have a PT-boat school at Melville.

Nothing more to report from here so—

Toodle-oo Bill

Dear Pop, 1 April 1943

I got your letter to Mr. Lippmann this morning and was very interested in it.[18] I thought your points were well taken and well expressed. I hope it does get to him.

I was amazed to hear that Mr. Crawford is still keeping his record of voting wrong on major issues intact.[19] To reject lend-lease at this time would seem to me so unwise as to be humanly impossible.

We in the Navy are not allowed to write our congressmen. On the whole, I suppose it is a wise rule. But it sure burns me up in this instance. Here we are, training to fight for a victory and for peace and guys like Crawford are willingly, even if *possibly* unwittingly, right now preparing to scrap our efforts.

Before you get to be a chaplain (if) please do me one favor. Write "our" representative and ask him just what is coming off.

Thanks also for the *New York Times* section again. It really does sound intelligent in its editorials. The one in this issue about the "time bomb" in the Senate was very good.[20] They sounded as if they were behind the proposals but they were rational about it rather than emotional like Bingay.

We've had a radio in the barracks for two weeks now, but this morning was the first time I heard a news broadcast on it. Mostly it's turned to Hill-billy or swing "music." At 2100 (9 P.M.), time for Raymond Gram Swing, it is turned off for the night.[21] I suppose I can afford some such sacrifices though as long as I'm not facing meat and butter shortages, etc., like the civilians.

It rained a little here last night but this morning the sky was cloudless. It is nice and warm here and should be from now on.

Now that the work week is over we are getting back to a regular schedule. Guard duty is rotating alphabetically again. I start off with the dog watch tonight.
Ho-Hum, Bill

Dear Pop, 7 April 1943

Boy things sure are going swell for me now. We had our service school lecture today. It was given by an ensign and explained what different schools trained a man for. We got our test scores and indicated our choices. Soon we are to get personal interviews before being assigned.[22] . . .

The C.P.O. [chief petty officer] just now told me I am high man in the Company.

I put aviation mach. mate as my first choice and gunner's mate as second choice. Then I volunteered for aviation machine gunner. That is open to men selected for an aviation school. I didn't put down photography as there was no way to indicate aerial photography and furthermore it has few openings.

Aviation schools are hard to get into, too, so I'm not saying definitely I'm in, but being top man I think my chances should be very good.

I got your letter today. It is very interesting to speculate on the whys and wherefores of the red tape in government appointments. Your last paragraph and closing line about "trying to get yourself into another war" are sobering and thought provoking.

What you say of the importance of Mr. Morganthau's proposals,[23] I agree with. I hadn't heard that any such proposals had been made and was glad to receive the clippings.

I would go farther (perhaps by steps, though) and advocate not only an international stabilization of currencies but also an overall international currency, not just for use in governmental negotiations but to replace present moneys.

Night before last I turned the radio here to Raymond Gram Swing. I didn't hear much of it though as there was a lot of noise in the barracks. It was the first chance I've had at that radio since we've been here.

Last night I was on regimental messenger duty down at the drill hall. Business was at a standstill, so I got to see the show: "Reap the wild wind." After that I had to go and empty a waste basket in the sound central room. The Petty Officer in there had a shelf of various books: Shakespeare, *War and Peace,* a French textbook, a book of synonyms & antonyms, some books of drama, etc. We had an interesting discussion of literature, history, science, etc. Some Navy.

Tell Mom she can stop worrying. Sub duty is not open to men under 21!!![24]

Bill

Dear Dad, 13 April 1943

Ask Mr. Place for a transcript of my credits and mail it to me as soon as possible.[25] . . . I have been recommended for V-12.[26] . . .

I'm not sure I want it but I would like to follow it up anyway. It is a 26 mos. College course leading to a commission. That would probably mean I'd be out of this war. However, V-12 is independant of the service-school set-up. My service school appointment would still go ahead and I'd *start* that, at least. V-12 courses are due to start in June. However there may be a bunch of delay like you are experiencing so that I'd start in a different bunch. It could conceivably work out so that I'd see some action and then come back for officer's training. If it means starting immediately it puts me in a tough spot like I was in when contemplating V-5.[27] The conflict is between immediate service in a small way; or future *possible* service in a big way.[28]

The interviewer yesterday was the one who recommended me. As to service school recommendations he put down my application for A.M.M. [aviation machinist's mate]. Also he made notes on my photo experience, including Redman's Address. He wrote down that I'd passed V-5 exams. At the end he wrote, "Wants to fly."

We are to know in a week or so what comes of it. Some of the guys who don't make service school were told definitely that they were slated for immediate sea duty. . . .

Here it is the middle of April and yet it is snowing today. It is only a very light precipitation, though, so it may not last, I hope.

Sunday night we had a "Happy Hour." The announcer was Lt. Bob Elson. They had a Navy band and then some amateurs from among the recruits. One guy did impersonations. He started off with movie stars; Cary Grant, Clark Gable, James Cagney, etc. Then he switched to radio actors and commentators: Gabriel Heater, Lionel Barrymore, Frank Morgan. He did quite a few like that and was really excellant. Then he finished off with Roosevelt and Churchill. They sounded just like they do on the radio.

How Elson rates a Lt.'s commission I don't know, although he wasn't bad just as a Master of Ceremonies.

Yours truly, Bill

Dear Dad, 18 April 1943

Yesterday afternoon my transcript came from Mr. Place so I got a pass from the battalion office and went over to the procurement office for an interview. It was a Junior Lieutenant who interviewed me. What it amounted to was him looking at my records and recommendations and putting down his own recommendation of me. Then I asked a bunch of questions to find out all I could about V-12. The next step, when and if I want it, is a physical.

If I take V-12 it will automatically take me out of service school lists and put me on general detail here at Great Lakes (after my leave) till about July first. Then I would get the equivalent of six semesters of technical training in some college which would give me a line officer's commission.

As it stands now I plan to wait and see what service school I am selected for before making a decision. V-12 dissatisfies me in these ways. It would keep me in school till Sept. 1945 by which time it is to be hoped the war is over and to be assumed that at least it will be in its final stages. The training I would get would be mostly technical, which as I see it, would not help too much in my hopes of having a share in the establishment of the peace.

If I can make my aviation Machinist's mate school I will have a very good chance of transferring to V-5 later on. That will give me the flight training I desire and will lead to a commission equivalent to what I'd get from V-12. If I could complete my service school training and get into action as a gunner I could really feel I was in it all the way. Then if I could come back later for pilot training I would be very well satisfied.

Of course this all depends on what the selection board says as to my service school assignment. My chief aversion to V-12 is that I don't want to be a parasite. To my way of looking at it I will be wasted on this war if I'm sent to school for two years. Of course I would then be well fitted for a career in the Navy. But the kind of service I hope to be able to render doesn't involve being in the Navy but rather, I think, would be hampered by such a condition.

As to the education offered by V-12: if I'm not going to stay in the Navy I don't think it reasonable for the Navy to educate me. I think that the time for me to go to College (if ever, although it seems more reasonable to me now than when I was in high school) is after the war. I would rather work my way through it than have the government spending its money on me.

I joined the Navy because there's a war going on. If I'd wanted to go to school I could have stayed out till drafted, or even have gone ahead into V-5 reserve and gone to school while waiting call. There is a job at hand to be done and I want to do it. I will keep my thoughts and hopes on the future and my eyes on the goals to be attained, but all things must start from the beginning. . . .
Yours truly, Bill

Dear Mom, 22 April 1943

Yesterday Afternoon we had another swim test, this time a more thorough one. We had to tread water, then swim across the pool overhand. Then we had to dive in and swim back across breaststroke (frog paddle). We went across again underwater and then all had to dive from the spring board. It was fun.

Last night we had our farewell party. We had to have it this week as the general detail men graduate next Wednesday.[29] We had a good meal followed by speeches. First were the three Chaplains from this Camp and then the Company Commander. After that each of us was called on for "a few remarks." I told of my delay in getting in and the attendant deep disappointment. I finished off by saying that all seemed to have worked for the best as I was sincerely glad to be in this Company under Chief Delk.

It was a significant occasion when it is realized that friendships so quickly but firmly made are soon to be parted. The general theme in mind seemed to be that if our teamwork aboard ship is as fine as it is here the war can't last long.

Tonight, I went to the show, "Chetniks."[30] It was a story of Gen. Michailovitch and his men. On the way down to the drill hall I got into a little argument with some of the fellows as to the importance of the Jap execution of our Tokyo raiders.[31] One of the guys got the mistaken notion that I was sticking up for the Japs. What I really meant was that war being horrible and dirty anyway what was the value of quibbling over the legality of shooting half a dozen prisoners of war. It seems to me that retaliation in kind on our part would be extremely unwise. It would only serve to remove the plea of righteousness from our cause and would not in any way help win the war.

If a man has an infectious disease, he fights it and endeavors to kill the germs. But he does not work up a violent emotional hatred for those germs. So should it be in our attitude towards our enemies.[32]

Tomorrow we have Good Friday Services and then I think are to hear our Service School Assignments. I will let you know how I stand.

Yours truly, Bill

Dear Dad, 23 April 1943

We just got the report on our Service School assignments. I am completely satisfied. I made Aviation Machinist's Mate School. Now if I can go on from that to aviation gunnery I may be into it in a few more months. In any case I am in an excellent spot to maneuver into V-5 later.[33]

I don't know where I will be sent when I return from leave in May. However, I understand they have schools for that at Navy Pier, Chicago, and in Detroit. Either wouldn't be so bad, especially Detroit.

This morning we had competitive drill with the other three companies in our battalion who are scheduled to graduate with us. The best marching Company is the Color Guard at graduation. The Battalion Commander deliberated several minutes between us and one other Company after all four had passed in revue. Then he had us two go through it again. They got it.

I got a swell new billfold from Grandmother and Grandfather today as an Easter present. They had forgotten to rub out the price tag ($3.50). It's a snazzy one with four celluloid photo pockets, coin pocket, bill fold, and identification card.

See you in May.

Bill

Dear Pop, 25 April 1943

How did church go this morning? Was the weather O.K.? We had early church here, at 8:15, the first shift. The day started out cloudy but warm and this afternoon the sun came out. They had communion service this morning, which seemed to me a bit incongruous for Easter Sunday. The sermon, though not exceptionally fine, was good. His theme was that the Christian principles for which we fight have not been crucified.[34]

This noon I tried to call you folks up. I waited in line an hour before getting into the phone booth. Then the operator got through as far as Lansing. The Lansing operator said they were very busy and there'd be a three- or four-hour delay. I decided it wasn't that important. . . .

Having made A. M. M. school my chances of going ahead in aviation are very good. As to being an officer, I'm not so sure now I would want it, except in connection with flying. When I consider the rest of these guys being in action soon, some within a few weeks, it would be exceedingly difficult to be left behind. Besides, having developed such keen comradeships here, it would be hard for me to be in the position of giving orders to guys just like these.

But the two important factors are that I want to get going in the war, and that in the war my main interest lies in Aviation.

During the war, planning the peace lies in the hands of civilians. We are going to have our hands full in the service. As to an education for peacetime service on my part, as I see it, action in battle is the most important feature thereof. As you said in your letter, it is not the actual courses of study but the personal experiences. Those should start as soon as possible.

As to writing, I have considered that possibility and found it not without interest. A position such as Swing's would certainly be something to be desired. It would take some luck to gravitate toward such jobs, but I've always been lucky.

Anyhow that's after the war, which by nature must be viewed in rather indefinite light.

Yours truly, Bill

Dear Mom, 28 April 1943

This morning we all woke up a bit early due to the excitement of the general detail men going home. That gave us time for a leisurely dressing and last-minute session of conversation before breakfast. All the g.d. [general detail] men had blossomed out in their dress jumpers without boots and really looked swell.

Last night I went up to the Hostess House and Canteen with the guy who sleeps—or rather slept—in the next bunk. He is from Detroit and is a pretty swell guy. I threw a private farewell party for him as we had gotten to be quite good pals. In the morning we went to chow together. I helped him fix his gear sea-going fashion, etc., and shook hands with him before he left. About half the Company left this morning.

The rest of us all stood out in front of the barracks as they were marching away and cheered them on. There were tears in the eyes of all of us, both the ones leaving and the ones staying here. All week there has been a lot of kidding about the whole business. The service school men ride the general detail men for not making school and the general detail men rub it in about us having two more weeks. This morning, however, we completely forgot that.

When the fellows left it wasn't just like acquaintances parting, it was almost a family breaking up. Constantly there was the realization that we'd never again see most of them; some of them would never come back at all. That is such a profound truth that we didn't even think of it. It just clung to our subconscious minds. . . .

Co. 262's service school men had a review with the rest of the battalion yesterday. We are to be the color guard at our graduation. Our general detail men came in second (close) on that competition. . . .

See you in two weeks, Bill

Bill completed his basic training on 5 May. He was granted one week of leave and went home to St. Johns, Michigan. On 27 May he was transferred to the Naval Training School, Navy Pier, Chicago, for a course of instruction in Class "A" Aviation Machinist's Mate School. In the meantime his father entered the navy and went east for training at the Naval Chaplaincy School, located on the campus of the College of William and Mary, Williamsburg, Virginia.

CHAPTER 2

Naval Air Technical Training Center, Navy Pier, Chicago

Dear Mom, 29 May 1943

Today is Saturday so there isn't much doing here. My work detail is in the heater-repair shop. I went down there this morning and swabbed the deck and hung around till after inspection. Then I was dismissed for the rest of the day.

At 4 o'clock this afternoon we have personnel inspection, after which we go on liberty. So far, life here is a "gold-brick's" paradise. I don't like that idea too well as it doesn't quite fit the notion of a man-power shortage. But there's no way of disputing Navy orders so I've learned not to care.

I am planning tonight on liberty just to more or less get acquainted with Chicago. I may also take in a show, if there are any good ones on. Tomorrow we have all day so I guess I'll go out to the Field Museum.[1] . . .

Yours truly, Bill

Dear Mom, 31 May 1943

I am enclosing a program from the church service we had here yesterday. Here it is not compulsory to attend as it was in boots but they had a good-sized congregation. The chaplain was fatter than Dad.

The service lasted about an hour, after which at 10:00 we went on liberty. I went with another [Company] 262 man (from Alpena) and we had a swell time. We went out to the Field Museum, Planetarium, and Aquarium. Then we saw the Memorial Day parade, which lasted better than two hours. We were busy saluting all afternoon as every formation carried several flags.

We went to a service club and had something to eat. Then I beat him four games in a row of checkers.

In the evening, we went and saw "Saludos Amigos," Walt Disney's technicolor cartoon of a Latin American tour of good will.

There are some British sailors here at Navy Pier for schooling. I overheard one today as he was reading of the Nazi bombing of that British Sunday school.[2] Our fellows didn't seem to be caring much about it, but he was taking it personally.

I'll quit now as I have to go to work pretty soon.

Yours truly, Bill

Dear Mom, 10 June 1943

This morning I got three pieces of mail [forwarded] from Great Lakes [Naval Training Station]: a letter from you of May 26, a card from Dad of the same date, and a letter from him on the 28th. I was glad to get the one from you which told about Spot.

Dad told about the physical fitness obstacle course they have there. He said he thought they ought to start charging admission when he went through it!

Last night on liberty I passed a little joint on W. Washington where they take free photographs of servicemen. They take one shot and send a 3x4 mounted print to the man's wife or mother. So you'll be getting my picture in a week or so. Let me know how it comes out.

I fear we are going on KP [kitchen patrol] tomorrow. One hundred men from our Company are scheduled for it. I had heard that due to some mix-up in a change of policy the messengers would stay on till Monday, so we might not be on KP. But that's too good to expect. However, in two more weeks we'll be starting school.

Tell Ruth and Butch to write.

Bill

Dear Puddle Mush, 11 June 1943

Guess what I'm doing now. Our section went on KP today and my assignment is washing dishes. Only we do it in the "Navy way." We have big dish washing machines that shoot sprays of hot water from above and below. All we do is stack the trays and bowls in racks and shove them through. It's actually fun. The poor fellows who serve the food have to wear whites, which get stained and must be washed every night. We wear our dungarees.

We don't get dishpan-hands because they don't get in the water. However, we do play around considerably with the garbage.

Hoping you are faring equally well, I remain
Yours truly, Bill

Dear Mom, 13 June 1943

Your letter, and the Shakespeare book came this morning. Thank you for sending it. The boy in the bunk above is reading it. I have just finished the library book I was reading and will start on it soon.

I decided not to go on liberty tonight as we didn't get off KP till 6 P.M. I decided it wasn't worth getting cleaned up and into my dress blues just for six hours.

Last night, however I went into town, ate at a service center, [and] walked down to the beach. Then I went back up to the WGN studio and attended the "Chicago Theatre of the Air" at 8 o'clock. It had some good music, which was at its best, being in a scientifically designed auditorium. Also, it was interesting to see how a radio show was put on. However, I had to sit through a talk by "Col. Robert R. McCormick, Editor & Publisher of the *Chicago Tribune*."[3]

We are allowed to have visitors here, every day I think. I don't know what the hours are, though. I do know that guys bring their girls, mothers or wives to chapel on Sunday morning and then go out on liberty with them. Why do you ask?
Yours truly, Bill

Dear Mom, 20 June 1943

. . . Last night I went to the "Chicago Theater of the Air" broadcast again. The musical background was "The Children's Prayer" from "Hansel and Gretel." Did you by chance hear it? It took me back to the days when I was in the seventh grade and we put on that marionette show.

Later I went to a Telenews theater.[4] In one scene showing the President, he had a marine escort. I could swear one of the marines was Bob Bailey. Mr. Bendle said when we were up there that he had joined the marines.[5]

I ate at three different service centers, bought this stationery in a drugstore and came back to the pier.

This morning I got Dad's letter about the trip to Norfolk. The lucky bum! I know how he feels about wishing he were through there and going aboard ship.

Thanks for the pictures of Dad. Tell Ruth the dark background doesn't set off the uniform too well, but it is a lot better than the usual brick wall or wire fence of the average snapshooter.
Bill

Dear Puddlemush, 22 June 1943

What are you kids doing to amuse yourselves now that school is out? Does mom keep you busy with housekeeping?

If you get time you might make me some more cookies sometime. Of course that's just a suggestion to keep you out of mischief; I don't really want the cookies! (Who said that?)

Enclosed is a $2 Bill to buy yourself some war stamps with. I got paid $14 today, a ten and two twos.

Scullery is still going strong.

Bill

Dear Mom, 22 June 1943

I am enclosing a little leaflet we were given today about Aerial Gunnery. I think you'll be interested. Our physical exams for gunnery will come next week. I should be able to pass having passed for V-5, unless they are very strict on the feet. However, I shall try my trick of walking on the sides of my feet again!

Apparently there are eliminations all the way along so that one who passes the exam and volunteers now won't necessarily be a gunner. However, I intend to try for it all out as that is the main reason I asked for A.M.M. school in the first place.

Have you read about the riot in Detroit? I saw the headlines this morning and didn't know what it was all about till I got to read the articles later. Apparently the whole city just went crazy over a rumor and started fighting.[6]

I had thought that the fights between Zoot-suiters and service men in Los Angeles was bad, but that doesn't begin to compare with this race riot.[7]

One writer in the *Chicago Sun* described it as a victory for the Axis. If this instance is at all typical of Americans we have, I would say, practically no hope for a decent, lasting peace. It is to be hoped that such is not the case.

It must have been mighty discouraging to the soldiers who were called in to stop it, to see the way in which the home folks were backing them up.

And we talk about "those awful union men who go on strike."

Yours truly, Bill

Dear Pop, 22 June 1943

. . . Have you read about the race riot in Detroit? I suppose you have. I saw the headline this morning and not knowing any more about it dismissed it from my mind. Later I heard a couple of guys talking about it so I hunted up a paper and read about it. One writer in the *Chicago Sun* described it as a victory for the Axis, and I would say he was quite right.

It's pretty discouraging to think that the success or failure of the future peace depends on a nation in which civilized, normally decent, educated people can suddenly go completely mad! Those soldiers who were called in to stop the fighting must have been pretty disheartened to think of the way in which the home folks were letting them down.

Apparently they had nothing to fight about. It was just mob psychology. A rumor started an individual fist fight which grew into a city wide tragedy. The paper said that whites and negroes side by side in the hospitals from their wounds, forgot all about the fight and comiserated with one another. . . .
Yours truly, Bill

Robert Catton responded to Bill on the matter of the Detroit riot.

Williamsburg, Virginia
Dear Bill; 25 June 1943

. . . The thing we need above most else is a sense of history, a perspective, a sense of humor.

Our country is not a perfect country. If the men who are fighting for it are going to be discouraged at every unworthy thing in the picture they are in for a lot of discouragement.

Our country is not perfect, but it is growing and it is improving. And I think more than for a perfect country even, it is worth fighting to preserve the opportunities of growth.

If you look only at the imperfections and think only of them, it's a pretty dark picture. But if you know the past and look back and see that, dark as the picture is, it's getting lighter, that's a different story.

There is race friction, it's true. A hundred years ago, there was perhaps less "friction" between whites and Negroes because the whites held the Negroes as slaves. At the first sign of "friction" the Negro could be flogged, legally. After all we're getting more civilized. And only a *little* time has passed. Give the thing another hundred years.

This college of William and Mary is 250 years old. A lot of things are much better now than they were 250 years ago. I'd like to see what they will be like 250 years from now. And by that time, looking backward, this whole 500 years won't seem like such a very long time.

We need a sense of humor and of proportion in the army and navy. The high command will make mistakes, for instance, and some of those mistakes will cost a lot of poor soldiers and sailors their lives. That will be a great pity. But don't let it get you down. It's inevitable. How could you organize a Navy of 2,000,000 men and not have quite a lot of fools in it, first and last? But read the history of the first world war, and of the Spanish war and of the Civil War. I think we are ever so much better organized and better staffed and know what we are doing in ever so much greater a degree than ever before. We're making progress. It's too bad we aren't 100 percent efficient, but it's splendid to be as efficient as we are. Poor Abraham Lincoln had enough experiences with inefficient generals and civilians, too, in the war department. The inefficiency had to be paid for in blood, a lot of it. But he didn't on that account give up. I'm glad he didn't. You could hardly have "blamed" Washington if, after his experience with fools and cowards and even traitors, he had said "Oh, what the _____!" and quit. But he didn't quit. He gave thanks for the good and brave men he did have and did the best he could with what he had, including himself, and finally won.

There's a lot in the picture that's bad, but there is a lot that's good. There are race riots in Detroit, and there's the *Chicago Tribune*, and Martin Dies[8] and Father Coughlin.[9] And there are gamblers and profiteers and "what is there in it for me" people everywhere. But think of all the honest and unselfish and far-seeing men there are in public life and in industry and in the army and Navy. You can fight for them, even if it is exasperating that at the same time you have to fight to preserve Bertie McCormick's right of free asininity. And if you ever wonder whether the war is worthwhile, think of Butch and Ruth and your Mother at home and ask yourself if homes like that are worth fighting for, and I fancy we'll forget the rest and go to it.

This sounds a lot like a sermon and maybe it will be one some time.

Dad

Raymond Gram Swing, the radio commentator, also responded to a letter from Bill.

Washington, D.C.

Dear Mr. Catton: 25 June 1943

I was delighted to have your letter and know what was happening to you. I can well understand your concern over the riots in Detroit. But you must not take affront at them. You must see that these riots were a consequence and not simply a burst of bad temper. Every intelligent observer has been predicting that this trouble would come in Detroit, and we are likely to have it in many other centers where the same conditions prevail. We have overcrowded the war centers with workers and failed to give them adequate housing and, in particular, recreational facilities. Congress likes to spend money on guns, but not on social welfare. This is one of the problems in intelligent planning and thinking to which our American democracy is still not sufficiently alive.

I hope all goes well with you, and please be sure I am glad to hear from you from time to time.

Yours sincerely, Raymond Gram Swing

Dear Mom, 1 July 1943

I went ashore last night in blues. We had a two-day cool spell here but are in whites again today. I met Stege at the Dearborn St. Station.[10] We spent the evening together downtown. He stayed overnight at his Aunt's house and reported for duty today. We are hoping that he will get liberty Sunday. By that time he will be in uniform and we can parade together.

I ate your strawberry jam tonight on some bread at chow time. It is the best, I think, I've ever tasted. Did you make it differently than usual? It didn't taste like jam at all, rather like *fresh* strawberries!

I got a letter from Dad yesterday about his adventure last Sunday. He says he doesn't care if he never gets back to Williamsburg. I sure envy him.

By the way, I think this entitles him to 50% extra "flight pay"! Not bad.

I did some more washing and ironing tonight. They sure keep us busy now. I'm enjoying phys. ed. although I'm very stiff from it.

Yours truly, Bill

Dear Mom, 2 July 1943

I forgot to mention in my letter last night that the box of cookies, when it arrived, was immediately divested of its contents. Keep up the good work! . . .

I read in the paper today of some Republican meeting last night, at which Col. McCormick was praised unanimously for a likely presidential candidate. Not only that but the speakers denounced and the crowd jeered the four freedoms and all hands booed the president, Willkie, and internationalism.

I wish I'd been there. There would have been a sailor suddenly appearing on the speakers stand and the whole Republican party wouldn't have been able to stop me from saying my ideas!!

McCormick's constituents certainly showed their hand. They don't even pretend decently, like Lindbergh[11] and [Sen. Burton K.] Wheeler, that isolationism is the way to protect our ideals. They just come right out and denounce those ideals!

I can't believe that an electing majority could sink to such depths. But Americans are unpredictable.

Bill

Dear Mom, 4 July 1943

Last night I went to the "Chicago Theater of the Air" and met Col. McCormick. What a man! I was just getting warmed up to start talking about world affairs when he said, "I'm glad to have met you" and *oozed* away! I never saw anyone so smooth.

He seems like a nice guy personally at first, but he impresses me as a bit of a moron. And of course, I think his political and social views are not only wrong but crazy.

I haven't heard from Stege since Wednesday so I presume he doesn't have liberty this weekend.

I got 100 percent on my Math test and on my drawing test yesterday so I'm doing O.K. so far. This week we have "hand tools" and make some of the things we drew last week. And of course, we continue to have phys. ed. I should be in pretty good shape by November.

Yours truly, Bill

Dear Mom, 11 July 1943

Another week went by—pfft—like that. Our subject last week, as I may have said, was hand-tools. It was new to me and I didn't get off to too good a start. But yesterday afternoon for a test we had a small fitting, the making of which contained some of each operation we had learned. I was the first one done with it. So I guess I'm doing all right.

Last night I did some washing after Captain's Inspection before going out.

Things seem to pile up over the weekend such that I usually have a big wash to do Monday night. And I wanted to cut that down. Also, I kept my whites clean enough last night so that I'll be able to wear the same ones today.

I went to the broadcast again. This time it was very good. There was a full hour of music as Col. McCormick is out of town.

Things look good in the Mediterranean right now. Yesterday when the headlines in the *Sun* said, "Sicily Invaded" the melodramatic *Tribune* headline was

"Eisenhower Strikes." They had an equally ambiguous headline the other day which said, "MacArthur Attacks."[12]

I got a little background for the Mediterranean war last night by seeing "Five Graves to Cairo," a movie about the turning of the tide from Rommel to Montgomery.[13] It was very good. . . .

By the way how is Spot? Tell Butch to write soon. How is the water in Crystal Lake?[14]

Yours truly, Bill

Dear Mom, 14 July 1943

Saturday, I guess I told you, I went and saw "Five Graves to Cairo." Sunday, I was baseball minded, but I was afraid the game was going to be rained out. So I went and saw "Pride of the Yankees" again. Afterwards I ate twice at the service center and then went out to Lincoln Park. I had a good time feeding the squirrels and pigeons. Then I rode back downtown, walked around for an hour or so and came back to the pier.

We had a lecture yesterday on poison gas. The three standard Navy gas masks were demonstrated and the effects and uses of gas were explained. In answer to the skepticism of possibility of use of gas in this war, the lecturing officer reminded us that gas has been used in Ethiopia and Manchuria!

We also had a talk and two movies on the importance of keeping our mouths shut. It impressed me that even a born gossip could keep quiet when his life possibly depended on it.

Our course of study this week is in "structures." We are working in the actual rigging of wing and tail assemblies. We work in some old 1928 or '30 Navy fighters. They sure seem primitive.

I'll enclose the last letter I got from Dad.

Just finished another wash. We're very busy and I'm way behind in my correspondence.

Yours truly, Bill

Dear Mom, 23 July 1943

I had thought you were going home this week so I wrote you there last night. I suppose the letter will be forwarded soon.[15]

This morning in swimming we had to jump off the 20-foot tower. 20 feet seems like a long way down, looking from above. I felt like a paratrooper. I jumped okay, but when I hit I was sitting down. I hit hard. It didn't hurt me but I was dimly aware while I was still underwater that "Gosh, I didn't do that quite right!"

Tell Butch thanks for his letter and to write again soon. I'll write him when I get a chance. We have field day tonight (barracks cleaning) and I'm on watch from 2100 to 2400.

The *Tribune* today had a cartoon promoting the dissolution of the British Empire and an editorial criticizing Russia for not attacking Japan. The cartoonist didn't indicate what would be preferable to the Empire. If he advocates giving some of it to the Axis, let him look to Burma, Malaya, and the Indies. I suppose he'd just as soon let the Japs control our rubber and tin supplies for always. Or if he merely means to "free" the dominions he is a very *blind* student of politics. Canada and Australia are as free from England as we are.

As for denouncing Russia, let us not forget the four million Russian dead, the territory lost, the suffering, and disrupted living. Would we under like conditions attack a nation with whom we were neutral. No!! Don't let our smug American "righteousness" fool us either. Even when we were at the height of national health and prosperity, not already tied up in a total war we were unwilling even to "offend" Japan by fortifying Wake Island!!

It's my bet that when Germany is licked Russia will fight Japan, perhaps not immediately but as is feasible. They have never said, like we did, "It's not our war!" They have merely contended that Hitler must be beaten first and that was a big enough job by itself. And who would envy them their position in that job. Certainly not Col. McCormick.

Yours truly, Bill

Dear Mom, 27 July 1943

Thanks very much for the cherries. I got them last night and they were all gone within half an hour. I ate about a quart myself and Co. 14 ate the rest. They were very good and much appreciated by all.

I went to the show last night. It was very good: "Bombardier," with Pat O'Brien and Randolph Scott.[16] Before the movie there was a singer (of whom I'd never heard) by the name of Mark Love. He made a speech just before leaving which was well worthwhile and very well spoken. He said that it was our (servicemen's) responsibility to see to it that a just and permanent peace was established after the war. We will be in a position of vast influence and have a great right and duty to exercise that influence. He said we must not be too hasty to "get back to normalcy."

It made me feel good, as I had said before enlisting that I wanted to enlist so as to have a say in the peace. Remember?

Today there was a campaign on here to sign men up for war bond allotments. Allotments were to be made in denominations of $6.25, 12.50, 18.75, etc. I decided not to change from my present allotment home as the only advantage would be in giving Navy Pier credit for it. The disadvantage would be the red tape, as the deductions on the new plan wouldn't start till October.

Today our group of five from Section E, removed, inspected and reassembled the empennage, tail wheel and gas tank from a Grumman FF1, pre-war fighter-bomber. We're getting good. We had the entire tail off in 15 minutes.

Things seem to be happening fast and favorably in Italy. Strange, isn't it, how even we Americans had come to regard Mussolini as a permanent fixture.[17]

Yours truly, Bill

Dear Mom, 1 August 1943

I finally located Stege again. I got a letter from him last night in answer to a card I had addressed: T. W. Stege, AS V-12, Ill. Inst. Tech., Chicago. He got it but is not at that school. He is at George Williams College, 5315 Drexel.[18]

I went out there on the bus last night. It is located in a very nice section of town and the ride out was very pleasant. I didn't get to see Stege, as he had already checked out on liberty. However he is going to meet me at the pier today. His school is a swell looking place, small, quiet, and neat. I should imagine it would be a very pleasant place to serve in the Navy, but I'd rather be at the pier for sixteen more weeks than there for two years.

I came in at 2130 last night, to get some sleep for a change. When I got here I found my bunk full of Grape Nuts!! Luckily I came in while lights were still on so I noticed them before turning in. Otherwise I would have had a very itchy night.

What day of the week does Dad get home? I haven't written him for several days because I didn't know just when he'd be leaving. I still don't know any further about my chances of getting home, so I'm rather assuming I won't be able to. I hope you folks can make it down here.

Yours truly, Bill

Dear Mom, 2 August 1943

I got a letter from Dad yesterday suggesting that I mention to the authorities that he would like to be able to see me come home before he goes to boot camp himself.[19] I gave it to the Co. officer just now. He says he'll try but he doesn't think it'll do any good. "Such things," he says, "just aren't done."

Yesterday I went out and met Stege at noon. We rode and walked out to Harold Marsh's house. He was glad to see us both.[20] We stayed for dinner there, swiss steak, etc., and water melon for dessert. Harold had to be at the P.O. at 4 P.M. so we rode downtown on the train with him.

Then we went to the service center and ate some more. We went out to Lincoln park later on. He has to be back in at 2200 on Sundays so I got in before taps myself.

We went to a stage show of some all-Negro band. It was mostly very good. Some of it was corny jazz "music." But there were some drum selections that were amazing. And then there were two baton twirlers who beat any I've ever seen. They twirled in such a manner that the baton almost seemed to be a part of their arms. I sure wish Butch could have seen it.

Stege likes V-12 very well but wishes like I do that he were out to sea.

Yours truly, Bill

Dear Mom, 2 August 1943

This afternoon we had a demonstration-lecture on "emergency equipment." This included parachutes, life belts, and rubber life rafts. We got to inflate, deflate, and repack a raft similar to the one in the epic 34-day experience.[21] I wonder if I will ever get the chance to use one. I found myself this afternoon rather halfway *hoping* the chance would come.

There is another fellow from Manistee here on the pier I think. He is a big tall lanky fellow who was in my speech class. His name is Jack Moran, commonly known as "Foozy." I haven't spoken to him yet but he went through Co. 14 area this noon as I was writing. He kept turning about every ten feet and eyeing me curiously. I didn't hail him as I was enjoying too much the puzzled facial expression. However, I shall have to look him up sometime.

Yours truly, Bill

Dear Mom, 4 August 1943

Yesterday morning the Chief was giving Co. 14 a lecture about "Request mast." He made the statement that no overnight liberties were granted except to married men whose wives live in Chicago (who get to overnight every week). He said that many requests have been made by men whose brothers are on leave before going abroad, or some such thing, but they were all refused.

The policy is that such liberty is granted only in case of emergency.

So, I guess I'm not coming home this week. When could Dad, or Dad and you, or as many of you as can, come down? I can get an extra liberty whatever evening you'd be here, from 1800 to 2400. All I need is a letter or telegram telling of your arrival to show at request mast.

It was cool yesterday, so we didn't swim. Instead they marched us about a mile or so down the beach and back. We were in perfect cadence all the way back and it was fun.

Yours truly, Bill

Dear Pop, 6 August 1943

. . . Today was again a beautiful sunny hot day so we were out swimming. We went off the 22 foot platform again and for the first time I hit square so that I cut the water instead of slapping it. All I did different was to keep my eye on the horizon. On the way down I could feel myself automatically straighten out.

Later while we were out there we could see three or four planes about three miles out practicing take offs and landings from the U.S.S. *Wolverine.*[22] They came in on the stern with the carrier into the wind and they only go about 20 yds. after they touch the deck. Prettier yet though is the take off. It doesn't seem possible that a plane could get off in such a distance. It was well worth watching.

Yours truly, Bill

Dear Mom, 12 August 1943

I met Grandma as scheduled last night and had about an hour and a half to talk with her before her train left.

She said she thought Dad looked swell in his uniform and was enjoying Navy life. She thinks this assignment at Bainbridge will be good for him, both to be with a large congregation and to be among the younger men.[23] I agree.

Grandma said that you were considering the possibility of coming down to Aunt Bobbie's the last of the month and spending the weekend with me. If you do, you could come down to the Pier on Sunday morning about 0800 and go to Chapel with me.

Let me know just what plans you make. I think Butch and Ruth would very much enjoy a weekend here.

Yours truly, Bill

Dear Mom, 16 August 1943

Yesterday I went out and met Stege about 1100. We went out to a Drug Store and got some ice cream, bought a paper and came back in. At noon, we ate chow at his place (pork chops).

Then we went to Comisky Park to the ball game.[24] The stands were pretty well filled up so we sat way around by right center field. The games were pretty good, six homers in all, several other good hits, and some swell fielding.

The second game was called in the eighth inning on account of rain. By the time we got out of the park, however, the rain had let up. I got some pretty grey polka dots on my white pants when a car hit a puddle in front of me as I was waiting for a streetcar!

In the evening, we went to the service center and ate. Then we visited the Army Air Corps exhibit by Tribune Tower. There was a P-47, B-24, B-26, parts of a C-54 and others.[25] Also, a 15-man glider. I would like to own the little auto trailer field darkroom I saw.

Yours truly, Bill

Dear Mom, 19 August 1943

. . . We had some very good chow tonight: tomatoes (fresh), chili, cabbage, peaches, bread and jam, spinach soup, cocoa. I am full.

I sure wish I could be in Manistee this weekend. Mitch is home now. Stege told me last night that he'd heard from him. Mitch has leave from Aug. 17 to Sept. 4. He has been to England, returned to Brooklyn about two months ago, and went right out again. His second voyage took him into the Mediterranean and he took part in the invasion of Sicily! The lucky bum! I sure would like to talk to him.

Tell Butch I was eating peanuts last night and even beat Spot at catching them. I threw some 20 ft. up and caught them in my mouth.

Yours truly, Bill

Dear Mom, 23 August 1943

. . . This morning we started in on "top overhaul." That has to do with engine repair, more specifically the cylinders and accessories. Also, 3rd and 4th periods we have ordnance. This week we are working with the .50 calibre Browning aircraft machine gun. This is one week I'm really putting all I've got into it, as I hope to be behind a couple such weapons next spring.

If you can't come down this weekend how about next? I see by the paper that school begins Sept. 8. Thus next weekend would make it one last bit of vacation for the kids.

It seems strange to think of *going back* to school. Remember how all through high school I swore I wasn't going to College. And then two weeks after graduation I did. And now this year at autumn I find myself again in school.

All that the end of summer means to me this year is that we'll soon be back in blues and I'll have some time to myself instead of always washing.

Tonight I took my dress jumper down to the tailor's to have new stripes put on. The old ones were rather frayed and a bit tattle-tale grey. I rather hated to do it though, for sentimental reasons. The stripes on the sleeves and shoulder were my own handiwork, done the last Sunday in boots. That was perhaps one of the biggest weekends in my life.

Yours truly, Bill

Dear Mom, 24 August 1943

I'm sorry if I neglected to write you for quite a while. As a matter of fact, I did write on Monday night, but I guess it wasn't picked up till Tuesday morning, so you wouldn't have gotten it till today.

It just illustrates what I've said before, though, that psychologically the war is harder on the folks at home than us in the service. We are kept busy so that we hardly notice the passage of time. You don't get a letter from me for four or five days and it gets you to worrying.

Last night Co. 14 moved! They are bringing in a large company of Diesel students soon in the Co. next to us. They are going to spill over into our area so we had to move east about 30 yards. I have a top bunk now.

Tonight is liberty night. Each Co. on the pier had ten tickets to the All-Star football game. There were 16 of us at the desk this afternoon asking for them so we drew lots. I missed. So I stayed in to wash and press some clothes. Now it's raining, so I'm glad I didn't go out. Anyhow we would have had to come away at the end of the third quarter in order to get back to the pier at 2400.

I wish I could be home to help you folks move, as you must have quite a job on your hands. Anyhow I hope I can get home before too many months and see the apartment.[26]

Yours truly, Bill

Dear Mom, 27 August 1943

This morning we had a speed test on the .50 cal. Browning. We were each placed at a gun, given the signal to go, and then timed in taking it apart (stripping) and reassembling it. I came in second in the class with a time of 3:10. I am really amazed with all that I've learned this week. My time was only five seconds behind the lead. If I can keep up such work (with luck) I'll make gunnery.

Last night I saw "First Comes Courage" in the auditorium here. It was very good. It was a picture of underground activity and a commando raid in Norway.

I am on duty section tomorrow till Sunday. I think I'll go out and see Stege. He was to have gone up to Manistee last weekend and I didn't go out on Wednesday, so I haven't seen him for some time.

I got a letter today from Mr. Redman in Detroit.[27] He says he was in Chicago a few hours a couple weeks ago, on one of these lake excursions. He was personally conducted around the Army Air Power show (down by Tribune Tower) by a Captain Lawson, whom he photographed last fall when I was at the studio.

He says business is pretty good and he could use me now and this Christmas season had I not enlisted. His customers are mostly girls sending pictures to their boyfriends in the service.

Yours truly, Bill

Dear Mom, 2 September 1943

How is the moving? Are you pretty well settled in the new home?

Last night I went out to Stege's place again (in whites). He was busy the early part of the evening as his outfit had to listen to the reading of "Regulations Governing the U.S. Navy."

After that we got together for a short time. He told me about having been home. He was there just a couple hours. He got to see Mitchell. Mitch wears two campaign bars now. One is for the American theater of action (North Atlantic) and the other is for the Mediterranean. One has a bronze star on it for a major engagement.

It seems he was in a battle up near the English Channel. As he describes it, "More went down than stayed up." And to think we were all high school *kids* together not so long ago.

The quality of our chow has picked up considerably of late. A cooks-and-bakers class must be about to graduate. This noon we had roast beef with excellent brown gravy. Tonight, we had cold meat, eggs on toast, blackberry jam and bread, sugar cookies, cocoa, tomato soup and to top it off a nice big ripe banana!

Just finished an evening of washing and pressing. It's almost time for taps so goodnight.

Yours truly, Bill

Dear Mom, 7 September 1943

The last you wrote me was Aug. 30, a week ago. I missed your letters but figured you must be very busy. Dad remarked in a recent letter that you folks must be missing him and me more than ever during moving time.

How successful were Ruth and Charlene in dismantling the darkroom? When I built it I never figured on taking it down, so its construction wasn't so designed. But I guess it was such that it would come apart fairly well. Tell Ruth to send me a plan of the darkroom they are building.

I'm glad to hear Butch's and my bed are in a double deck form again. If, as, and when I get home again I will feel right at ease in the top bunk.

I won't be having any leave before graduation and possibly not then. Perhaps I should even say Probably not. Those who aren't shipped out right away are given overnight liberties after graduation and may go home if they live near enough. But as I understand it the ones who are going to advanced gunnery school are shipped out right away.

So by all means come down and spend the weekend here, as there's no telling when I'll be home again. I'm not going ashore tomorrow night as I want to see the show that's on here at the pier. But I'll call Aunt Bobbie from the phone booth in the canteen.[28]

If you get in here in the morning it will give you most of the day to "shop around" or see Aunt Bobbie or anything else. We get off on Saturday right after inspection which makes it anywhere between 4 or 5. So I believe the best bet would be for you folks to meet me at the gate about 4:30 as that's the time we usually get out. You can get a Navy Pier Street Car on either Grand or Wabash Avenues. It will bring you right to the gate.

The chances are I will be in blues. Last night was very cold and the boys who had liberty last night said the whites felt like no clothing at all. If it's at all like that Saturday, blues will be [my] uniform.

Sunday morning if you get to the pier about 0800 you can say that you want to attend church with W.R.C. (me) 14–136 and you'll be admitted with visitors' buttons. I believe they have a bus to get you to the east end of the pier, but if not it's only half a mile to walk. Chapel is held in the big auditorium which you can easily find. I will plan to be by the gate to meet you. After chapel I can go ashore with you at 1000.

How are Butch and Ruth looking forward to school? This used to be my *un*favorite time of year.

See you Saturday.

Yours truly, Bill

Dear Mom, 8 September 1943

I just got through calling Aunt Bobbie. She said to write you that she thought the best bet would be to stay at their place. The Aurora & Elgin makes it just as accessible to the Pier as Oak Park would be. Also, we are all to be at Aunt Bobbie's for Sunday dinner.

Seeing as how I have until 1:00 A.M. Liberty, Saturday night we can spend the evening in town. I can take you out there about 11 P.M. and still get back to the pier on time.

On Sunday morning, you are all to come in for chapel service and then leaving here at 1000 we can get out to Glen Ellyn about noon or somewhat before.

I always remember Pearl Harbor's bombing as the date of Dad's candidacy in St. Johns. We can now remember Italy's surrender as the day Navy Pier went back into blues. It's a great day all around.[29]

See you Saturday, Bill

Bill's family rode the train from Lansing, Michigan, to Chicago on Saturday, 11 September, for a quick visit with Bill at Navy Pier and returned home late the next day.

Dear Mom, 14 September 1943

Sorry I didn't write last night. I went to the show.

It was sure swell to have you folks down here. I hope none of you lose too much sleep by it.

It rained yesterday and this morning so I guess Sunday's rain just couldn't be helped. It's clear now, and it looks like tomorrow will be a good liberty night. I think all danger of it warming up to "whites weather" is past.

I have written Dad about your visit, about Uncle Pete kissing you at the station and about buying the mop at Fields.[30] So you can expect some kidding when you hear from him.

I got a letter from Jane last night. Among other things she mentioned that Ed LaValle was married—to Betty Stordahl, the secretary of the camera club the year I was Pres. They were married in Chicago this weekend.

I have some washing to do so I'll have to close. Cold much better.

Bill

Dear Mom, 17 September 1943

Today we had our test in recognition. We had 20 American planes to give name, number and wingspan. I got all three counts on all 20. We also had a test in Range estimation. It seemed very easy and I was the first one finished so I guess I don't need to worry about its outcome. . . .

I was officially notified yesterday that I had passed those gunnery screening tests I told you about a few weeks ago. So far so good.

Monday we start target practice on the Range. Here's hoping I make good.

Yours truly, Bill

Dear Mom, 26 September 1943

I was amused at your last letter, by the little "sales talk" in which you tried to get me to "avoid the risks" of flying. You needn't worry. The instructor with whom we flew has been detached and transferred to Aviation Cadet training.

Last week and the next three we have one period a day of shooting out on the range. We shoot skeets with a shot gun. The purpose is merely to give us practice leading a moving target, etc. Those who qualify in that, then, are the ones who go on to gunnery school. That would follow this immediately. I don't know how long it lasts as I have heard various statements ranging from four to eight weeks. If the former, I might be home for Christmas, but forget it till the time comes.

The Navy now has an exhibit down by Tribune Tower where the Army Air Corps show was previously. They have an SBD Dauntless, F4F Wildcat, TBF Avenger, F4U Corsair, and SNJ Texan trainer down there.[31] Also, displays of Naval small ordnance, guns such as we've been working with. Tied up in the river is a destroyer escort, I guess built at Manitoac.[32]

The whole affair is a bond selling campaign. The prices of everything are prominently displayed. The TBF Avenger (the torpedo bomber in which I someday hope to be a gunner) costs $150,000. Every time it drops a torpedo it costs $11,000. So you can see why the government is anxious that bonds be sold. I'm glad you folks are buying what you can. Has Ruth given up the idea of a bike if she put those stamps into a bond?

I went out to that football game as scheduled last night. Yes, I wore my peacoat. It was a pretty good game but it seemed to me there wasn't much enthusiasm among the spectators. Half the stand on one side of the field was filled with sailors and we made our share of noise. The home team cheering section also did its bit. But the crowd as a whole didn't get very excited.

On the train going out some of us got talking to a couple sorority girls. An

amusing and distinctly modern twist came out in the conversation. It seems the whole sorority is going to join the Marines when it graduates! How wars have changed!!!
Yours truly, Bill

Dear Mom, 28 September 1943

The box of cookies and taffy came today with the razor and razor blades in it. Thanks for sending all aforementioned items. The jam will be consumed tomorrow night on bread in chow.

Last night I put off some washing to go to the show. It was Sonja Henie in "Wintertime." There was quite a bit of fancy skating in it. Also there was a short released by the War Department to be seen by military and naval personnel only. It was a detailed picture of just what's going on and how we're doing it. Very good.

This week we are in Ignition II, going more into detail on the timing and maintainence of magnetos, care of spark plugs and wiring, etc. It isn't bad. We are kept quite busy in shop so the afternoons pass very rapidly. The instructor, at first appearances, seemed like an utter moron, but turned out not to be at all.

In gunnery on the range I am getting into the swing of it and beginning to do O.K. It's quite enjoyable, too. We shoot skeets (clay targets) with 12 gauge shot guns. It is a rich man's sport in peace time but the Navy spares no expense in trying to make good gunners out of us. I'd certainly like to have the price of the ammunition and targets I used up in an hour.
Yours truly, Bill

Dear Pop, 30 September 1943

Thanks for sending the *New York Times* sections. I was very interested in the round table on postwar organization. Particularly I liked Clarence Streit's part in it.[33] You will remember perhaps that I read his book, *Union Now with Britain* last February while waiting for the Navy to "want me." It seemed to me that of the eight, he was the most straightforward. The rest all seemed to be more or less beating around the bush with a theme of "some form of world police . . . etc."

He, however, made a clear point which I have for some time thought should be so presented. He said that the police force, though necessary, was by no means the only or even the most important feature of the peace organization. I have thought for quite a while that the main trouble with the League of Nations and with most contemporary ideas is that they are meant to *settle* disputes rather than to prevent them. By now we should have learned that the sort of disputes that need settling of this nature cannot be settled except by violence. Therefore, they must be prevented, or to say it differently, settled before they arise.

He also remarked on the word which seems to be the crux of all American postwar thinking: sovereignty. He said that too many of us have been brought up on the belief that our own sovereignty (personal) was dependent on national sovereignty. I think that about adequately expresses Bingay's attitude. Whereas, Streit says, we have not had personal sovereignty. Instead we have had to abandon our way of life in favor of war.

Did you, by the way, read the article about Willkie's growing proximity to candidacy?[34] The article therein mentioned from *Look Magazine* I read in the library at the service center the other night.

I like Willkie's thoughts and policies, but I'm still afraid of what might happen if he and Roosevelt oppose each other again.

This morning we took our first shots with the .30 Cal. machine gun. It is really quite a weapon. We fired 20 rounds, one at a time. That is done by flipping the trigger with the edge of your thumb rather than pressing it firmly.

One fellow had his gun feeding wrong such that one cartridge went off just a hair before the bolt was forward. That split it in the center driving the forward half firmly into the chamber. Then as the bolt came forward on the next round, it brought the cartridge up inside this first one. The gun jammed and he had to hand charge it to extract this freak. The old broken cartridge had not split fore and aft but had stretched enough to fit over the live round.

The cost of our 20 rounds was $2. Normally a .30 Cal. gun fires 20 rounds per second. So, you can see where the taxpayers' money goes.

This noon I got a request from the chaplain to come down and see him after chow. This I did, wondering what I'd done now. When I got there, he asked if my father was a chaplain. I replied yes, but that it was the first I knew he had such a widespread reputation. Then he read me the letter he'd gotten from you. It was, I must say, quite complimentary. Then we just talked about this and that for a while and he gave me a slip to get back into class. I guess he more or less wanted to see what kind of a guy this was who liked the Navy.

Yours truly, Bill

Dear Mom, 11 October 1943

Today we began the subject "Power Plant Trouble Shooting," commonly known as "live engines." As the name implies: it involves work on running engines, or recently run, or to be run engines. This afternoon we spent in learning the proper procedure for correctly starting, revving up, and stopping an engine.

It was quite a thrill to be in control of such vast power. The roar is deafening but exhilerating and the whole pier seemed as if it were throbbing.

I have begun to read the Raymond Gram Swing book that Dad sent me. It's quite interesting, and I think will be increasingly so as I progress into it. Some of the chapters are past broadcasts and I shall probably be familiar with quite a number of them.

It is swell summer weather here now, and I hope it stays so when we get out on the line. I wished yesterday that I could be up around Onekama in the woods with Butch and Spot.

Yours, Bill

Dear Mom, 18 October 1943

It's too bad you folks didn't come down this weekend instead of six weeks ago or whenever it was. Butch could have added one more to his list of conveyances ridden on. The new subway opened Saturday. I rode on it yesterday on the way out to the Jackson Pk. Museum with Stege.[35] It is really a marvelous engineering feat.

We spent the entire afternoon at the museum. They have one exhibit which interested both Stege and me and which again Butch would have enjoyed. It is in an area of about 30 x 60 ft. built up with a model landscape of the Grand Canyon area and with an extensive model railroad system. We stood there quite some time getting a great kick out of watching the tiny trains, proving that nobody ever really grows up.

After that we thumbed back downtown, went to the service center and ate. Then we attended a showing of a Soviet film "We will come back" showing the activities of Russian guerillas. It was very interesting. All the talking of course was Russian but there were English translations across the bottom of the screen.

I am wearing the sweater you knitted me last spring. It is very effective. The V neck is just right such that it doesn't show at all under my dress jumper. And I believe I shall be able to use the wristlets when we get out on the line next week.

Yours truly, Bill

Dear Mom, 8 November 1943

How has your "career in the Navy" seemed to you? Quite pleasant I hope. Most of what you got to see and do at Bainbridge I imagine is almost identical to what I had at Great Lakes. Only of course I was the lowly boot and not the Chaplain's wife. You have been very fortunate in your visit there with Pop to see both what he is doing and what I did.

Yesterday, I went out to the Bears vs. Packers pro football game with Stege. There was standing room only, and little enough of that, but they were still letting servicemen in free. It occurred to me that just outside the gate would have been an ideal spot for a recruiting officer to situate himself.

The game was very good in spite of the rain and mud. The Bears won 21–7 but I think had it been a dry day the story would have been different.

We hitchhiked back down to the loop and ate heartily at the service center. Then we got photographed together, in a joint like Dad and I got our picture taken in. We went to a show in the evening and then I went out to Stege's place with him, as he had to be in earlier than I did.

He was home last week and by a swell coincidence so was the rest of the old gang, or most of it. Lt. Alex Topping was back from bombardier school, Sgt. Frank Slachik, AS [Apprentice Seaman] Bob Mauzy, etc.

M.H.S. beat Ludington while he was there, too.

We have only seven more days "on the line." It's hard to realize so much time has passed since I came here. Two weeks from now I should be in Memphis.[36]

When you come down be prepared to take back some books, the iron, and other miscellaneous stuff. And by the way, don't be disappointed if I don't make a rate. The quota has been cut to 10 percent of all graduating men.

Yours truly, Bill

Dear Mom, 11 November 1943

Today, on the line, our section went into the "black" squadron. That is the one with all the up-to-date planes in it. We worked on a Grumman Wildcat and got to handle some TBF "Avenger" torpedo bombers. It's quite a thrill to work on some of this modern stuff. We were working on 03u's from 1930 approximately.[37]

When we took off the cowling on the Wildcat, I was quite impressed with the engine. Here, instead of an airplane with an engine mounted in it, we had an engine with an airplane mounted behind it. And the Wildcat itself is *becoming* obsolete.

Tomorrow we have our test in blinker signals. I got them perfect in class today at test speed, so I'm not worried.

This afternoon in the hanger I was called into the squadron office, among others, and [was] asked some questions about what I did before enlistment, how I liked aviation, what did I want to do from here on, and would I like to remain at the pier as an instructor in squadron operations. I answered the last, "Not if I can possibly avoid it." The Lieut. put down "no." But I won't feel safe till I see my name on the gunner's draft next Saturday.

It would have been a good deal, this instructor's spot. I would get liberty four out of five nights, overnight (to come home) every other weekend. And I'd be in line for a second-class rate in six months.[38] But nothing other than gunnery will satisfy me.

By the way, reveille at gunner school is at 0645 instead of 0600 as it is here.

Yours truly, Bill

P.S. Have you written for your hotel reservation?

One week later Bill's mother, sister, and brother arrived in Chicago for his graduation ceremony, which took place on 19 November. Bill placed 7 in a class of 120. His "maintenance of a fine scholastic record" (as reported in his hometown newspaper) earned him the rating of aviation machinist's mate third class (AMM3c).

Next, he was transferred to Naval Air Technical Training Center, Memphis, Tennessee, for two weeks of instruction in airborne-radar operation. Before leaving Navy Pier, he was examined by a medical officer and found to be physically fit for service as an airman. Following completion of the two-week course in radar, he received another transfer to Naval Air Gunners School, Hollywood, Florida. He boarded a train in Memphis on 5 December and arrived in Hollywood the next day.

CHAPTER 3

Naval Air Gunners School, Hollywood, Florida

Dear Mom, 7 December 1943

There really aren't words to express what this place is like. To begin with, it's summer down here of course. The grass is beautifully green, the sky is blue, and the sun is hot.

We got here just in time for chow last night. Then we mustered and were assigned to rooms. Yes, rooms!! There are four men to a room. Each room has a private bath. We have spacious lockers, a table and chairs in our rooms besides two double deck bunks.

It used to be a boys' military academy, this place.[1] Thus, it is quite luxurious. They have an excellent canteen, tailor shop, barber shop, soda fountain, etc. Those, the post office, the mess hall, officers' quarters, and the offices are all right in this building. There are only a few hundred men here altogether.

We are about two miles from the town of Hollywood, which in turn is on the ocean. Buses took us over to the beach this afternoon and we had a good swim. It was calm, almost like Crystal Lake. The temperature was perfect. The extra buoyancy of the salt water is fun but the taste is putrid. You can't help getting a little in your mouth and then your instinct is to wash it out!!

While we were at the beach there were squadrons of TBF's flying over. They were practicing diving runs. In about six weeks I'll be up there if all goes well. This first week we are on work details (only part time, and not KP this time). Then we have two weeks of school, followed by three weeks on the range. After that we go directly to squadron operations, which will be about 60 days. Then we either go to our embarkation point by delayed orders, giving us a chance to go home in the meantime, or a definite leave. So it'll be about 3½ months yet before I get home again. But it's going to be a very pleasant 3½ months.

The uniform here on the station is dungaree pants and skivvy shirts. Very comfortable. Uniform for liberty is optional. It's plenty warm enough for whites in the day time but it does cool down a bit in the evening.

It's hard to believe it's December 7th. It's quite different from last December 7th or the one before—not only in the weather but in the situation I find myself in and in the whole world situation. Who'd have thought two years ago I'd be here now? And who'd have thought a year ago that Berlin would be half destroyed?[2]

I'll close now as it's almost time for chow.

Yours truly, Bill

P.S. I have a brush cut again. It's practically a necessity in this climate. They have an enlisted barber here and he really trimmed it so that I think even you would admit it looks O.K.

Dear Mom, 12 December 1943

Yesterday we went swimming again. The wind was off shore so the ocean was quite smooth, and warm as usual. We had to swim 80 yards backstroke before our free swim. I made it O.K., even though I've never swum backstroke before.

While we were on the beach a TBF flew over on a practice torpedo run, about 20 feet off the water. It was close enough to see the faces of the pilot and gunner. I can hardly wait till I am doing the same.

I went in town last night and saw "Behind the Rising Sun."[3] I hadn't thought from the previews that I was going to like it. It looked too vicious, too hate-inspiring. I can't yet see why we need to hate the enemy to fight him, any more so than we hate the germs of disease that we willingly destroy. But it turned out differently, expressing the need for understanding the Japanese now and after the war.

I went to church this morning. Services are held in the gym. There weren't too many there but I guess attendance was proportional to the population of this base. The chaplain is a young [lieutenant] J.G.; used to be a Presbyterian minister in Pennsylvania and New Jersey. He has a very good voice and is quite interesting.

Starting tomorrow, our first day of school, we are in a section-squadron organization instead of battalion. I am a section leader on account of my crow.[4] I don't care for the responsibility but it gets me out of standing guard and it gives me liberty every night till 2200.

That doesn't start till tomorrow, though, so I do have another midnight-to-four watch tonight.

I have a pair of blues drying in the sun. Guess I'll go bring them in and then get some sleep.
Yours truly, Bill

Dear Pop, 24 December 1943

Your book has not yet arrived but I did get a package from home which Mom says contains pictures. I'm saving it to open tomorrow just for the sake of Christmas atmosphere. The fountain pen came tonight. It's hard to get used to the feel of it but I like the much thinner line it produces.

Thanks for sending the clipping of Sir Stafford Cripps![5] I read it before reading the letter and immediately got the connection. I like the sermonette on the back of your Christmas Sunday program. I wrote somewhat the same thing in a letter to Mr. Swing last week. I was telling him of my appreciation of "Preview of History," especially the broadcast of last Christmas eve, wherein he defined war as "the breakdown of peace." I told how I'd found myself standing guard under the palm trees humming to myself "I'm dreaming of a White Christmas." I said that meant not less but more this year, etc.

Incidentally that definition of war as the breakdown of peace illustrates what Sir Stafford and I mean. Rather than considering peace as "not being at war" you should consider war as "not being at peace." Peace is the positive goal to be attained for its own sake; war is the evil we lapse into through weak efforts toward peace.

I applied earlier this week for two days leave this weekend to go to Gainesville. No could do, though, so I guess I'll spend Christmas here. We are to have no reveille tomorrow. I wonder how late I shall sleep! Remember at home how we used to be up early on Christmas, we kids all impatient to get down to the tree. It's quite different this year.

I've heard and read a lot of sympathy for the servicemen recently about how poor a Christmas we will have. But I think it's the other way around. I think Mom will have a harder time of it than either you or I will. I'm glad there are Ruth and Butch to make it Christmasy for her.

However, I think it was just that idea of a Christmas "for the children" that has always obscured the real meaning of Christmas for me in the past. This year it's not a matter of Santa Claus, snow, family dinners, etc., all of which are very much worthwhile, but it's more a matter of working towards the goal of "Peace on Earth." I feel as though I had a part in the effort towards that goal not only because of being in the Navy but also because of my hopes for the postwar world. . . .
Yours truly, Bill

Dear Mom, 27 December 1943

Thanks very much for the pictures of the family. They turned out very well. Where did you have them taken? It's an especially good one of Butch.

I went down to Miami both Saturday and Sunday. Saw "Bambi" and "Fantasia." Sunday, hitch-hiking back, I was picked up by a car full of "Spars."[6] One asked me right away if I was "in the Coast Guard or are you a sailor?" A little later I happened to use the word "bulkhead" in conversation. One of the girls said, "It's good to hear someone who talks our language!" I was quite amused at that. They were just out of boot camp. Remember how salty I was then? When I got back the boys all asked if I'd gotten their addresses and couldn't understand why I hadn't.[7]

We started at the range today. It's quite enjoyable. About the middle of the morning we stripped to the waist and soaked up Vitamin D all day.

Yours truly, Bill

Dear Mom, 3 January 1944

After chow yesterday noon (steak, incidentally) I caught the 1300 liberty bus in town. Set out from there via thumb for Pompano. The first car that picked me up contained a family whose son will be 17 in March and is enlisting in the Navy. So they asked me how I liked it and would I do the same thing again, etc. I said I certainly would. He, it seems, has had his mind made up since last spring and has had to wait like I did to become old enough.

Then I got a ride in an oil truck to Pompano. From there a couple of Army officers gave me a lift over to the beach. Then I walked to the Barnes' Cottage from the corner.

I had a swell time there. They were glad to see me, I guess, and we sat around and talked for a while. Then I played some shuffleboard with Kay. A little later Lt. Bill Snorbach and his wife, from a nearby Army air base came and we all went to supper.[8] After supper, we sat and talked some more. I read a couple copies of the *News Advocate*, one of which had PFC Norval James' address.[9] Then Bill and I struck up an argument as to whether the Army or the Navy had better planes! All the others were interested but mystified spectators as we talked in terms of piston displacement, octane, airfoils, etc.

I left there about 10. Bill drove me over to the highway. I soon caught a ride from there all the way to Hollywood. Quite a pleasant day, all in all.

This morning we had to go to the Naval Air Station, Miami,[10] for "Low pressure chamber indoctrination." They put us in a big air tight tank and by exhausting the air from it they simulated changes in altitude. First we went up to 18,000 feet. We sat there for 15 minutes. Then we put on oxygen masks and went on up to 30,000 ft. We spent another 15 minutes there. Then we started to descend. All the way down we had to keep "popping" our ears by holding our nose and mouth and blowing hard. Got all the way down without mishap. It was quite an experience.

This afternoon we fired .50 Cal. guns. Boy, what a sensation. The old 30's went dadadadada! These went BUB-BUB; BUB-BUB; BUB-BUB!

They seem so huge and their voice speaks with undefiable authority.

There were some officers (blimp pilots) out there shooting the same guns after us. They didn't do nearly so well, but it was the first time they'd been out there. We were talking to them afterwards. I don't think anybody saluted all afternoon. And nobody said "sir." We all just talked as one of the gang. They asked us about gunnery and we asked them about flying.

After school we had to go swimming. It was raining and the air was cold but the water was swell.

I got a book from Pop tonight as a Christmas present. *The American* by James Truslow Adams. I hope I can finish it before we can leave here. It's pretty big to put in my sea bag.

Yours truly, Bill

Dear Mom, 11 January 1944

Sunday, I got a letter from Arnold Flynn, that Alpena guy I used to go out on liberty with in Chicago. He is stationed at Miami N.A.S. So I hitchhiked down there to see him. I had excellent luck, getting a ride all the way down on a Navy truck. It took a couple hours to find him after I got there. But we finally got together and went into town.

Coming back, I got a ride out to the edge of town right away. After thumbing two cars unsuccessfully I saw a jeep coming. Figuring it might be SP's [shore patrol] I didn't thumb it. But it stopped anyway. The occupant turned out to be a mere soldier on his way somewhere under orders. He gave me and a marine a lift all the way into Hollywood. I thought all the way along what a kick Butch would get out of such a ride.

Last night I went to the show here on the base. It was "Gung Ho" with Randolph Scott, the story of Carlson's raiders (U.S.M.C.) on Makin Island.[11] Again, I was very amused at the assortment of U.S. planes used by the Japs in the movie. They made one raid with a squadron of TBF's!

I got a letter today again from Lt. Hook Topping telling all his adventures since he left Manistee. He also mentioned a couple other guys of the old gang. Ace Gutowski was wounded (he doesn't say how badly) in the landing on the Gilbert Islands. He also gave me Frank Slachik's address.[12]

He says they are having snow and bad weather there. He said, "Ever hear the song, 'Beautiful, Beautiful Texas'? Well don't believe it!"

Also, I got a Christmas card from Mrs. Von Hagen at Montrose.[13] It had been sent to the Pier, forwarded to Memphis, and thence to Hollywood.

Yours truly, Bill

Dear Pop, 12 January 1944

That certainly must have been a dull Christmas for Uncle Bruce's family.[14] It kind of makes this business of us servicemen away from home pale beside it.

It's interesting to hear Bill Bruce's plans.[15] What does his mother think of his idea for submarine duty if he doesn't make V-12? Remember how I used to kid Mom about sub service before I enlisted! . . .

This morning we had an A.C.I. [Army Council Instructions] lecture on the Pacific area. 60% of our TBF's go there. I hope I'm in the 40% till it's over in Europe. The lecture was quite interesting. It concerned the geography, history and general strategy of the Pacific war. Then we had a lecture on Geopolitics. I should like to take a course in that after the war.

I don't know what the connection was between all this and gunnery, but I think it's a good idea for all servicemen to be exposed to it. I was quite surprised at the number of men in my section besides myself who expressed their interest in the lectures. One or two, of course, said they could hardly keep awake.

As to your next duty, how much "applying" can you do, and for what would you apply? According to what they told us this morning about the number of carriers in our fleet, you'd stand a good chance of getting one if you applied for it. By the same token our chances of being on the same one are slim.[16]

Yours truly, Bill

Bill satisfactorily completed the ground course in naval air gunnery and was designated a naval air gunner. On 15 January he was transferred to US Naval Air Station, Miami, to train as an airman.

Dear Mom, 25 January 1944

I haven't been up again since that flight last week but I'm going to try to get another hop tomorrow. One guy here has got nine hours in already, just since we came here. He spends most of his time down by the flight board asking for rides. Maybe I should!!

We had a B-25 on the field overnight.[17] When it took off today I couldn't help wondering how they ever got them off a mere carrier deck to raid Tokyo.[18] That B-24 also left here. We get to see quite a number of different types of planes what with this Navy base and the Army field farther north.

I got a letter from Pop in which he says as a tail gunner I'll be a "typical reactionary, trusting to fate as to where I'm going and concerned more with where I've been." Which reminds me I got a letter from Col. McCormick "thanking" me for a letter I wrote him a few weeks ago. . . .

It looks now as though I'll be home *about* Easter time, almost a year from the last time I was there.

Yours truly, Bill

Dear Pop, 27 January 1944

Pardon the postcard again but I haven't gotten around to buying any stationery yet.

We went up again this evening for another hour and a half. There were clouds over the whole sky between two and three thousand feet. Coming out above them was a wonderful sensation. They looked like the ice on Lake Michigan at Manistee but stretching endlessly into space. We did a few of those gunnery dives, on two of which I partially blacked out.

When we got back I again had that cramped feeling on the ground of being unable to see enough of the world at once.

Bill

Dear Mom, 30 January 1944

. . . We are in barracks here but they are small, only a couple dozen bunks to each one. VSB-5 means as follows: V is the Navy designation for heavier-than-air-craft. SB is for scout bomber and 5 is the squadron number.

I got a letter from Frank Slachik (former M.H.S. quarterback) now cpl. in Army Engr. corps. He expects to ship out soon.

Night before last I went up on a night hop, from 9:30 to 11. We just flew in formation over Miami and vicinity. It was certainly beautiful. My pilot told me I should go up some moonlight night if I really wanted to see something beautiful.

We are on night duty now, from 3 P.M. till 11 P.M. So this morning at reveille we did something a service man always longs for: turned over and went back to sleep. . . .

Yours truly, Bill

Dear Mom, 1 February 1944

I got three days' issues of the *News Advocate* today. Thanks for the subscription. The service columns contained several familiar names. Next years' football schedule was given. M.H.S. plays Alpena, so I was kidding Flynn about losing the championship.

Yesterday was my day off, and Flynn's also, so we went into town together. We set out thumbing south, no destination in mind. We got one ride out to the PAA base.[19] That was a very interesting place, teeming with flying boats. Then we went a few miles farther to a swell little bathing beach. It was a county park and it was really beautifully laid out. But we didn't have our trunks with us. We headed east and then back to Miami. In the evening, we saw "Ali Baba and the 40 Thieves."

I saw several photo studios in town I liked better than the one in Hollywood. But it's a little too soon to get shot again. . . .

Tell Butch thanks for his letter. Tell him yes, I still like the Navy. For his benefit, "SBD" means Scout Bomber by Douglas. It is known as the "Dauntless." Dad had a hop in one at Norfolk.

Yours truly, Bill

Dear Pop, 4 February 1944

Your letter about your early flights was very interesting. In some ways, I think you probably had more fun, being in a balloon I mean instead of a plane. As you say there was no noise and you were apparently motionless. However, the view is the same, and the new sense of perspective. Then, too, you didn't make dive-runs on a sleeve target.

I think your idea of transferring the new sense of perspective to other things than geography is quite correct, too. You do see things in their relation to each other, and quite apart from their relation to you.

I doubt if flying can yet have had so much effect on me but something makes me view many things quite differently than most of the other guys around here. For instance, this latest splurge in the news of Jap Atrocity stories. Of course, they were obviously released to have an effect on the war bond drive. But that in itself is a reflection not on the stories but on the American public. In reading I haven't been able to see yet what the atrocities were. The papers speak of "these inhuman actions," etc., but the few examples cited seem to me nothing more than is to be expected. And anyway, what's so new about it all. Haven't these things been going on in China for years? Which brings us back to the idea of perspective again. Instead of thinking anything about the millions of Chinese dead, we get all burned up over a few thousand American lives lost. Not that those lives are insignificant, but by comparison their effect on us should be.

If the publication of atrocity stories will sell war bonds, O.K. But what other effect are they going to have. I hope we shan't stoop to reprisals. Congressmen are speaking in terms of revenge. One said we should "assemble the entire fleet and send it to Japan to blow Tokyo to Hades." Good oratory in an election year but obviously the Admirals know better. If we are determined to win the war the quickest way possible, what more can we do!

The net effect is to inspire hatred for the enemy. This will affect not the war but the peace.

Anyway, what do we expect; what constitutes an atrocity? As far as I can see there's no such thing as a "clean" war. It isn't like a football game. We talk of "rules of war" but that's silly on the face of it. War consists of an infraction of rules, the rules of diplomacy. If a nation decides to throw off the rules, that is the atrocity, not the individual violations thereafter.

Well I guess people are entitled to their own points of view. But I do think mine is based on reason and the majority on emotion.[20]

I have finished *The American* and will return it to you as soon as I get around to it. On the whole, it was quite encouraging. The isolationist attitude of the American seems based on his background, rather than an inborn stupidity. Maybe it can be overcome then.

That other chaplain's son you speak of in the paratroopers deserves a lot of credit in my opinion. I love flying but to step out of that seemingly solid support into nothingness is not my idea of a day's work. However, above the clouds, I did have the screwiest desire to jump onto them and go to sleep in their softness.
Yours truly, Bill

In early February Bill's training in the air abruptly came to an end. His official record indicates that he received a medical examination on 17 January and was found by the medical officer "to be NOT physically qualified for duty involving work as Aircrewman" owing to a diagnosis of tachycardia (faster-than-normal heartrate). The official record also states that on 19 January he was dropped from the training program by direction of the commanding officer. Yet Bill was not informed of the disqualification until he was reassigned to an aircraft ground crew three weeks later.[21]

His disqualification as an aircrewman came as a shock and disappointment to Bill, but it had a silver lining: he received a twelve-day leave. Characteristically, he focused on the good news and hid his disappointment when he wrote to his mom of what had transpired.

Dear Mom, 8 February 1944

Things sure do happen fast in the Navy. As of Feb. 9, 1944, I am transferred to Casu 21 (Carrier Aircraft Service Unit), NAS, Norfolk, Va. I am traveling under delayed orders (ten days) and two days travel time. So I'll be home about Friday or Saturday.

I plan to come back (to Norfolk) by way of Ann Arbor, Washington, [and] Bainbridge.

They tell me over at the personnel office that this should mean sea duty, before many more months. I hope so, but I'll believe it only when I actually carry my gear aboard.

Don't tell Butch or Ruth I'm coming. It'll be fun to surprise them. I only wrote you to be sure somebody'd be there when I arrive.

Luckily, I've been spending moderately down here, and have the dough to cover the trip. Some of the guys would be out of luck if they had so far to go.

See you soon.

Bill

Bill's sudden return home was not the only surprise for the family. Robert Catton managed to get leave and come home at the same time. After a restful four days in Michigan, Bill rode the train with his father to Washington, DC, for a short visit with Uncle Bruce, Aunt Hazel, cousin Bill, and Grandma Catton. He passed the weekend with his father and grandmother at his father's base in northern Maryland, then made his way by train and ferryboat to Norfolk, Virginia.

CHAPTER 4

Naval Air Station, Norfolk, Virginia

Dear Mom, 22 February 1944

One year ago tomorrow I was sworn in. It's been a short year, yet a very full one.

Dad and I and Grandma spent the day last Friday being chauffeured around Washington by Bill Bruce, who had skipped school to do it. It was quite an interesting day and I think I probably saw as much as the class of '42 did. We visited Congress in the afternoon and I was quite disgusted with what I saw. Dad can tell you about that.

Dad went on up to Bainbridge that afternoon. I stayed over and went up Saturday afternoon with Grandma. Saturday morning Grandma, Aunt Hazel, and I went through the Supreme Court building on a guided tour. The guide was a colored fellow[1] who seemed to know as much about the building as I would know about Manistee High School. It was very interesting.

Dad met us at the station that afternoon and took us out to the base. We went up to the Ad[ministration] building and met the senior Chaplain. Then his yeoman took me down to the ships company barracks to his bunk, where I slept that night. Meanwhile Dad and Grandma went out to the "village" where he got her a room.

We had supper in the cafeteria and went to the show that night. It was amusing riding around on the bus with Dad. All the boots would stare amazed at me, as much as to say, "Who is this guy who talks thusly to an officer?"

Sunday morning, we all met at the cafeteria and had breakfast. Then we went down to the gate to meet Aunt Ione.[2] When she got there who should be with her but Uncle Tubby! So we all went to church together. I had to leave right after church to catch my train.

I got to Newport News about 10 P.M. and came across the bay on the ferry. It was the first time in my year in the Navy that I'd been on a ship of any kind. It was kind of amusing to think of that as we came across.

I got here and got quarters about midnight. Yesterday morning I went up to the personnel office and checked in. I got a typhoid and a tetanus refresher shot at sick bay. In the afternoon six of us went in town on a truck to get our sea bags. I got all my gear into my locker last night and did all my washing this morning.

I went to the show last night. It was Orson Welles in "Jane Eyre." A typically Orson Welles picture and quite interesting.

I start work tomorrow in the engineering shop of a fighter outfit. So I guess I'll not be able to get any hops.

I don't know how long it will be before we go to sea. Too long, I'm afraid. I think Pop will be out there before I will.

From what I saw of Norfolk Sunday night and yesterday afternoon I think I'll spend most of my liberties on the base. They have a swell ships service dept. here and a beautiful theater. But the base is too big for comfort. I've gotten used to a little place like Hollywood and Miami.

The F.P.O. [Fleet Post Office] address doesn't mean I shall move soon. It is just an address to cover this unit wherever it is.

Yours truly, Bill

P.S. I had a letter from Topping. He says Dick Mitchell's ship had a run in with a sub. Mitch got a shrapnel wound in the hand and may get an M.D. [medical discharge].

On 23 February Bill began duty as an airplane mechanic, working on fighter aircraft at Norfolk Naval Air Station. For the next five months, he would work on planes there and at nearby Fentress Field while awaiting assignment to an aircraft carrier. Though he smarted over the navy's decision to disqualify him from serving in an aircrew, he would not let it get him down.

Dear Mom, 23 February 1944

Just a year ago tonight I was sworn in. A lot of water has passed under the bridge since then. I have been at six different bases, hit ten new states plus Washington D.C., had two leaves, advanced three pay grades, learned a trade, flown, and in all thoroughly enjoyed myself. Due to my age, had I been of a different temperament, I might have had a year of college instead, which some of my revered relatives suggested would do me more good. But looking back I'm glad it was a year in the Navy instead. Thanks for permitting it. . . .

I'm beginning to get used to the base and like it fairly well. The chow is good, the quarters are excellent, and I've already run across five guys I know. . . .
Yours truly, Bill

Dear Mom, 5 March 1944

I got a letter from Pop yesterday telling about his ship. He says he will be going back to Newport for a while. I wonder how familiar the place will seem to him. It should be a lot of fun for him, like going back to Oberlin or Benzonia. He must feel a lot younger again, reliving old experiences. I wonder if I'll be at Navy Pier or Miami or some such place 25 years from now.

I went over to the canteen tonight for some ice cream. There I met one of the fellows who was in our line at Miami. He got here last Wednesday. He wasn't so fortunate as I and didn't get a leave. I guess Dad and I really had phenomenal luck. The rest of the boys have started operations—two weeks ago, I guess.

I still wish I were a gunner but all things considered maybe it's just as well. They have almost a surplus of gunners now from the looks of things and I'd only have gotten into action as a replacement anyway. And I may do that yet. I have a hunch I'll at least handle a deck gun before it's over.

The show tonight was one of the best I've seen in some time. It was "The Sullivans," the story of the five brothers who enlisted, fought, and died together.[3] It was very well done and very inspiring. Be sure to see it.

Dick Mitchell's address was in the *News Advocate;* he is at the Naval Hospital, Long Island. I guess I'll close now and write him.
Yours truly, Bill

Dear Mom, 7 March 1944

I had the day off again today. It was a dreary day so I didn't want to hitchhike anywhere and I didn't want just to go into Norfolk. So I went over to N.O.B. [naval operating base] to the piers and saw some of the Navy.

There wasn't any big stuff in, but there was more than I'd seen before anyway. I saw a "baby flat-top" that hardly seemed as big as the *Wolverine* or the *Sable.*[4] It had TBF's and F4F's on it. There was a queer looking ship close by, with an industrial air about it which I judged to be some kind of a fleet tender, perhaps like what Dad is assigned to.[5]

In the next dock were a small training ship and some destroyers. They were interesting to see. They were loading crates of fruits and vegetables aboard, and the crews were having a field day.

Beyond them were some DE's [destroyer escorts], mounting numerous antiaircraft guns, and a French ship of about the size and description of a Corvette. Also, I saw a mine layer, minesweeper, and tanker, plus some sort of large landing craft.

It was quite an interesting morning. At noon it began to rain, so I spent the afternoon in the library. I've been reading H. G. Wells' *Outline of History.*[6] I'm just past Caesar. I also went through a book of Gluyas Williams cartoons.[7]

What did Butch & Ruth think when Dad came home the second time?

Yours truly, Bill

Dear Mom, 15 March 1944

Your box of cookies, cakes, and candy came today. It all tasted very good, especially the cookies. Thank you very much.

There have been a lot of rumors on the local grapevine about various drafts going various places at various times with various numbers of third class mechanics wanted.[8] But so far nothing has materialized. Should a draft come in, I think my chances of getting on it are good. There are only one or two 3/c's ahead of me in our shop and they're not anxious to go to sea. One has already had a year of sea duty. So far, though, we've had no news but scuttlebutt.

Yesterday I was called up to the personnel office to hash out this allotment business. It seems I had listed you as Mrs. W. R., whereas I should have called you Mrs. Helen W. So I changed my application. In doing that I asked the yeoman if you'd get two checks or one. I mentioned the new address. He said you'd probably get two checks. Then I put in two requests: one to cancel the old allotment of $20, and one to start an allotment of $44. So beginning the end of April you should get one check for $44 at 404 S. Oakland. I'm glad to have gotten it straightened out.[9]

I wrapped up my Navy Pier notebook and three "pocket" books I'm through with but would like to save, tonight, and will mail them tomorrow. You might keep the Navy Pier notebook with your scrapbook on my "career."

Thank Butch for me for his letter. That was a cute poem he enclosed. I'll try to get around to write him soon.

I am up as far as the U.S. Civil War now in H.G. Wells' *Outline of History.* His account of that conflict is very interesting, being written by a non-partisan. He has a very great respect for Mr. Lincoln.

Today was my day off again. I spent both morning and afternoon reading. I have suddenly developed the ambition to get an education on my own hook. There are dozens of books in the library I want to read. I hope the desire lasts. It's a good idea.

Do you remember Harry Sheridan in Manistee? He went into the army about two months after I enlisted and within nine weeks he was in Australia. Now he is home with a medical discharge.

Well I've got to do some washing so I'll sign off.

Yours truly, Bill

Dear Mom, 25 March 1944

Your box of cookies came today. They are very good; I still have some in my locker which I shall eat before going to bed. Thanks a lot for them. Who made which ones? What kind of fruit was in that one kind besides raisins?

I went to the show tonight. There was a one reel "travel talk" short subject about Colorado. It showed the Garden of the Gods, the Royal Gorge, the palisades. I could have picked much better scenes: Red Mountain, Box Canyon, Black Canyon, Grand Mesa, etc.

Dad wrote that his ship will be commissioned on April first. He expects to be in here at Norfolk about the 15th. That's only three weeks, so it's quite likely I may still be here then. I hope not, though. I should like to ship out before he does.

I heard from Dick Mitchell today. He wanted me to meet him half way at Philadelphia and spend a liberty with him and Kurt Illig. I wrote to him that I'd like to, but it was too far, and out of the question. His survey becomes effective in about a month.

You're right that Harry Sheridan did usher in church at Manistee. Also, he's the one who owned that big old '27 Buick he called "Nellie." So far as I know all the guys who ushered when I did are now in service. Norval James, Johnny Peterson, Dewey Bucher. Sheridan is in and back out, Mitchell is in now and will soon be back out. And I believe I heard somewhere that Bill Nungessor is in the Army.

One of the guys in our shop with whom I've been working, and who's eaten with me frequently, left today for Atlantic City. He has been here three weeks longer than I have. However, he is second class. No 3rd class have yet left VF Engr.

Did I write you that I'd been all signed up for a hop to Washington on my day off Thursday, and weather canceled it? I think I'll get an out-of-bounds pass and go up by train next Friday, hoping Dad can be there too. I wrote him tonight.

Dad was telling about Uncle Bruce's visit to Newport. He said he found himself thinking of Uncle Bruce as me, because he identified us both as 17-year-old sailors. I found myself trying to think of Butch and me in a similar relationship years hence. But I thought of Butch as a "little" brother. Then I realized that Uncle Bruce was a "little" brother to Dad. It's funny how till you grow up you regard all

grown-ups as equivalent [to each other], just because they're on the other side of a line between childhood and adulthood.
Yours truly, Bill

Dear Mom, 26 March 1944

There's one respect in which I definitely can't complain about this place: the chow. Ruth would have enjoyed our dinner this noon. I had a great big chunk of chicken. They don't try to carve the meat off but just break the chicken up into good sized portions, which you devour in the most convenient manner. For dessert, we had lemon pie.[10]

I worked all morning this morning. A squadron of Wildcats was in to have a certain change incorporated in their engines. To perform the operation the cowl rings and all the exhaust stacks have to be removed first. That's what I was doing on one of the planes. This is about the fourth or fifth squadron that's gone through our shop for that change. It looks like we're going to alter the whole Navy Air Force.

In chow line tonight I was talking to a TBF gunner. I happened to mention how I'd bunged up my thumbnail in a gun down at Hollywood. He showed me one of his fingers which had the whole tip missing. He'd been clearing a jam in the air and the bolt slammed forward, removing his fingertip and jamming on it. So then he had to start all over again, this time not to get a shell out but a piece of himself.

It's been beautiful and sunny here the last three days. The whole day today reminded me of Miami.

I sent that picture of Dad and me by the train to Aunt Nellie. The one of Butch & Dad is good. Was it taken on Dad's "second leave"?
Bill

Dear Mom, 29 March 1944

Yesterday three issues of the *News Advocate* showed up at once. I read through them one at a time in order. There were various items of interest in the Service columns and "Locals," but nothing important. However, in the third one was a little article which I almost didn't read. It said, "Among those entering the Naval Training Station at Great Lakes this week were eight new recruits from Manistee County," and proceeded forthwith to list them. The first seven were from other towns in the county. Number 8, however, was Warren Thomas Stege.

So apparently he's out of V-12. How come I don't know. I haven't heard from him since I got here. I wrote him yesterday, just: U.S.N.T.S., Great Lakes, Ill.

It would be rather awkward going through boots after eight months in the Navy, three liberties a week, a couple week long leaves, etc. But on the other hand, it might be fun. He's already had his shots. The drilling, saluting, standing watch, and all that is already familiar to him. I'm rather anxious to hear from him. . . .

I saw about eight or ten Pullmans being pulled onto a siding here this evening. Somebody apparently is going somewhere. Wherever it is I'd like to go along. I've now been here darn near as long as I was at Hollywood. It's time I was seeing new places. . . .

I saw an interesting show the other night. It was called "The Hour Before Dawn," a story by W. Somerset Maugham. The main character in it was a conscientious objector, an English Farmer. It was a good presentation of the mental conflict in a man's mind trying to reconcile himself to the necessity of killing in war. . . .
Yours truly, Bill

Dear Mom, 2 April 1944

I saw a show tonight which I would recommend you seeing when you get a chance. I think you will especially enjoy it, having visited Bainbridge. It is "The Navy Way" photographed at Great Lakes. There were a good many familiar scenes. The receiving station, the clothing issue room, several shots on the drill field at Green Bay. I spotted the drill hall, the canteen, our old barracks, etc. The Ross Auditorium was shown, where I attended church in O.G.U. [outgoing unit]. And there was an interior shot of our O.G.U. barracks, showing the same old coxswain calling off the drafts.

It ended with a draft marching down the road and out the main gate, singing lustily "Anchors Aweigh." Well do I remember a similar scene. May 27, 1943, Navy Pier bound.

I had quite a time on my day off in Washington. Washington is certainly a beautiful city after Norfolk. I got out to Uncle Bruce's house just in time for breakfast, pancakes. After Bill and I came back from driving Uncle Bruce downtown, Dad called up from the station and shortly thereafter he came out to the house. We spent the morning together. At noon Aunt Hazel had to go to a blood donor, so Dad and I went downtown and had lunch. I asked Aunt Hazel what type of blood she had. She didn't know. Dad said, without thinking, "Well, isn't it on your dogtag?" (Needless to say, it wasn't.)

Dad came part way back with me, for the ride, and to visit the town of Fredericksburg. Afterwards I talked to another sailor on the train, formerly of Bainbridge, who recognized Dad. He hadn't spoken to him, as he said Dad probably wouldn't remember him.

I had written Dad previously of my doubts as to the advisability of you and the kids visiting us in such a place as Norfolk. But he says there is an excellent hotel, just across in Portsmouth, reserved for families visiting Navy personnel. So if I don't ship out I'll look forward to seeing you folks about the end of the month.

Dad said he'd told Butch he might be able to take him aboard his ship. He said it would be worth the price of a trip down here just to see the expression on Butch's face at such an adventure. I agree.

Tomorrow is pay day. I'm on the list for the usual 25 bucks. So I don't think my new allotment has gone through yet. It may get through before the end of the month and I'll draw one dollar next payday. Did you get the check for March O.K., the usual $20?

Yours truly, Bill

Dear Mom, 4 April 1944

I had a chance last night to get a transfer away from Norfolk—and turned it down. They asked for a volunteer 3rd or 2nd class mechanic to transfer to CASU [Carrier Aircraft Service Unit] 27, somewhere in Rhode Island. I was tempted to take it, not only to get out of Norfolk, but just because I'd like to move on general principles. Six weeks is long enough to stay in one place.

Two things made me pass by it though. First, it would probably mean a delay in getting to sea. I'd have to start in waiting my turn all over again. And second, if I'm not going to sea within the next few weeks I'd like to be here when you folks come down to visit Dad.

Today about five of us had to go over to a part of the base called "the graveyard." We were detailed to find a wrecked FM-2 and remove the cowl ring, to be used on another plane.[11] A truck took us over and drove all around the lot looking for such a plane with an undamaged ring. It took us about an hour and a half to find it and about fifteen or twenty minutes to remove the part we wanted.

During the search, we saw a lot of interesting aircraft "corpses." Also, I got oriented a bit better with the geography of the base. I think I vaguely recognized the area that constituted the entire Air Station shown in that picture of 1919 with Dad in it. Saw two big flying boats (Martin Mariners) come in and another take off. They are very graceful with all their 115 feet of wingspan.

Yesterday noon I mailed that photograph of Dad and me on to Grandmother. At the same time, I mailed Butch a small package of gum. He will probably have gotten it by the time you receive this letter.

Saw the technicolor movie "Cover Girl" last night. It was pretty good. There was some excellent photography in it, especially in one scene where the male lead did a dance with his own ghost. The timing of the two parts was perfect.

Here's the latest GI gag: Angry father: What's the idea of bringing my daughter in at this hour of the morning? Sailor: I have to muster at 7.
Yours truly, Bill

Dear Mom, 10 April 1944

I guess yesterday is the first Easter I didn't go to church. In our outfit here any one man can only go to church once every eight weeks. That's because we have every eighth day off, so that the day off falls on Sunday every seventh time. What kind of a day was it in Benzonia? It was warm, clear, and bright here, but there were no Easter bonnets!

Saturday I went up to the flight office about 0700 and waited till 1030 without getting a hop. It was perfect flying weather, but there just wasn't anything scheduled to Washington. So I went to the waterfront to find out if the U.S.S. *Oahu* had come in yet.[12] It hadn't. But I rather enjoyed inquiring. One of the places I asked was on the quarter deck of a three-star (vice admiral) flagship. They asked to see my I.D. card before they'd tell me. Dad is now a military secret. I now have 3½ minutes of sea duty.

I also saw quite a few other interesting ships. A baby flattop was in, also a big first line British carrier. It was a beauty. There was a squadron of destroyers in, plus several auxiliary vessels and a British corvette. A gang of English sailors on the dock were playing rugger football [rugby].

In the evening, I met a couple of Canadian sailors, one from Vancouver and one from Montreal. They were going on liberty and were trying to exchange some Canadian money. So far, they'd gotten $1.30 together. They asked me where they could go and have a good time for a buck thirty. I told them there was no place in Norfolk, that the best place was the fleet recreation park just outside the gate.

I hope you had a good time in Benzonia. Where did you have Sunday dinner and what did you eat? We had very generous helpings of turkey, potatoes, bread, butter, cranberry sauce, celery, olives, salad, peas, apple and raisin pie. Quite filling. Did Butch get to play with Spot? How is he?

Work has been pretty slack here the last few days. The liberty sections secured at 1100 yesterday. And there is only one plane in the hangar now.

I got a letter from Gillespie at Miami. They graduate this week. He will get fifteen days' leave. He says he had a thrill the other day on a glide bombing hop. They pulled out just five feet above the water. They were so low that their propeller blast kicked up a wave which swamped the patrol craft that was acting as target. Nobody was hurt, but his pilot, a big husky football player, was pulling on the stick with all he had down to bring the plane out of the dive. The pilot said that it was the first time in all his flying he'd ever been scared.

Gillespie always used to be broke when I was there, and borrowed money from me. Recently he won enough at a poker game to send his girl a present, send his mother some money, and buy himself a pair of tailor-made dress blues. Also, he is drawing some 150 bucks pay before going home.

Dad wrote that he'd sent for my camera. I hope he can get it fixed. It's doing no good in its box at home, and it would be interesting to have some pictures of his travels. He, at least, is soon going to bear out the old slogan, "Join the Navy and see the World."

Yours truly, Bill

Dear Mom, 17 April 1944

Dad pulled in sometime the middle of Saturday afternoon. He came over to our hangar about 4 and found me working on a Hellcat. I got off at 4:30, had chow, took a shower and changed in to my dress blues. I got over to the waterfront shortly after six. He met me on the pier, and we went up to his quarters aboard the ship. He showed me all around the ship and then we went back over to the Air Station to try to call you up. There was a "one to two hour" wait so we cancelled it.

Yesterday, Sunday, I finished work at 4:30 but had to stand by for muster till 6. In the meantime, I ate and got cleaned up and into blues again. After muster, I met Dad up at ship's service and we put in the phone call. While waiting for it to go through, we went over to my barracks, and I got some letters out of my locker to show Dad. They were from Ohio U. & University of Chicago, concerning Armed Services Institute correspondence courses.[13]

Then we went back over and completed the call.[14] Afterwards we returned to the waterfront, watched part of a movie on an open-air screen on the Battleship *Wyoming,* and went back to Dad's ship. Talked a while, and drank a cup of bullion (he lives in luxury) and I came away at 10:30.

I am to meet him at 9 this morning. We both have the day off.

Bill

From Robert Catton to his wife:

My Dearest; 18 April 1944

I shudder to think of the bill that the five of us ran up for you Sunday evening: I trust you think it was worthwhile. I hope you will think it worthwhile to spend the money to visit us down here, also. I think we have been able to fix up pretty good arrangements. But already it is necessary to change the schedule, because of unforeseen delays here. Will you now leave St. Johns Monday, the 1st of May, to arrive here Tuesday, the 2nd? I shall have the rooms at the Chamberlin reserved for the 2nd, and you do all the rest as I said before. Be sure to buy round trip tickets; there is a considerable saving over buying one-way tickets. If you decide to go home by way of Washington, your ticket will still be good from Washington by paying the one way from here to Washington. And there is a convenient overnight boat for that.

Bill and I had much of the day together Monday. First, I did some errands, including buying a gray uniform for myself. Then we visited the docks a bit and found out about boats to Old Point Comfort. Then we went to the Navy Yard in Portsmouth and looked at ships there. We get temporary apartments in a rather nice housing project, that would just about have room enough for us. They are housekeeping apartments and we can get our own meals, or eat at the Officers' Club at the Navy Yard. Probably we would eat out a good bit, but bring your ration books. Bill can visit us three evenings out of four, which is all I can do myself. He will have one day entirely free while you are here, and two if you stay that long. We thought that he and you three could take a trip to Williamsburg that day, and I will go if I can have that free also. I shall try to have one day entirely free while you are here. He and I rode about through a different and nicer part of Norfolk, after visiting Portsmouth, and then came back to the Air Station, had supper and went to a movie together in the evening. It was a very nice day we had, or at least I thought so. He very much enjoyed planning for your visit etc.

My thought is for you to come directly to the Chamberlin when you first come. That is the most convenient, and it is such a nice place to be that I want you to have at least a little time there. Then if that is not entirely satisfactory for your whole stay, we can get one of those apartments for the rest of it. Both accommodations are nominally priced, and you need not worry about expenses, and can stay as long as you like. It is lovely spring weather down here, with lilacs and other things blooming in people's yards, grass green, leaves out on the trees etc. I think you will enjoy it.

I suggest you arrange to check the largest and heaviest of your baggage. By the route you are coming there seems to be little or no chance of delay in getting checked baggage through.

Bill seems even taller than when he was home in February. He is quite well, and I guess as satisfied as ever. He has finished all of his studying and assignments for his second-class rating, but has his final examination yet to take. But he will have no trouble getting a good grade on it. He thinks there is much more chance of getting a carrier assignment when he gets a second-class rating. As he watched me pay out money for uniforms and stuff he said he thought it better to be an enlisted man. But I think there is a great advantage in being an officer.

I suppose he has told you he increased the allotment and wants more bonds bought. You should get the first check of an increased amount on the first of May. This morning I made an allotment for a bond, which will have your name and Ruth's on for safety (but which is to be for our future savings as a family) and the first of those should come in June or July. I have also made a small cash allotment for Mother.

There will be lots to talk over when you are here, but don't save it all for then. I think an answer mailed at once upon receiving this would reach me.

All my love, Robert

Dear Mom, 21 April 1944

Last Night I went over to the pier again and went aboard the *Oahu*. Dad and I walked around at the waterfront looking at the ships that had most recently come in. There was a British baby flattop on one side of Pier 7 and a U.S. ditto on the other side. They were nearly identical. Apparently, the British job was a specimen of lend-lease.[15]

Then we went up to the canteen and bought two pints of ice cream, which we later ate in his cabin, together with some fruit cake from the officer's galley. (Pop lives well.) We finished off the evening reading aloud James Thurber and Robert Benchley.

Dad is to meet me at my barracks tonight and we are going into town to eat. We will probably take in a show or something.

This afternoon I went up to the educational office and signed up for a correspondence course in American Government, through the Armed Forces Institute, and Ohio University. The only reason for choosing O.U. is because they were the only good school on the list offering that particular course. The Navy pays half my tuition.

It's hot here today. I worked up a sweat this afternoon, playing ball.

Yours truly, Bill

Dear Mom, 23 April 1944

Friday afternoon Dad called for me at the barracks about 4:30 and we went out together. We rode the bus over to Gate 4, the other side of the seaplane base. From there we went out to Ocean View, and took the ferry over to Old Point Comfort. When we got there, we walked up to the Chamberlin Hotel. Dad inquired to see if we could eat together there. It turned out we couldn't. Then he asked if the situation would be the same when the family is here. It will except that I can visit you in your room.

We went down to the ferry dock and ate in the lunch room there. Then we walked around Fort Monroe, which is a very interesting place. It seemed very quiet and peaceful. Presumably there is more activity in the daytime. There were some destroyers, auxiliaries, and the battlewagon *Wyoming* out in the bay.

We took the ferry back and then went aboard the *Oahu,* first stopping at the Ship's Service for a couple of pints of ice cream. We ate that and Pop wrote a letter for me to mail, while I read an old *Reader's Digest.*

Last night I had the duty again so we won't get together again till you're down here.

The last two days there have been no planes in the hangar so we've had no work to do. I've been reading some. Started a book called, *The History of American Democracy.* Also we pass the time playing volley ball, and another fellow and myself have been playing a lot of checkers. He is an expert at the game and almost seems to have the whole game planned from your very first move. I finally beat him one game today.

It seems a kind of funny way to be spending time with a war going on. But I guess it can't be helped. The nature of this organization makes the work come in in spasms. Thus, in order to have enough men available to take care of all the work when it comes in, at other times there is bound to be an excess.

Yours truly, Bill

Dear Mom, 26 April 1944

It is fortunate for the two Millman boys to get home together.[16] Like Dad and me. Who is the one at West Point? Is his name Bill?

Friday was the day Dad and I went over to the Chamberlin. While we were there we went down to the Cape Charles ferry dock and looked up schedules. There is a ferry leaves for Washington from Old Point Comfort at 7 P.M., every other evening. I could go up with you and come back on the train, except for the fact that my day off doesn't jibe with the "every other day" part of the schedule.

Anyway, I think you should probably stay here as long as Dad's ship is in, even if that keeps the kids out of school two weeks. It will doubtless be quite a while till you see Dad again but the kids can afford to miss school. I can well imagine Butch wanting to stay out as long as possible. Ruth probably isn't so anxious.

When you come, you might bring the old iron and a cord, if you have room for it in your suitcase. Bring it in a box in which I can mail it home if I ship out. I will probably need it here when we go into whites, which will be soon.

See you next week, Bill

At the beginning of May, Helen, Ruth, and Edward rode the train to Hampton, Virginia, and took up residence in the Chamberlin Hotel while Robert's ship remained moored at Norfolk Navy Yard. On 13 May the chaplain was called aboard Oahu *as it prepared to embark for the Pacific theater. On 14 May, Mother's Day, Bill met his mother, sister, and brother in Washington, DC, parted company with them in the evening, and made a late-night trip back to base.*

Dear Mom, 16 May 1944

We got down to the bus depot about 8 o'clock Sunday evening in the taxi. I got right in line for the bus which was a good thing as the line soon extended about two blocks behind me. They ran several special buses for servicemen only. Being such, they didn't stop at every little burg along the way. So whereas the schedule read Arrive Norfolk 5:10 we actually pulled in at 3:45. I got out to the base and checked in at 4:15 and went to bed at 6.

The bus was crowded but I had a seat, way in the back. It was stuffy, but I slept most of the way and didn't mind it. It was swell to be up there for the day and to go to church with all of you on Mother's day.

Dad apparently shoved off Monday instead of Saturday. All that time we were speculating on his being seasick he was still anchored out in Hampton Roads. He came in Sunday evening looking for me. The MAA [master-at-arms] in the mess hall told him I'd gone to Washington. I figured if he were still here he'd come in again Monday evening, but I didn't see him. So I guess he finally did get under way.

This afternoon I got out the iron at 2 o'clock and pressed two pairs of whites. Then another guy used it, and another, and another. It is now almost 8 and it's still going.

I got a letter yesterday from Aunt Ione. She doesn't know yet what I'm doing now. She asked various questions about when I'd go to sea, etc. This morning I polished brass fixtures in the WAVES' mess hall.[17] It was a big help in winning the war!!!

Tomorrow is payday. I haven't seen the pay list yet but according to my figuring I should be drawing 30 bucks. I missed last payday when we went to Williamsburg. Have you bought the first $50 bond yet?

Well, I've got to get some reading done so I'll close.

Yours truly, Bill

Dear Mom, 23 May 1944

Your letter just came telling of your trip home. I'm glad you were able to go on the B & O [Railroad] and I guess you made it O.K. All in all, you must have had an interesting two weeks. Did the kids get to see enough of Washington?

I also got a letter from Grandma Catton today, thanking me for a letter I'd written her about going up to Washington. I told her about waking you folks up and Bill answering the door. Also about Butch's timely remark in the afternoon, "Wouldn't it be simpler to take the car?" I wrote her another letter today enclosing a map, with Portsmouth, Norfolk, N.O.B. [Naval Operating Base], N.A.S. [Naval Air Station], Ocean View, Willoughby, Fort Monroe, etc., all marked on it.

Last night I went to the show here and saw Gary Cooper in "The Story of Doctor Wassell." It was an excellent picture. Makes me feel all the more like a 4-F.[18]

This present life is pretty much a routine, so there's not much to write about. An amusing observation can be made however regarding a comparison between the WAVES and sailors. The sailors all ask, "C'n I have some more, mac?" And the girls all say, "Just half of that!" Sounds like home, doesn't it?

Are the kids thoroughly reinstated in school now? How badly in arears were they on assignments? I read in the *News Advocate* today about the J-Hop in Manistee. Butch will be interested to know that Donna Lee Hornkohl, now a senior, is to lead the grand march.

My text book [for the American Government course] came the other day. I have read the first chapter, which was very interesting. Haven't written any assignments yet, though. I should knock it off and go do that now.
Yours truly, Bill

Dear Mom, 1 June 1944

I hadn't heard anything from Bill Bruce yet when I got your letter. What do you mean he's "*in* the Army"? Has he actually been sworn in yet? It is a raw deal. He definitely comes from a Navy family with Uncle Bruce in it last time and Dad and I now. And Dad and I visiting up there has made him very Navy-conscious. In spite of my raw deals, I guess I've had a lot better luck than him. And all simply because of graduating so young from H.S.

In spite of the humiliation of working the Waves' mess line, it's sometimes kind of fun. Tonight, one wave whom I served looked familiar so I asked her, "Didn't you go through the line once before?" She said, "This is the third day you've asked me that and I'm getting tired of it!"

I explained that I hadn't realized it was the same one I asked each time, and that I was sure there was some other girl who looked just like her who had come through a few minutes before. Shortly after she'd gone and sat down I spotted the other girl. So I caught the angry one's attention and pointed the other character out. They were almost enough alike to be twins. But she didn't like the other girl's looks and considered it an insult and was madder than ever! Women are funny. . . .

I had a letter tonight from Grandmother Willard. She enclosed last Sunday's church program. It had the "World Order Compact" in it.[19] I hope that becomes overwhelmingly the stand of our church as it is a position which needs support.

Have you read of the State Department's latest reports on peace schemes? The newspapers haven't given a very complete account of it, but from what I've read I'm rather disappointed. I still can't see how we can have a World Organization which will be worth anything and still maintain full national sovereignty. I can't see how anything short of an actual world federal government will work. And such a government requires the delegation of a portion of national sovereignty. But if anyone can make it work it is Mr. Roosevelt. I wish the word "sovereignty" had not become so popular and the idea so precious. I've got to have a part in this business. I think it will eventually make a politician of me for better or worse.

There was some very choice scuttlebutt going around last night. Stories were quoted from various sources saying that CASU 21 was being broken up. One guy said some of us would be going to New York. Another rumor had it that the whole outfit was to be moved to California.

I did the only logical thing, but a thing which for some reason is seldom done. I went up to the personnel office and asked the yeoman what was the dope. Absolutely nothing to it, was the answer. But it was a lot of fun imagining!!

Pay day again tomorrow. I draw $15 again. Not much, but I don't spend much. I already have a ticket to Washington. And I have about 50 bucks or so in my money belt as a reserve. Your statement of my financial status sounds good.

According to the *News Advocate,* Stege is in a pre-radio school in Michigan City, Indiana. He is seaman first [class] now.

Yours truly, Bill

Dear Mom, 6 June 1944

I don't know what the dope is but I got off mess cooking today. Tomorrow, several of us are to be transferred to Fentress Field. That's where Pop had church last summer. I don't know what my address will be, but will let you know immediately.

Big news today.[20] I wish I were in it!

Bill

Dear Mom, 7 June 1944

This morning we packed our gear onto a truck plus ourselves and came down to Fentress Field. The ride down through the woods and farm country and swamps reminded me of the ride from the gunnery school out to the range at Hollywood.

The field here reminds me of the VSB-5 field at Miami. There is just one small hangar. We have small wooden barracks. I have a window right at the head of my bunk. There is an electrical outlet for the iron nearby, too.

I still haven't the slightest idea how come the sudden change. But I'm not kicking. All the men relieved from mess cooking were mechanics. Several ordnance men and other rates whose three months were up did not get relieved. As a matter of fact, nobody relieved us. We were just pulled off the list and the mess hall has to get along with a smaller crew.

I am assigned to the night engineering crew. We go to work at midnight and work till whatever time in the morning we finish up. We get two weekends a month. The weekend runs from Saturday morning to midnight Monday. So I'll be able to get up to Washington.

We'll be working on Wildcats, TBF's and SNJ's here. How long we'll be here and what's next I don't know. But this is a part of CASU 21 so I guess all the old dope applies.

Last weekend I got off at 1000 on Saturday and got a ride with one of the mess hall M.A.A.s [master-at-arms] as far as Richmond. There I had to wait about half an hour before getting a ride but finally got a lift all the way to Washington, getting there at 3:30 P.M.

Bill had a date that evening so I spent the evening just visiting with Uncle Bruce and Aunt Hazel. Sunday morning Bill and I went to Church. Spent the afternoon after a very good dinner visiting again and in the evening Bill drove me over to catch my bus.

I got to the bus depot at 8 o'clock to catch a 9 o'clock bus. But with [the] bus company inefficient at its highest I didn't get out of there till a quarter of eleven. I really thought for the first time in my Naval career I was going to be over leave. But we got into Norfolk at 5:15 and I checked in at the base at 5:45, my liberty expiring at 6:00.

I was interested to hear the dope on Bill. It seems he was sworn in the day he took his physical, with no time for dickering with them. The quotas that day were five to one for the Army. And the fact that he was a hay fever patient had much to do with keeping him out of the Navy. Why, we couldn't figure out. Where, aboard ship, are you going to find Ragweed? He was quite disappointed but took it well. He doesn't like the idea of seventeen weeks of basic training, but figures even so he might get overseas quicker than in the Navy. Also, he doesn't care for the idea that he will probably go to some southern camp for his basic.

We listened to the president last night and the night before in the barracks on some guy's little pint-size radio. Also heard the King of England yesterday afternoon.

Wish I was aboard the U.S.S. *Augusta* in the English Channel.[21]

Yours truly, Bill

Dear Mom, 10 June 1944

This is turning out to be fairly good duty here at Fentress. It's much better than working in the mess hall and I think better than VF Engineering. At VF we used to spend most of the time doping off in the shop, working only semi-occasionally. You never get anywhere that way. Here we keep busy. The first night I was here we pulled a 60-hour inspection on an FM-2 (that's a check of the condition of the aircraft which is made after every 60 flying hours). Night before last we did the same on a TBF. Last night it was an FM-2 again.

With four or five of us working on a plane, such a check takes seven or eight hours. The plane gets a thorough going over and I get a little more knowledge of what makes it tick.

So far I haven't been on liberty from here yet. There are only two ways to get in town, which is quite a distance. One is to take the liberty bus which runs three times a day. The other is to hitch hike, but there's not much traffic out past here, so that's not so good. We're off from whatever time we secure in the morning till midnight but I spend a good deal of it in my bunk.

I guess I wrote you that we get two weekends a month. That's not strictly true. We get two 48-hour liberties a month, but not necessarily on the weekend. I have next Thursday and Friday, I believe it is. I have written the Washington folks to expect me.

The slight case of sunburn I got the other day turned out to be a bit hotter than I first thought but it's on the down grade now. The duty section has to stand by till 3 P.M. and man the crash truck. Nothing was doing the other day so we all took off our shirts and lay down on the rear of the truck in the sun. Next thing I knew the driver was waking me up to go to chow. I was beautifully pink. In the afternoon I did the same thing but on the other surface. So when it does cool down into a tan it will at least be a solid over all color.

We eat pretty well out here. We get up at midnight for breakfast and then go to work. About 0400 we have a light snack. Breakfast again at 0800. Lunch shortly after noon, and dinner about seven in the evening. The breakfasts are the best. Cereal, milk, fruit, beans or bacon & eggs, and this morning we had pancakes with syrup and melted butter.

There is a canteen here which sells mainly cokes, also soap, tooth paste, and razor blades. To supplement this some farmer across the road runs a little general store, which stocks a little bit of everything. There is a one chair barber shop on the field. No movies, etc., though.

I remarked to some guy yesterday that if there weren't a war going on and me wanting to get to sea this would be a swell place. He said, if there weren't a war on we wouldn't be in the Navy anyway. To which I replied, and he agreed, that it would be a swell place to spend that six months after the duration.

Well I'm getting tired of writing, so I guess I'll quit.
Yours truly, Bill

Dear Mom, 13 June 1944

I have a two-day-plus liberty starting tomorrow when we secure from work. I am going to Washington again. I wrote them last week that I'd be coming but told them Thursday instead of Wednesday. I only found out today my error. So they'll not be expecting me.

The scuttlebutt I told you about had nothing to do with us coming to Fentress. And the duty here is not quite what the scuttlebutt was going to offer. But it is better than mess cooking. One of the guys who came down here with me and who happens to be a gunner is being transferred tomorrow to a squadron. I wish it were I that was going.

I hope you have a good time this summer at Crystal Lake. I do wish I could be there, but I wouldn't feel right if I were. Does Butch plan to pick cherries, too?

What did you and Butch do in Lansing last week? Did he get to buy some records? What ones?

I ironed some whites today for my trip to Washington. I wore my bathing trunks while doing it. Still I was so hot, I had to keep applying a towel to prevent dripping on the uniform. The sun was very hot today. Hope it cools off tomorrow.

I bought some starch and tried starching my whites. It works pretty well and I got a beautiful, sharp crease in the pants and the collar.

Sunday I went back up to the air station. I saw all the mess hall gang and let them know what kind of deal I was in. Also I went up to the hangar and saw the rating list. No mech[anic]s of any class were rated this month. A bureau order came through limiting CASU to its complement in rates. And it was already way over rated. Had it not been for that situation I'd be second class now. I got a recommendation from the Chief in the mess hall and passed my board test. Oh well 3/c is a good rate.[22]

Well I better sign off and go to chow.
Yours truly, Bill

Dear Mom, 17 June 1944

Wednesday morning, we secured from work about 5 A.M. I took a shower and got into my whites and went up to the personnel office. To my dismay I found my out-of-bounds pass hadn't yet been signed. The previous day had been the personnel officer's day off. So I had to wait till about 8:30 when the duty officer got up.

It was a little after 8:30 when I finally did put my thumb up outside the gate. I got a ride in town shortly, caught the Naval Base car out to the dock and made the 10:15 ferry to Newport News. There I had poor luck at first getting out of town. But finally a soldier from Fort Monroe picked me up. I rode as far as Fredericksburg with him, going 60 most of the way. There I was stranded again for a little while.

While I was standing there thumbing a cop across the road asked, “How far are you going, sailor?” I told him to Washington, and he proceeded to stop cars and ask if they were going to D.C. About the third car squeezed me in. They already had a soldier and a marine in the back seat.

I got to Washington about 4, and out to the house a little after 5. It had just started to rain.

Bill had a dinner date that night at the home of a young lady who worked adjacent to him till he quit. When he got there, he found one of the guests unable to attend so he nominated me to fill his place. I was called for and spent a pleasant evening there. For Ruth’s information, we had fried chicken. The people were native Virginians but not from Norfolk.

The next morning, I woke up thinking I heard Uncle Bruce just going to work so I promptly got up. I looked at my watch and concluded it had stopped during the night. The voice turned out to be Bill’s and the watch hadn’t stopped. The time was 11:30.

That evening Bill had “class-night,” a dinner for class members, followed by a program of music, comedy, and horseplay.[23] He had two tickets to that which he gave to me, and arranged for a girl around the corner to go with me, “to show me the way.” When he called her up and propositioned her she said, “How old is he?” “18.” “Is he in service?” “Yes.” “Oh, boy!!” It was quite an amusing evening.

Yesterday morning we went to the zoo. We spent a good deal of time in the reptile house seeing snakes and things. They had one glass cage of some species of cockroach about as big as a mouse. I asked Bill how he’d like to find one of those in his bed. There were some friends of ours there, too: green spotted frogs, ribbon snakes, and mud turtles. Also, saw some cute little rock lizards like we used to see in Colorado.

From the zoo, I went to the bus station and caught the 2:30 bus for Norfolk. Got in at 10:30 and went up to the Navy Y to catch an 11 o’clock liberty bus to Fentress. It had left early (a new driver who didn’t know the schedule) so about six of us were stranded there. We called the station and gave them the dope and then waited for the 2:45 bus. By the time I was in my dungarees it was time for our nightly snack. After that there wasn’t much work to do and along about 6 o’clock we secured and I went to bed.

The evening of Bill's class night we went to a Dairy Bar after the performance. I had the first *good thick* milkshake I've tasted since boot leave. While there I bought a paper telling about the bombing of Tokyo.[24]

I wish I'd been a gunner in one of those planes. The day I visited the Barnes in Florida we saw one fly over. Bill Snorbach who was also there told of having flown one. He was highly enthusiastic over it.

Aunt Hazel asked me to ask you if you had received a package from her. She sent some pictures Butch wanted and some other things.

If you can find it, I'd like you to send me my baseball glove.

Yours truly, Bill

Dear Puddle Mush, 22 June 1944

Yes! As an AMM3/c I could definitely be called a "grease-monkey." That's what the term means—a guy who monkeys around in grease.

You amuse me with your statement: Your little brother is somewhat different from you. Do tell!!

The cookies came day before yesterday and were finished today. They were enjoyed by all hands, including the cockroaches in my locker. Even the fudge was good.

Where did you get the snazzy one-piece stationery? This cheap stuff I'm writing on came from the little general store across the road. They had some better stuff, but it cost more, so I bought this. Anyway, it's paper and can be written on.

Hope you have a good time at Crystal Lake. Enjoy it for me. Be sure to get me some more pictures of Spot. As I understand it you are planning to pick cherries. (Hint!!) (Sweet ones please!)

Yours truly, Bill

Dear Mom, 23 June 1944

Yesterday morning we had a check job which took a little longer than usual so I didn't get through in time to make the 9 o'clock bus to the beach. Today I had the duty (stand-by till 3 P.M.) so I missed it again. I hope I can make it tomorrow. I'm getting started on a good tan.

I had intended to get a hop this afternoon but was too lazy to walk up to the squadron office. Maybe I'll try for one tomorrow.

While I was working this morning there were some FM-2 wildcats flying around overhead making strafing attacks using a gun camera. They would dive about like this at the control tower. [Diagram drawn on letter.] As they came down we'd be looking right straight into the nose. You don't hear much noise as

they approach but just as they pass over there's a loud "Pheeeee—ew—ooooo" followed by a whistling sound as they pass away. Their speed is exaggerated by the sound, the angle, and the nearness. I'd hate to be a jap and realise those guns were loaded. . . .
Yours truly, Bill

Dear Mom, 26 June 1944

I just got back from another TBF hop. This time it was a radar search hop. All I did was watch, but what I saw made me wish I weren't stuck here in Norfolk.

I got a letter today from Stege. He is now in Radio Technician school at Texas A & M. Whom should he meet there but Herby Holland of Cadillac, one of our Mt. Pleasant buddies. They'll be shipmates for at least the next three months.

Also, I received a V-mail from Cpl. Frank Slachik, class of '42, M.H.S., dated 31 May.[25] It was in answer to a letter I had written him Feb. 24. He is now in China, the lucky bum.

Interesting things seem to be happening in Chicago now.[26] Perhaps the whole future of the entire world will be decided there. I'd like to be there the next few weeks to take in both conventions.

It cooled off here for a few days after a big rain last week. But it has warmed up again with very bright, hot sunshine. The water today was a very clean, beautiful blue. We were out of sight of land.

I now have ten hours in the air.
Yours truly, Bill

On 12 July Bill was granted sixteen days' leave. He rode the train to Michigan to visit his family, who were spending the summer with his Grandmother Willard in Benzonia, near Crystal Lake, thirty miles north of Manistee. His high school girlfriend, Jane, was back in Manistee for the summer, and they had a romantic time together. Bill returned to base on 27 July.

Dear Mom, 28 July 1944

It's hard to return from heaven to earth and even harder to return to Norfolk. But all things must come to an end.

This past 16 days has been the shortest 16 days of my life. On the way up from Detroit I passed a sign on the road saying "BOATS" which caught my eye because of the large "B" in comparison to the skinny "OATS." Coming down

Tuesday it caught my eye again. I suddenly realized, "Why, it's been two weeks since I saw that." It seemed like just yesterday.

Of my 16 days away from Fentress, 12 were spent in the old stamping grounds, one in Detroit, and three traveling. Of the 12, seven evenings were spent in Manistee, five of those with Jane, four of those with the car.

I guess you really didn't see much of me, did you? Even so I had ten days at the cottage and five evenings. But that time in Manistee meant a lot to me, more, I think, than my additional presence could have meant to you.

I really had meant to be at the supper Monday evening but after Sunday evening I never could have forgiven myself for going away without one more evening in Manistee. I don't know what it was, the music in the movie, the flickering firelight, or the gentle sound of rain on the roof of Illig's cottage or what, but I felt differently Sunday night than I had Sunday morning.

All we did Monday night was drive around a bit. Up Dunewood road, through the woods, back to town and down to the beach. There was a beautiful crescent moon over the water. The ocean isn't nearly so beautiful as Lake Michigan. Then I took Jane home. I never in my life found it so hard to say goodbye to anyone.

I hope you have enough gas to last you. I guess I really did use a lot, 23 gallons wasn't it? But they were well used I think. Be sure to accept Uncle Dayton's offer if you run short. I'd have done so had I not had your coupons.[27]

The trip back was quite uneventful. It was very hot when I got off the train. I enjoyed the ferry ride. It rained last night just before time for the bus to the base. Both squadrons are at some other field for a few days so we secured right after muster. So I got a night of sleep.

I guess I left you rather suddenly Tuesday. The ride you saw me get took me to Manistee (M-55 corner). Then I got a ride with a discharged soldier in a truck to Cadillac. I got a ride immediately to a junction about 15 miles out. Then a gas truck took me to Clare. There, a guy gave me a lift to Saginaw. A woman took me out past the city limits, where a man gave me a ride to a junction your side of Flint. Then a family took me all the way to Elmhurst in Highland Park. Eight hours total.

In the evening, while Aunt Belle was at the Y[WCA],[28] I went down to the General Motors building and saw their "Arms for Victory" exhibit again. It has been revised since a year and a half ago. And of course, I see all the guns and engines in a different light now.

The carload of Navy Recruits we had on the train on their way to boot camp were amusing. They were as worried as I was 17 months ago, and trying not to show it. But they were full of questions. I did my best to reassure them, saying the Navy is mostly what you make it. I think my haircut worried them no little.

It's almost time for chow so I better quit.

I took my film to a photofinisher yesterday in town. It will be several days till they're ready. I'll send you some. Send some of the others as soon as they're finished. And write soon. Wonderful as leave always is, it's hard on the morale when the time comes to go back, especially to Norfolk.

Much as I feel like a 4-F here with Dad where he is and much as I'd like to be at sea, I'm not quite prepared to say I'd have forgone this leave. Not even to be a gunner, I think.

Yours, Bill

Dear Mom, 2 August 1944

. . . My luck seems to run in strings. After 16 swell days of leave I came back to Fentress to find myself due for a "48." But instead of the usual trip to Washington I decided to spend it in the barracks. Which was a good thing.

Sunday a draft came through for the *Ticonderoga*.[29] The AMM 3/c whose name was on the list was on leave at the time. So they asked for a volunteer. Naturally that meant me. My divisional officer didn't want to let me go. He said he hated to break in a new man. I finally persuaded him to consent to the toss of a coin. I won, checked out that afternoon, and went up to [censored] Monday.[30] The whole draft came aboard Monday afternoon.

We mustered and were assigned bunks and lockers. After chow, we got squared away in our quarters. Saw a movie on the hangar deck in the evening.

She's a big ship, a first-rate carrier of the *Essex* class. I paced the length of the flight deck and it's simply unbelievable. Today I was one of many detailed to sweep down the hangar deck. Here again the bigness is impressive.

Tuesday morning, not having been aboard a day yet, I met someone I knew. Do you remember A. J. Davis, of Manistee? He's an electrician's mate second class, and shows the movies on this ship. I guess we hadn't seen each other for three years.

It's hot in the crew's quarters, but not too bad. The bunks are comfortable, and the lockers adequate. I won't be quite as well off as Dad but I think I'm going to enjoy it at least as well. I'd better after volunteering for it.

We get liberty every other evening and no days off. So I won't be getting up to Washington again before we shove off. Guys who have had no leave recently are getting ten days. I'm glad I had my 16.

Had I not just returned from leave, I would undoubtedly have gone to Washington last weekend. In which case, I'd have missed this draft. Funny how things all work out in the end. Had I not been assigned mess duty last May I wouldn't

have gone to Fentress, I wouldn't have had my leave, and I wouldn't now be on the *Ticonderoga*. . . .
Yours truly, Bill

In early August Bill was granted another ten days' leave while Ticonderoga *underwent alterations and repairs following its shakedown cruise. As he would be shipping out to the Pacific soon, he made another trip home to Michigan. He got back to base on 13 August.*

Dear Mom, 15 August 1944

That car you saw pick me up outside of Cadillac took me clear to the R.R. Station in Toledo. The people in the car live in Erie, Mich., ten miles from Toledo. They had been at their cottage at Lake Leelanau, up past Traverse City. We got to Erie about 3:30 P.M. EWT.[31] He owns a little orchard, so he filled the corners of my ditty bag with apples and pears. They gave me supper and then drove me on down to Toledo in time for my train. Their son is 17 and wants to join the Navy. Naturally I put in a good word for the service.

I occupied a seat on the train next to an armed-guard sailor. He lived in Toledo. He was wearing his whites. It was rather warm in blues when we got here but looking at his whites I decided it was better to be in blues anyway.

I had quite a little mail waiting for me when I got here. Two V-mails from Dad, one dated July 20 and one July 26. In the first he hadn't yet heard from me since I'd written I was to get leave. In the latter, he had gotten my letter written from the cottage. By now I suppose he's got my new address but hasn't heard of my second leave yet.

I had letters from Grandma Catton, Harold Marsh, Lee Redman, and Mrs. Eleanor Richardson.[32] Eleanor is in Florida now with Ray.[33] Harold was in Manistee the latter part of July. I guess I just missed him both ways. Also, I heard from Frank Slachik and Alex Topping. Hook told me that he'd just heard Bill Tennant (M.H.S. '42) was killed in the crash of a Helldiver. He was a Marine 2nd Lt.

Last night I ate, went to a show, and got a room at the Navy Y. Came back to the ship this morning. There's some of the juiciest scuttlebutt around as to where we're going. I think it's anybody's guess, though, for all any of the men know.

It's hot here again today and I miss Crystal Lake. Last night I thought ruefully of the contrast between the dirt and vulgarity of Norfolk and the serenity of my six days at home. The show I saw helped me to forget all about Norfolk, though.

It was "Going My Way" with Bing Crosby. I highly recommend it. It's entertaining and heart-warming. . . .
Bill

From Robert Catton to Bill:

Dear Bill; 16 August 1944

Congratulations! I didn't think you were necessarily going to have to wait at Fentress as long as you feared. Of course, I never could have foreseen the train of circumstances that led to your assignment on the *Ticonderoga.* I have seen her, and have seen several others of her class. I know how you feel. She is a beauty, and it seems to me you have gotten as good an assignment, at last, as you could possibly have had. You're quite right, you won't feel like a 4-F the next time you see me. The roles will be reversed; I shall. By the way, I'll be looking for you. I wouldn't be at all surprised if we were to meet up some day.

Now, how good it was you had your leave when you did. Everything seems to be working out. It frequently does.

Your letter took a little time to reach me. Curiously enough on the same mail I had one from Grandmother C. saying she had just heard from you and that you had been assigned to the Ticonderoga. So it would seem your letter to her could reach her and give her a chance to write me and still have her letter get to me as quick as yours did.

Look up the chances for your 2nd class rating now as soon as possible. I wouldn't be surprised if you discovered that on this new ship there could be some advancements, for those qualified, I mean. I trust that what you already did got entered in your service record. Did you get to finish that correspondence course before you left? We have rated men and advanced men on this ship since coming out here. But don't waste any time. The ship could get rated up to her full complement and then your opportunity is shut off again.

You will have the same experience we have now. You will be seeing new things and having a lot of experience you would like to write about very much only to find that what you would like to talk about the most is censorable. Don't blame it on the censors; they are subject to the same rules you are and they don't like it better. What you can write, of a personal nature, go ahead and write. The censor can't pay very much attention to what you say, other than to make sure it is permissible, and he has forgotten your remarks as soon as he is in the midst of the next letter.

Hope you get this somewhere before too long. Keep writing me whatever you can. Good luck!
Dad

Dear Mom, 23 August 1944

I had a letter, air mail, from Dad yesterday 12 days in transit. However that included forwarding from Fentress Field. He had written it in reply to my detailed account of the leave in July. He mentioned similar experiences and similar feelings on a leave he had from Pensacola in 1918. I suppose you remember.

He also had some things to say concerning the current political campaign. Some of his statements I find myself disagreeing with. He said for one thing that he had hoped the Republicans would make good their promises to keep foreign policy out of the campaign, but feared they couldn't. I feel that foreign policy not only should be *an* issue, but should be *the* issue. I would rather see a clear-cut, out-in-the-open fight between isolationist Republicans and internationalist Democrats than to have both parties soft pedaling foreign policy. If we do not concern ourselves with foreign policy in the campaign how are we to avoid another Henry Cabot Lodge–Warren Harding play. If we fail this time to build a sound peace as dismally as we failed last time we might not have another chance. After all, we could have lost *this* war. Look at Dunkirk, Stalingrad, and Pearl Harbor, all close calls. And even granting that we should win another war, why purchase another chance at such a price?

I wish there wasn't going to be so much opposition to Roosevelt over the fourth term. Opposition is going to be dangerous in the establishment of the peace. And I do think Roosevelt is the man, unless Dewey opens his mouth and begins to say where he stands in clear and precise words.[34] I don't doubt Dewey's ability as a leader, it's just that nobody knows his thoughts toward our policies in the future.

This perhaps isn't the usual sort of letter a serviceman writes to his mother but I'm feeling rather powerless in all that's going on because I can't vote.[35] Request cards for absentee ballots were passed out the other day to all those over 21.

I don't know how Navy men as a whole feel politically. A good many people who have given me rides while hitchhiking have asked me how the Navy "feels about Roosevelt." I've always told them I thought opinion was divided in about the same proportion as it is among civilians. After all, what difference does the uniform make? In case anyone asks you, that's what I think is the answer. . . .
Yours, Bill

Dear Mom, 25 August 1944

I had a refresher in gunnery today, and was checked out in firing 20mm anti-aircraft. What a gun!! Remember how I used to describe the feel of the .50 caliber at Hollywood? This makes you feel even more as if you had something powerful in your hands. And you should see the sky when a whole bank of them is firing at once. You wonder how an enemy plane could ever come through it.

I had a letter today from Donald Norton. He is in the Hospital Corps school at the Naval Hospital in San Diego. Also I heard from Flynn, my Great Lakes–Navy Pier–Miami acquaintance. He is now in an advanced mechanics school at Oakland, California.

Two days before he was supposed to have gone on a 20-day leave he was transferred out there. So I guess luck doesn't always get properly distributed.

A. J. Davis had a nervous collapse the other day. He is to be transferred to a Hospital and may get an M.D. [medical discharge]. It's a tough blow, but less so for him than it would be for me. He's had more time in the Navy, some sea duty, and on top of that he is now a family man.

It has warmed up again some but it's not uncomfortable yet. I see by the Manistee paper that you had quite a storm up there a week or so ago. Was that the day you lost Butch in the outhouse?

Thanks for sending the pictures. The one of the monument turned out well. Where did you have them finished? It's a very poor printing job. The shadows are all blocked up—no detail. The *prints* were overexposed it looks to me, maybe even too soft a grade of paper. I like the one of Butch and you at the picnic table though. Be sure to send me the ones of you in swimming.

That's all for now I guess.

Yours, Bill

Dear Mom, 29 August 1944

Do you remember about two years ago now? It was toward the end of August that I finished up that course at Mt. Pleasant. The 23rd, I think, was the Sunday I spent in Manistee. The following Thursday you folks came up in the car and got me, and I told you of my decision to join the Navy.

A lot has happened since then, and to me it seems like more than two years ago. To you I suppose the time seems short. Little did I picture then being on a ship like the "Big T." I really didn't picture, too clearly, what might be ahead. All that mattered was that I had reached a major decision and wanted to enlist in a big hurry. At that time, I don't think it had occurred to any of us that Dad might be in it too.

I had two V-mails from Dad today, one forwarded from Fentress, and the other finally addressed to the ship. He mentioned the visit with Paul and says it would not surprise him at all to see me someday. He asked where Stege was now and asked if I were going to bet with him on this election. It was hard to realize it was only four years ago that I was working at the Marsh Photo Shop. Stege and I were arguing politics in the darkroom one day and it ended with a three-dollar bet. It was about a week later that I quit there so I could go out for football, all 105 pounds of me.

I wrote Dad that the next time I saw him I wouldn't feel so much like a 4-F now that I was on a ship. In his letter today he agreed and said at such a meeting he would be the one to feel like a 4-F, as he did when visiting Paul's ship.[36]

What would you and the kids like for Christmas this year? This seems a ridiculous time of year to be thinking of that. But I should receive any requests as soon as possible because my chances to do any Christmas shopping are definitely going to be few.

I believe you said you'd be going home September 2. That being only four days from now I'll mail this to that address.

Yours, Bill

CHAPTER 5

USS *Ticonderoga,* the First Voyage

[Atlantic Ocean]

Dear Mom, 31 August 1944

Thanks for sending my driver's license. It does seem rather useless now, though, doesn't it?

Today I put in more hours, I think, than I have since the last couple of weeks of Redman's. From General Quarters this morning till 8:00 this evening it was almost continuous physical exertion. I'm in a plane handling crew and we move the planes around on the hangar deck. We push the outgoing ones onto the elevators and take the incoming ones off and spot them in their places. It's too bad I'm not going out for football this fall. This would be good training.

Last night I watched the sun set. It reminded me strongly of the days in Manistee. The white foam kicked up by the ship could have been the ice on Lake Michigan in the early spring. The water was an ink blue nearby, fading into a bright silver on the horizon. It was a clear evening with just a slight haze on the horizon making the sun a ketchup-red.

You've no idea how blue water can be till you've seen deep ocean. Looking out over the ocean it might just as well be Lake Michigan. But looking down into it the richness of the color is indescribable.

Once, when we passed through a slight rain with the sun still shining the ocean didn't even look wet. The gentle swell of the surface was hardly broken by a wave. Its smoothness was vaguely pebbled by the raindrops. It looked like nothing so much as shiny-smooth, blue leather. I wish you could have seen it.

One of the guys said he saw some flying fish today. I didn't. Perhaps I was too busy.

Yours, Bill

[Panama Canal Zone]

Dear Mom, 3 September 1944

The other night there was a little affair aboard the "Big T" that made her seem like a Lake Michigan excursion steamer instead of a ship of war. It was a beautiful moonlit night with broken clouds here and there in the sky reflecting the silvery light. The water was smooth with gentle swells on it. The ship was, of course, blacked out.[1] The band, assembled out in the cool breeze on the flight deck, had a jam session, playing their own arrangements or disarrangements of various songs. It was most enjoyable.

The skipper made an extemporaneous speech to the whole crew this morning on the flight deck. He brought home the fact that this type of ship is, of itself, not an offensive weapon; that its sole purpose is to get the aircraft where they can do the most good.[2] He told us, "We're not going out to play marbles." It seems the top boys in Washington were pretty complimentary towards him about the shakedown and the general organization aboard. I guess I really got a wonderful break that Sunday at Fentress when I got on this draft.

It's been several days since I had any mail. But I've been busy enough not to mind much. I imagine there'll be times when it will be several weeks between letters.

I attended church again this morning but had to leave before the close of the service on account of flight quarters.

Pay day today. I drew twenty dollars.

Have the kids started school yet? Who were the people Uncle Dayton had working for him?

Yours, Bill

[Pacific Ocean]

Dear Mom, 5 September 1944

The billfold you sent came today. It was a good idea, sending it first class. It looks like a good species, almost too good to use. I'm glad to have one with celluloid pockets for pictures. Thanks very much, even though you did spend too much for it.

I also had a letter from Aunt Ione today. She, like Dad, gets a lot into a V-mail. I'm hoping for letters from "others" next mail call. Since we left the U.S. I haven't fared too well on mail.[3]

I just happened to think this morning, today is the Tuesday after Labor Day, the first day of school. How I used to hate it. The first few days of a new routine have always irked me. Then for a few weeks, after I get in step, I enjoy it. Then I get restless for something new. That was true each new year in school and it has been true at each new base or new phase in my Navy career.

However, that's the beauty of sea duty. You can stay in the same outfit yet have a frequent change of scenery. By the same token, such a life is necessarily educational. I wish Butch could be having these "adventures" with me.

Have Ruth and Butch write about what they're doing now, what subjects they're taking, etc.

In a recent *News Advocate* there was a schedule of football games for M.H.S. I clipped it and taped it up on my locker door. The accompanying article gave Manistee quite favorable prospects for the season.

Incidentally, note the change in my address. Both grandmothers and some others have asked me to try and give them "some idea" of where I am from time to time. Such is, or course, out of the question. But they've even asked if there was any way I could just let them know which ocean I was in. All they need do is look at the FPO address.[4]

Yours, Bill

[Pacific Ocean]

Dear Mom, 11 September 1944

Recently I've been reading a library book on football. It's a manual put out by the Navy Department for use by coaches in the Navy's pre-flight schools. This time of year, it makes appropriate reading. As September rolls around football rather gets in your blood. Two games I should like to see this year are M.H.S. vs. Ludington, and the Bears-Packers pro game.

It occurred to me that there should be some good college football a year or two after the war. Many of the players will be rehabilitated servicemen on government scholarship. They will be two to four years older than college men usually are, and proportionally bigger and huskier. That might even include me.

The other day, I actually had a chance to vote in this year's election! A shipmate had received his ballot but was none too enthusiastic over voting. He wasn't particularly politically minded. Rather than throw the ballot away, however, he offered to let me mark it and he'd send it in. Strictly illegal, of course, but I think my conscience is elastic enough to have permitted me to do it had my mind been made up as to whom I want to vote for. It's too early in the campaign for that, though.[5]

I have to hurry down to the ice cream stand now, before it closes.

Yours, Bill

[San Diego, California]

Dear Mom, 15 September 1944

Would you like to be able to come aboard the Big T for a day and see how things are done, what the life and routine is like? You can almost do it! See the movie, "Wing and a Prayer" with Don Ameche and Dana Andrews. Take the kids. It's about the most authentic war movie I've seen in a long time. Many of its scenes were taken aboard a carrier of our class. They show the daily routines, planes landing and taking off, men working, the layout of the ship, etc. The scenes, actions, and words are an accurate portrayal of our daily life.[6]

I had a letter from Jane today and one from Kurt Illig written on the 30th and 29th of August respectively. The letters must have chased around Robin Hood's barn to catch me. The letter from Kurt enclosed the pictures taken with his camera that evening in July. The best one, of Jane, I have in my new billfold. The others I'll send to you for the scrapbook. One, I'm sending to Dad. It's of Jane and me.

Had our first rough sea today. It wasn't, I guess, what an old salt would call rough, but it wasn't placid either. Our escort ships were tossed around a bit. The Big T, though, rode it like an elephant walking through a mud puddle.

I was issued a helmet and gas mask today. Some of us had been doing general drills, etc., without them, till now. When I first put the tin lid on, I felt like a little kid playing war. I guess that's really what we all are, just kids playing war—for keeps. . . .

Yours, Bill

[San Diego, California]

Dear Pop, 17 September 1944

Due to the noise and confusion aboard this morning there were no church services. Instead the skipper sent three sections ashore on liberty at 0900. All liberty expires on board at 2400. The noise and confusion were due to loading a bunch of cargo to be taken somewhere west of here.[7] So far, we are following in your footsteps, so to speak.

I came off the ship with the intention of giving another try at finding Donald Norton. I went out to the Hospital Corps school, but O.O.D. [officer on deck] looked up his name on the list and said he was on liberty. So, since I was out in Balboa Park, I paid a visit to the zoo. I stayed there about 2½ hours. I went through the snake house, past the monkey cages, saw the cat-animals, bears, etc. In front of the moat around two huge Russian brown bears a crowd was watching a lady make them perform. She claimed to have no connection with the zoo, just a frequent visitor. She said she'd been coming there regularly for eight years and had watched one of the two bears grow up. He performed well under her direction and was rewarded with bags of food.

As this was going on a little boy and his mother walked up. The little boy pointed to the bears and asked, "What are those?" The frequent visitor replied, "Grapes and peanuts!"

At two o'clock a trained rhesus monkey gave a performance in a little amphitheater. It was very amusing. I wish Butch could have been there.

This morning, as I was walking up the liberty boat landing, a sailor hailed me with, "Where have I seen you before?" He was Bill Burnett, AMM3c, one of the guys in my section at gunnery school. He had just flown down from Minneapolis in a Liberator.

I can't yet see any comparison between Norfolk and San Diego. I've heard a lot of guys say they were two of a kind. True, they're both cluttered up with hordes of sailors. But there the similarity ends. San Diego has a more prosperous look to it. The buildings and streets are all clean, there are more decent places of amusement. It reminds me more of Miami than of Norfolk.[8]

Yours, Bill

[Pacific Ocean]

Dear Pop, 19 September 1944

I got your letter, written 9 Sept., today; ten days in transit. If that were the longest it would ever take, we would have no cause to gripe. I imagine it will soon be a matter of weeks instead of days.

I also had letters from Ruth and Jane today. Ruth told about her new bike, about starting school, what subjects she's taking, etc. Jane gave me some home news including, "I suppose you've read in the paper that Ed LaValle was killed. . . ." After reading her letter I opened the copies of the *News Advocate* which had come in the same mail. There on the front page was the enclosed article.

I was thoroughly shocked by the news. When I was home in July, I had called on the LaValles, including Betty, Ed's wife. I had known her in school. They gave me his address and I wrote to him when I got back to Fentress. I had told his folks in July that I wished I could trade places with him. I guess that still goes. At least I wouldn't leave a young widow. It's too bad, though, that it has to be an acquaintance like that to wake you up. What I mean is, why shouldn't we be just as concerned over the death of some Chinese, Russian, English, French, German, or Jap? Human nature is too narrow.

To change the subject, I'm also enclosing another picture of Jane and me. Kurt took it with his camera that same evening in July. It came out a bit better than the one on Ruth's Box camera. He used a swell German Voigtlander job. It used to be his Dad's. I just got his set of pictures the other day. The best one of Jane is in my billfold, the others I sent home to Mom for her scrapbook.

I had an argument today about everything under the sun. It started when one guy asked if you could take a taxi from one certain town to another. It ended up with a discussion of race relations in the south. As it evolved to that subject I began to back out. In speech class in high school, Henchey told us never to enter a debate on either religion or politics. I would broaden it to say, never debate on a subject involving deep prejudice.

But some of the guys from Virginia and Georgia, etc., started bragging about how in their states the penalty for killing a "nigger" was a mere fine. I stood it as long as I could but finally got so disgusted I just asked them, "Are you proud of that?"

It then started in earnest as a mere controversy of prejudices but as I cooled off I was able to cool them off enough so that intellect began to enter into it. I have found in such debates that southerners will usually put up a stock question: "Would you sleep with a "nigger." I explained that the question as stated was too broad and thus irrelevant. I said I would have to be told what "nigger." Then another Virginian took my side and said that he had known many with whom he'd rather sleep than some whites. Another typical question then came out: "Do you think a 'nigger' is as good as you." I said this too was irrelevant. Actually, I believe nobody believes anyone is as good as he is. He may admit it academically but inside any individual thinks himself tops. I know I do. The point is not whether colored people are as good as I am. The point is that as human beings they are entitled to equal rights with me. Here I met, for the first time, a new kind of opposition. One man actually denied that "niggers" were human beings!

It wasn't settled. We finally quit and went to chow. When it ended it was still based on prejudice, as by nature it has to be. But I had persuaded my opponents at least that I had a right to my point of view.

Mom sent me a blotter the other day with the word Ticonderoga printed in big letters across the top and an advertisement for Dixon's Ticonderoga pencils on it. I don't know whether she thought it had any significance or not. The pencils were named long before the "Big T" was even authorized.

Incidentally, if it's any consolation the old *Oahu,* [a] river gunboat, was a sister ship of the ill-fated *Panay,*[9] which should have gotten us into the war. We would probably be home by now if it had.

I am wondering if you voted for Roosevelt or Norman Thomas.[10] I'm pretty sure it wasn't Dewey. His campaign reminds me more of Landon than of Willkie. However, I know a certain party who will vote for him. She lives in Benzonia. We were discussing politics when I was home. She made some statement about "thinking she voted for Willkie in 1940." I somehow restrained myself from saying, "I know darn well you did!"

Yours, Bill

[Pacific Ocean]
24 September 1944

Dear Mom,

The other morning, I was up on deck before the sun came up. The sky was clear and the sea was calm. As the light grew brighter and brighter its whiteness was reflected by the water. It can't be described, you'd have to see it. But it reminded me, except for the gentle motion, of nothing so much as a field of drifted Michigan snow. I could almost picture Butch and I and Spot plodding through it on the way to a "weeny-roast" in the Sand Hills.

This morning I was up on the fight deck while waiting for the chow line to get shorter. I watched the sun come up. I don't know why people usually consider a sunrise less spectacular than a sunset. This was as beautiful as one could ask.

Yesterday afternoon we had a double feature movie on the forward end of the hangar deck. One was a story of life in Brooklyn, starring William Bendix. It was moderately funny. The other was a good old rip-roarin', shoot-em-up-bang western, with Tim Holt. Apparently, most westerns are produced on the same lot at Hollywood. I could recognize the hills, rocks, trees, and roads as if I'd seen them all before. The whole show reminded me of the home town on Saturday afternoon. Kids lined up in front of the theater, waiting for two o'clock to come around and open the doors. Each has a precious dime clutched in his fist, and keen anticipation of hoofs, bullets, and ukuleles in his heart. Solid American.

The Chaplain's sermon this morning was based on the question, "Is religion a bargain." He said it was, in the sense that in the long run you get more back than you put into it. But, he said, it loses its whole meaning if you approach it with that attitude.

Last night I dreamed I was in Ann Arbor. (Mission obvious.) I was walking up the street on my way to a certain dormitory when reveille blew. It certainly is a vile bit of music.

Yours, Bill

Later this day, at 3:39 P.M., USS Ticonderoga *entered Pearl Harbor and moored alongside Ford Island. It remained in Hawaiian waters for the next three weeks, conducting air-operation drills and munition-transfer tests.*

[Pearl Harbor, Hawaii]

Dear Mom, 25 September 1944

I hit the jackpot at mail call last night. Seven airmail letters, three of them from you. They were postmarked Sept. 16, 17, and 20. In other words that last one reached me in four days. Not bad. Also, had a letter from Frank Slachik in China which got here in 16 days.

I really got more than my share of the mail last night. I'm not kicking, of course, but it was tough to watch the few who didn't get any mail look at me with envy each time my name was called. A mail call that doesn't bear fruit is worse than no mail call at all.

You asked where I was when I got the billfold. That was while we were in Panama. Your ideas of our progress move faster than the ship. When Dad was on his way out I pictured him always two weeks ahead of where he was. Perhaps it's just error, perhaps it's wishful thinking, like thinking the war will soon be over.

Thanks for sending Walter Lippmann's column. I wish you would continue from time to time to send clippings of his and other columnists. We have a little daily paper aboard that carries concise radio reports of the major news items. It has pretty good coverage, so we get a fair idea of what's going on in the world. But I miss editorials and such-like.

I just saw some pictures today of the effects of the hurricane in Norfolk. It almost made me wish I were back there. They must have had an exciting time for a while.[11]

I hope you didn't get the impression I was serious in my kidding Dad about the difference in our ships. That's all it was intended for, a bit of ribbing. Like Butch's remark about "There's our old Ford!" Anyhow, with him getting the *Oahu* and me the Big T, I'm glad they came in the order they did. Suppose I had come aboard the Big T in March and he got the *Oahu* in July. He'd have felt as if he'd been dealt a low blow.

A letter from Lizzy says you're cutting down my blues to fit Butch. I hope you made a pattern of the cut first as I strongly dislike a sailor suit that's "non-regulation." Are you leaving them as undress or are you going to put stripes on them? If the latter, don't forget the cuffs. Can you get 13 buttons on such a small pair of pants? Do you know how to press a sailor uniform?

I don't know when my *News Advocate* subscription expires. You'd better write them. It will probably be very slow in coming. Such matter rates a very low mail priority. But home town news, even if ancient, is always welcome.

You said the Mackinnons haven't heard from Frazer in nine weeks.[12] They shouldn't worry. It simply means "the line is busy," so to speak.

Yours, Bill

P.S. Start writing some of your letters V-mail to see how they come through.

[Pearl Harbor, Hawaii]

Dear Mom, 26 September 1944

I went ashore today, though I can't say where. My objectives were mostly sightseeing, etc. First thing I did, though, was go into a drugstore and get a good thick malted. We have ice cream in abundance on the ship but you know how I thirst for malts. Then we, myself and a Virginian by the name of Gregory, just started walking around to see the town. After an hour or so we got hungry. Went into a little restaurant and ate. Had a very good meal, meat loaf, potatoes, peas, tomatoes, bread and butter, and two glasses of fresh milk. That, too, tasted good after our powdered variety.

Then we got on a bus to head for the beach and a swim. I remarked to Gregory that the people in Michigan would appreciate it if I could send them a little of this hot weather as a souvenir. A lady in the next seat asked, "Did I hear you say you were from Michigan?" I replied in the affirmative. She asked what part. I said, "Did you ever hear of Manistee?" She said, yes, she used to live there, and taught school in Filer City. She spent summers before the war in Northport. The world is small indeed.

I had a good swim in some very nice, warm, mellow, salt water. But it wasn't like Crystal Lake by any means.

I do wish I could write more about today. I shall give you all the dope in a few weeks. Anyhow we're getting around and I'm having a good time.[13]

I had intended to do some Christmas shopping today, but didn't. There wasn't too much about that would instill the Christmas spirit. And anyway, I didn't get around to it. I guess I shall send you a money order soon and some suggestions.

Yours, Bill

[Pearl Harbor, Hawaii]
Dear Mom, 29 September 1944

Last night after the show I went up on the flight deck for some fresh air. The moon was up, about three quarters full. Bits of cloud here and there reflected its silvery beams. Some planes were having night practice. As they would approach the ship all that was visible was their red and green riding lights. The wind blowing aft carried most of the engine sound away till they passed right overhead. It was quite eerie watching those two little colored lights grow bigger and farther apart, accompanied by a whistle-like sound.

The sea was a bit rough today. Really it was more choppy than rough. The ship hardly felt it. But waves were sending spray up onto the hangar deck. The water was its usual deep blue, which made the splashes quite pretty.

Tomorrow is payday. I'm drawing 40 bucks. Last payday was advanced about a week so the boys would all have money in San Diego. Consequently, we only received a partial pay. So, we get a bit more this time. I think I'll send you a money order and shopping list in a few days and let you do my Christmas shopping for me.

Until the censor says we can write about our last liberty I'm afraid my letters will be short. There isn't much to tell. We're back on the same old routine.

I have to go help unrig from movies pretty soon.

Yours, Bill

[Pearl Harbor, Hawaii]
Dear Pop, 5 October 1944

You overestimated the distance already covered by the Big T. I do think there is a strong chance I shall see you in the future but not so soon as you had supposed might be possible. We are certainly a fast enough ship to have reached where I think you are by now but we've been doing a lot on the way. It's all been interesting though and I wish I could write about it.

Thanks for letting me see the snapshot. I don't remember the precise occasion on which it was taken but I believe it was the summer I was five and Ruth two. It is a strange thing to think of this little ignorant squirt being me!

I showed your letter to a shipmate whose dad is also a minister. He was quite interested in your point and in your manner of writing it. Some of the other guys here, knowing of your occupation, began calling me "deacon." Then when they discovered this other character was also the son of a minister they had to make a distinction. He happens to be about four inches shorter than I. So I am "big deacon" and he is "little deacon."

I got a letter from Stege today. He is, of all places, stationed at Navy Pier in Chicago. He finished primary RT [radio technician] school in Texas. None of them got rates. He now has six months of advanced radio and radar school to go through. Navy Pier has no more aviation or diesel school. It's all radio and LST now.[14]

Mom wrote asking if she should send along my sleeveless sweater which I mailed home from Norfolk. A sleeveless sweater here would be about as useless as a footwarmer in the Sahara Desert. Apparently, she's still worried about her little boy catching the sniffles.

Of all places for me to wind up, I am now doing duty on the Big T's master-at-arms force![15] I'm afraid it's more or less permanent. Here's how it came about. Our air department was over-complemented on rated men. (I guess the whole Navy is.) So a draft was drawn up to be transferred at our last port and be replaced by seamen. Somehow my name got on the list. I went up to see my division officer to see if I could be permitted to remain with the ship.

The only outfit on the ship with room for a rated man was the M.A.A. [master-at-arms] force. So I had to take it. I don't like it. It's quite a comedown from aerial gunner. But I'd have been willing to take even mess cooking to stay with this ship.[16]

Yours, Bill

[Pearl Harbor, Hawaii]
7 October 1944

Dear Mom,

It's funny how scuttlebutt goes around on a ship. It's worse than a women's knitting circle. Most of the time it's amusing.

When we were in Norfolk, for instance, speculation ran wild as to where we'd be going when we shoved off. It would start out with one guy saying, "I *think we might* go here"; the next guy that repeats it says, "I *wouldn't be surprised* if we went there." And it grows until some guy says, "I *heard* we were going such and such a place."

One guy even said it was straight dope that we were going to ferry some planes to England and then go down through the Suez Canal.

Well, all that is harmless, *if* you take it with a boxful of salt. But it can get out of hand.

Scuttlebutt started the other day that the Japs had already claimed to have sunk us. We all had a chuckle at that. But it has been growing. The next time I ran across the rumor, some guy was saying he had heard it over the radio. Then it was in "some newspaper." Finally, that got more specific. The latest story I've heard is that the *New York Times* carried an article about the Big T being lost.

I can assure you we've not been sunk!! And in case such scuttlebutt ever should get into the newspapers back home, here's the way to look at it: if it were true it wouldn't have passed the censor.

It's like the old game of "telephone" we used to play at the dinner table.
Yours, Bill

[Pearl Harbor, Hawaii]

Dear Mom, 9 October 1944

I hadn't had any mail for several days but this evening I had letters from you and Ruth, written the 5th of October. So, they got to me in a bit over four days.

Thanks for sending me the various clippings. I haven't yet read Dewey's speech but when I get time I'm anxious to study it. The other day on liberty I happened into a little souvenir shop where the radio was carrying one of his speeches. I didn't like it.

His acceptance speech last July had actually impressed me favorably. He is a good orator. But his subject is much too petty. For about ten minutes the other day I heard violent criticism of the New Deal but not one word of what Mr. Dewey would have done or would do instead. His whole theme was: It's time for a change.

I hope you had a good time in Benzonia again. I don't suppose the trip on the old Ann Arbor train was any too pleasant, though.

I attended church yesterday morning and again heard a very good sermon.[17] The Chaplain preached this time on the question: "Is Religion an Opiate?" His ideas seemed to coincide pretty much with mine. He said that some religions have been and are an opiate to the people in that they cause men to resign themselves to their "fate." But, he said, religion does not need to be so. If we discard a fatalistic attitude toward it then it can be a very vital inspiration to humanity. . . .

Thanks for the Stephen Leacock book.[18] I've been reading bits of it and enjoying it very much.

I heard the final game of the World Series this morning. The Browns disappointed me by losing, but all six games were exciting and topnotch baseball. I should like to have seen them.[19]

Yours, Bill

[Pearl Harbor, Hawaii]

Dear Ruth, 9 October 1944

I got your letter today telling about being home alone while Mom and Butch were at Benzonia. In the same mail, I got one from Mom telling about getting back from her trip. I couldn't dope it out as both were postmarked 5 October. Then I noticed yours was written 2 October. Does your bike have a flat tire or something; or were you just too lazy to go down to the post office?

Why doesn't Dad want you to join the WAVES? Maybe it's because of the time I did mess duty for them. He's afraid to let you eat what guys like me dish out. And why don't you like the WAVES? They can now serve overseas, you know. Of course, by the time you get old enough to join up, there may not be any WAVES. Incidentally, it just goes to prove I'm better than you. I got into the Navy at 17, whereas they won't take you till you're 20.

From the address on the envelope your handwriting is beginning to bear a marked resemblance to Dad's. Fortunately, Dad has a typewriter.

It still puzzles me how you could have gotten that A on your chemistry test. Did you "bank ears," as they say in the Navy? By the way, you probably have discovered by now that my lab apron leaks at waist level. Constant exposure to hypo and gold toning at the Redman studio as well as friction against the darkroom table wore off some of the rubber. Hope you didn't ruin a dress finding this out.

I note Michigan beat Minnesota the other day. Fine. Keep me posted on local football scores. Also, find out about the Bears-Packers professional games.

Yours, Bill

[Pearl Harbor, Hawaii]

Dear Pop, 13 October 1944

For the last four days ship's company has been enjoying (one section each day) a picnic on the beach. Yesterday was my turn. We had a lunch of beans, potato salad, celery, bread and jam, and fried chicken. To drink we had our choice of beer or coke. Believe it or not they ran out of coke first. I don't know whether they had less coke or fewer suds guzzlers. It reminds me of the old gag of the white horses eating more than the black horses.

After chow, some of the guys played tennis while others went for a swim. I got into a softball game, the first I'd played since last December in gunnery school. Playing right field (where I figured I'd do the least harm) I managed to make three errors out of three attempts, all overthrows. At bat I got two hits for four tries. One guy said I ran like a plow horse, which was probably a fairly accurate description.

Anyhow they all had a good time, some returning to the ship slightly inebriated. We ate a good chow and soaked up some sunshine.

Last summer while I was at Crystal Lake the boys were having similar festivities on their shakedown cruise to Trinidad.

Do you remember my telling of a radar hop I flew from Fentress on which I saw an *Essex* class ship? I found out recently by comparing dates that it was the Big T. At that time, I looked down at her with a feeling of envy, but little thinking I'd soon be aboard.

I read recently in the St. Johns paper about Dick Clark receiving his commission and wings at Pensacola. He will go to Jacksonville next for fighter operational training. In a way, I envy him. But I don't regret the decisions I've made or the career I've had so far.

Do you remember that time in Montrose it took me four hours to walk five blocks home? Today I had a guy working for me missing for about half an hour. When he finally showed up I asked where he'd been. He said he was up topside getting a drink of water. I said, "Why didn't you use that scuttlebutt right over there?" He replied, "It was being used at the moment!"
Yours, Bill

On 18 October Ticonderoga *left Pearl Harbor and shaped a course for the western Pacific. On its way to the forward base at Ulithi in the Western Caroline Islands, the ship stopped briefly at Eniwetok Atoll in the Marshall Islands, where Robert Catton's repair ship had been anchored since July. When Robert learned that* Ticonderoga *had arrived at Eniwetok, he went to visit his son.*

[Eniwetok Atoll, Marshall Islands]
Dear Mom, 26 October 1944

Talk about a small world—it sure is. Last evening who should come aboard looking for me but Dad. Somehow, we had both been rather expecting that we'd meet ever since I left Norfolk. But to look at the vast Pacific on the map and to consider the number of ships in the Navy, it does seem a bit of extreme good fortune.

I spent the late afternoon and evening showing Dad all over the Big T. We had a couple of sodas together and caught up on all the things we had to say to each other since we last met. Then, as it began to get late, we went down to the quarterdeck for Dad to get a boat back to his ship.

As we were standing there talking the Captain came along. He noticed that Dad was a stranger, so he spoke to him. Dad explained his presence and introduced me. The skipper shook hands with me and asked if I'd been telling Dad all about the ship. I replied that I'd been bragging about it.

Then the skipper made an offer that struck me dumb so that I couldn't even thank him. He said, "Why don't you go over and spend the night on your Dad's ship?" So, with his permission I logged off the ship in dungarees, and we went in the whaleboat to Dad's ship.

We sat in his stateroom eating sandwiches and looking at snapshots and shooting the breeze for a while. Along about midnight he rigged a cot beside his bunk and I slept on it with no mattress. This morning, they brought me back in the whaleboat. There is much more to tell, but it will have to wait awhile I'm afraid.[20]

Dad seemed quite favorably impressed with the Big T. It wasn't all new to him, of course, having seen Paul Brown's ship. We went down to call on the Chaplain but found he was not in. We judged he was at chow. Dad did get a look at his quarters, though, and left his calling card.

The first thing Dad said to me when we met was, "I can see you've been below decks!" What I had thought was a fair tan shrank beside his brown to an almost sickly pallor. Even his bald head was a deep chocolate color. I don't believe I've ever seen him looking better. He said he hadn't lost any more weight, but I believe he has shifted some of it to new positions, so to speak.

I got a very good picture in my mind, both by talking to him and just by observing, as to what their ship's work has been the past few months. I wish it were possible for you to obtain such a view of it all. Even if we could all revisit these scenes again after the war it wouldn't be the same. There will certainly be many experiences to recall in the years to come.

I think my mail will probably be more irregular in getting to you from now on. That's one advantage Dad will have. But as the skipper said way back in Norfolk, "we're not going to fool around; we're going out and have us a good time!" I told you then that I thought we had the best skipper a fellow could want to serve under, and after last night that goes double.

Dad got quite a kick out of telling his officer-of-the-deck how come I happened to be with him. We both very much enjoyed the whole day.

Yours, Bill

Ticonderoga *reached Ulithi Atoll in the Caroline Islands on 29 October and joined the US Navy's other fast carriers and their numerous support ships in Task Force 38, also called Third Fleet, the main US naval strike force in the Pacific.*[21] *The many ships already anchored at Ulithi were undergoing repair and resupply following their great victory over the Japanese fleet in the Battle of Leyte Gulf, 23–26 October.* Ticonderoga, *still not battle tested, was about to enter the fray in the western Pacific.*

[Ulithi Atoll, Caroline Islands]

Dear Pop, 30 October 1944

Yesterday morning the Protestant service was made a memorial service in honor of some of our pilots who didn't come back from a hop. It was very impressive. An officer representing the friends of each of the pilots read a few paragraphs in memoriam.

Then the chaplain's sermon dealt with "honoring those who are lost" and "how we should think of death." He spoke of death being a lie; he said that a man always has some "unfinished business," and he asked if it were possible to believe that man should never be permitted to attain all his ambitions.

In closing, he said that our lives should be rededicated to the principles for which these men sacrificed theirs. The closing hymn was, "I Would Be True."

The service was held on the foc's'le, which seemed much nicer than the hangar deck somehow. I have never been so impressed in a civilian church as I was at this service. I wish some of the people back home could have been there.[22]
Yours, Bill

[Ulithi Atoll, Caroline Islands]

Dear Mom, 1 November 1944

Your letter of 15 October came tonight. Mail isn't coming quite as fast as it used to, but that is to be expected I guess. The delay is less important than the fact that it does get through.

Thanks for sending the clippings. The one by Lippmann on the results of the Dumberton Oaks conference is very encouraging.[23] I shall send them on to Dad I guess.

The other night the ship received a very meager batch of mail. It consisted of thirteen letters. I got one of them. It was from Dad, written just before I saw him. So it can be said that at mail call the other night I received approximately 7.7% of all the ship's mail. You can see what a big shot that makes mail.

I had another letter from Dad tonight which I shall enclose. I should like you to put it with those letters I wrote.

So far only the one Christmas package has arrived from you. There is still a margin of considerable time before Christmas, which is why Uncle Sam set the mailing dates so far ahead.

I just got a letter in a second mail call from Hook Topping. He is a bombardier as you may know. He was an instructor at Midland, Texas but is now in a B-29 crew. When I read his letter the first thing I said was, "The lucky bum!" Then upon reflection I decided I'm just as lucky myself.
Yours, Bill

On 2 November Ticonderoga *weighed anchor and steamed westward with Task Force 38 to provide naval support for General MacArthur's much-heralded return to the Philippines. Bill enjoyed one more tranquil night before his ship entered the combat zone.*

[Western Pacific]

Dear Mom, 4 November 1944

Last night I was up on the flight deck as usual getting my evening breath of air. One of the fellows who works in the ship's post office was with me. We got to talking about this and that, just passing the time of day. We were lying on the deck looking up at the stars. He said, did you ever have nothing to do and start counting the stars? I suppose he meant like counting sheep or twiddling your thumbs. Then casually he said, "You know, it's almost impossible to count the stars!" Well, naturally I laughed at that. But thinking it over I decided that if the emphasis were put on the word "almost" his statement could be the basis for a bit of philosophizing. It's like what the reviewer said about that book "The Raft."[24] "It is a story our grandchildren will be telling their grandchildren to illustrate man's ability to master any fate."

Yours, Bill

On the morning of 5 November, Ticonderoga *launched its first airstrikes against enemy airfields on the island of Luzon in the Philippines. In the late afternoon of that day, its task group was attacked by kamikazes. The Americans had had their first encounter with this shocking new weapon of war just days earlier at Leyte Gulf. In this kamikaze attack—Bill's first enemy engagement—*Ticonderoga *had two near misses while the carrier USS* Lexington *(CV-16) suffered a hit. Following two more days of action on 6 and 7 November, Bill got letters off to his folks. Though he was proud to have been in action at last, in his letters home he could only make veiled reference to "adventures" and things he would like to write about but couldn't.*[25]

[Philippine Sea]

Dear Pop, 7 November 1944

In a letter from Mom today was enclosed a church calendar with the picture of divine services aboard your ship and the article by you. I suppose she sent one to you, too. If so, did you notice the article next to yours? Mom's letter came through in two weeks.

Also I had letters today from Grandmother Willard, Aunt Nellie,[26] you, Ruth, and Jane. They're taking a little longer than they used to to reach me, but all in all Uncle Sam does a bang-up Postal job I think.

Aunt Nellie wrote that she was voting for Dewey. She said she admired Roosevelt but thought that even in midstream it was advisable to start a new man going. In a sense, she's right. Because of age, health, etc., this must obviously be Roosevelt's last term (assuming he wins this one). And in view of the crucial times to follow this four years, it would be a good idea to work in a new man for the job. But this next term is itself going to be a crucial time. I only wish voting against Roosevelt didn't mean voting for Dewey. The issue is still as I see it between isolationism and internationalism.

Also I had a letter from Grandmother Willard discussing politics. I'll enclose it, although you will probably know without reading it, what it says.

Mom says Ruth has striped the collar of my undress jumper and it looks fine on her. I wish I could inspect it and see if she did a job up to Navy standards.

I wish we could write without restraint of all our adventures and experiences. I was thinking some more the other day of the Chaplain's sermon at that memorial service. He put the question: "Is it possible to believe that these men are to be denied by death the opportunity to fulfill their aspirations?" I applied the proposition to myself, and discovered that that was a pretty good way of looking at it.

I was amused at my own conclusion. It was impossible to imagine that any eventuality could bring an end to my mind and thoughts. And then I found myself assuming that should this concept be wrong and life does cease at death I should be able to tell someone about it. Which seems to me proof enough of the conclusion the Chaplain drew. . . .

Yours, Bill

[Philippine Sea]

Dear Mom, 7 November 1944

I got a laugh out of your facetious remark about Grandmother and Grandfather probably not going to Florida till after 7 November. I presume you are voting about now. Grandmother wrote me all about why she was voting for Dewey. I'm afraid it all amounts to nothing more than voting against Roosevelt.

Your letters of the 15th and 24th came today. Also, a letter from Aunt Nellie, Ruth, Grandmother W., Dad, and Jane.

The picture on the church calendar you enclosed I had seen before. Dad had an 8 x 10 print of it in his room on the ship. Did you read the article next to the one by Dad?

There is much I wish I could write about but can't. I am making many interesting acquaintances. The seven men working under me have changed one at a time till I now have a new seven. My battle station is in a magazine with some colored steward's mates.[27] They are interesting men to know. I shall be an authority on race relations when I return.

Yours, Bill

[Philippine Sea]

Dear Pop, 11 November 1944

The other day during a spell of rough weather a word was passed which by nature reminded me of your "All officers who have done so, please do so immediately." It was, "At 1220 the band will play a concert on the fantail of smooth music for all hands with upset stomachs."

Following election day when the results were announced they began by saying: "All good Republicans—break out your pocket books." Frankly I was relieved at the results of said election. I had expected it to be much closer.

I was interrupted by lights out last night. So here it is Sunday evening. Church was held this afternoon on the fo'c'sle again. It included a baptismal service for a couple of men, one of whom was a big rugged marine captain.

Talking with a BM1/c [boatswain's mate first class] on the MAA [master-at-arms] force today, the subject of religion came up. He claimed to be a heathen. He said he believed every man had a right to "go to hell in his own way." Then he said his idea of religion was Shakespeare's: "This above all, to thine own self be true and it must follow as the night the day, thou canst not then be false to any man!" I never expected to hear a two-hitch Boats quote Shakespeare, especially like that.

Bill

On 11, 12, and 13 November, Ticonderoga *launched attacks on Japanese warships in the Philippines. Its planes destroyed the light cruiser* Kiso, *four destroyers, and seven merchant ships while sharing credit for sinking most of a reinforcement convoy. On 17 November* Ticonderoga, *together with the rest of Task Force 38, retired to Ulithi for refueling.*

[Ulithi Atoll, Caroline Islands]

Dear Pop, 17 November 1944

Your letter, 4 November, came today. Altogether in last night's and this morning's mail calls I accumulated 15 letters. Six of them were from Mom and two from Jane. Three of Mom's six letters were written since she received the news of our get together. She seemed overjoyed at our good fortune and was full of questions as to how you looked, seemed, etc.

Soon after I saw you I was assigned a new battle station. It's in one of the magazines with some colored steward's mates. It's fun to talk to them and listen to them talk to each other. I shall come home full of humorous anecdotes.

We have no such announcement system as you mentioned and it is at times annoying. However our Chaplain does perform a function the boys much appreciate. Every morning and every noon he reads a newscast over the P.A. system. In the evening the war correspondent aboard gives an analysis of the days news.

Chaplain Gilmore has started a Bible class, which meets weekly in the library. The subject studied is the Parables. For the first couple of meetings it was mostly lecture and rather dragged. But this last time there was considerable discussion which made it very interesting. Though it is primarily for Protestants there were a few Catholics with whom I am acquainted in attendance last time. All hands agreed afterwards that the meeting ended too soon.

The other day I had to appear as witness against my first mast report. While I was glad to be on that end of the lever rather than the other, it was an experience I did not relish. The man was on report for shirking duty. When the skipper asked me for the story I told him what the score was and then added that since the report was made the man had straightened out and was doing good work. The skipper asked the guy if he thought he'd learned his lesson. After the obvious answer he was dismissed with a warning.

The man involved was 28 years old and was disturbed no end by my youth. However, there were no hard feelings afterwards either way.

You asked if I was still in V-2 division. I don't know if they still have my name on their books or not. My duties are entirely with the M.A.A. force. I just retain the same mailing address for want of any good reason to change it.

Yours, Bill

[Ulithi Atoll, Caroline Islands]

Dear Pop, 19 November 1944

A year ago today Mom and the kids were in Chicago for my graduation from Navy Pier. I seemed to myself quite a big shot with my new crow. Next morning, I left with enthusiasm for Memphis radar school and on from there to Hollywood for gunnery school. A lot has happened since then.

This being Sunday I went to church as usual. It was a communion service and was held again up on the fo'c'sle. The quiet, the fresh air and sunshine, and the blue water on either side combine to make a very religious atmosphere. I think after the war I shall never be quite satisfied with a civilian church.

The "boats" [boatswain's mate] who quoted Shakespeare to me the other day came around today and said to me: "Catton, you probably know something about the Bible having had it shoved down your throat since you were so high." Then he asked me if I was familiar with a certain quotation. I was not but I looked it up for him. It was one of the parables. It seems he had run across it in a book he was reading and not being familiar with it failed to get its full significance.

One of the guys here with whom I am quite friendly is a little Chinese kid. He only came to the states about four years ago and at that time could not speak English. Now, to hear him, you'd never know it was not his native tongue. How he got into the U.S. I don't know. I thought Chinese were excluded.[28] Early in the war his parents lived in Hong Kong so they may not have been Chinese citizens. Now his mother and sister live in a small Chinese town that has jockeyed back and forth between Chinese and Japanese hands. When it is in Allied hands he hears from them regularly.

He has a very pleasant personality and is very easy to get along with. About the only thing that will get him mad is to call him "little Tojo." Even then it is a good-natured anger.

Another kid I like very well is a 17-year-old from Arkansas. He is a simple fellow, not much schooling, I think. But he has a sense of humor and enjoys life. He never gripes about his work, but gets it done well and promptly. When I think of him I am reminded of the boy from Tennessee I used to write to in high school.

One of the colored mess stewards at my battle station with whom I'm acquainted is 35 or so, and has four children. He doesn't know quite how come he was drafted. He used to run a filling station in Ga. before the war, hopes to have a garage someday. He is an all-around good egg.

It takes all kinds of people to make a world.

Yours, Bill

[Philippine Sea]

Dear Pop, 22 November 1944

I had letters today from Mom and Bill Bruce, written 6 and 7 November, respectively. Mom told about Butch's new clarinet and such things.

Bill's letter was mostly about his girl. I hardly blame him. He apparently is quite serious in all his thoughts these days. He hopes to try again at voluntary induction about the first of the year. He wrote me his views on the war and politics and I guess we pretty much agree. Here's what he says: "By the way, how do you feel concerning the election? Willkie or any other half-decent Republican, could have won my vote (if I had one) without trouble this year, because like a lot of other people, I think it's time for a change. But not Dewey. No sir. Roosevelt is far and away the better man, I believe, and even at the expense of a fourth term, I'm for him. It's a pity isn't it, that Willkie died? I really believe he'd have made one of our finest presidents. The Governor of New York, though, had better stay in Albany. It's about his size and speed."

My thoughts, too, have been serious of late. When news reports come in of ships sunk and casualties I think to myself, that could just as easily have been us. Then I wonder why I am not worried about it, kid that I am. The other day I decided that it was because a man is so accustomed to being able to plan ahead and anticipate the pleasures of tomorrow that it is impossible to conceive of there being no tomorrow. As Shakespeare said: "Cowards die many times before their death; the valiant taste of death but once."

I have been reading some more Shakespeare lately. I started with *The Tempest.* In it I found three quotations apt for political debate on preparedness. They are as follows:

Sebastian says and I would quote to the Know-nothings:

"It is a sleepy language and thou dost speak out of thy sleep."

To which if my opponent were bright, he would reply that farther down Sebastian says:

"Thou dost snore distinctly—there is meaning in thy snores."

To which I would say that still further along Ariel says:

"While you here do snoring lie,
Open-eyed conspiracy
His time doth take.
If of life you keep a care,
Shake off slumber and beware:
Awake! Awake!"

At present I am engaged in a very pleasant sort of job. It consists of supervising the efforts of some extra duty men. They are scrubbing paintwork. All I have to do is look up now and then and count noses. Then I resume my correspondence. "One man's meat is another man's poison."

Yours, Bill

On 22 November Ticonderoga *returned to action in the Philippine Sea. In one day of combat, its aircraft sank the Japanese heavy cruiser* Kumano, *the escort ship* Yasoshima, *a merchant ship, and three landing craft while also shooting down fifteen enemy aircraft and destroying eleven more on the ground. On that same day the ship's crew manned battle stations against another onslaught of kamikazes. While* Ticonderoga *came through the attack unscathed, the aircraft carrier* Essex *was hit and set afire; its returning pilots had to ditch their planes in the water.* Ticonderoga *assisted in recovering the aircrews.*

[Philippine Sea]
Dear Mom, 23 November 1944

Enclosed you will find a menu of our Thanksgiving Day dinner today. In all points, it was excellent. I doubt if it was better, but it was as good as those we used to eat at Grandmother's. Everybody enjoyed it and we all got well filled up. It occurred to me that this would have been a particularly bad day to have had rough weather.

Although the food was as good as any, the absence of plates, white tablecloths, and napkins, and the lack of the usual holiday dinner table conversation made it different from former years, at home or invited out.

Still, with all the men on this ship that had to be fed we all ate in less time than a similar dinner at home would take. From the time the first man sat down till the last man got up was about two and a half hours. If you will recall, at Grandmother's we used to sit down about 1 P.M. and usually secured around 4. That, I would say, illustrates Navy efficiency.

Put this menu in your scrapbook. We had a Thanksgiving Day service on the Foc'sle this morning. It was very well attended with men standing in all available space. It was conducted by Chaplain Gilmore but there were both Protestant and Catholic men present.

Remember in Manistee how we used to make a full day of Thanksgiving? Ruth and I would get our skis waxed up as there was usually snow. Impatiently we would sit through the all-afternoon meal and finally when excused we would go out for a short fun-fest in the snow. You and Dad and all the aunts and uncles would sit around shooting the breeze. Finally, about eight or nine o'clock, some killjoy would say, "Well, we really *must* be going." Then we'd all pile into our heavy coats and spend an hour saying goodbye. When we got home, Spot would appear from under the back porch to greet us as the car drove into the garage.

I take great pleasure in writing about skis, snow, winter coats, etc. Today, it was like having Thanksgiving Day in July.

Yours, Bill

[Philippine Sea]
Dear Mom, 27 November 1944

I'm enclosing a money order for $18.75 with which you can add another war bond to my collection. What is the local quota in this drive? I don't know why but I have a feeling it won't be met.

Church services were held yesterday afternoon on the foc's'le. The Protestant service began at 1545. The Catholics held theirs in the mess hall at 1600. We were right in the midst of a hymn when church call sounded again on the bugle at 1600. Naturally everybody got off key and there was quite a mixture of sour notes. Contrasted with the solemnity of the occasion it was funny.

I developed a new type of practical joke yesterday which is now spreading like wildfire. Our chewing gum out here comes wrapped in tinfoil. So yesterday I took a piece of that tinfoil, cut a circle out of it just the size of a 50¢ piece. I laid that on a half dollar and impressed the coin's image on it with my fingers.

Then I carefully laid it on the deck in a place where guys walking by could easily see it. Several of us stood by and watched. Pretty soon, sure enough, some sucker, thinking he had just had a stroke of luck bent over to pick it up. As he grabbed it, it of course crushed in his fingers. The gag itself is not particularly humorous, but the embarrassed expression on the victim's face, really brings a laugh.
Yours, Bill

[Philippine Sea]

Dear Pop, 30 November 1944

I am writing this at night up on the flight deck. The moon is almost full, the sky is clear, making the light plenty bright enough for letter writing.

Your book came about two or three days ago. I began reading it immediately and have read so far a hundred or so pages. Before starting it I was prejudiced against it by the picture of the author on the jacket flap. She looks very dull. However, both the subject and its presentation are very interesting.[29]

I had a letter from Mom the other night telling among other things about Butch being in a fight with some kid on the way home from school. It reminded me of that picture I took a few years ago which won a camera club prize. The one I'm referring to was entitled, "Well, ya see Mom it was like this!", the one with the false black eye and the expression of complete innocence.

I hope you can read this letter. The wind is beginning to play havoc with the paper.
Yours, Bill

[Ulithi Atoll, Caroline Islands]

Dear Mom, 2 December 1944

I don't believe I ever wrote you about the close call I had at Pearl Harbor. The air department on this ship was overcomplemented. So at P. H. a transfer list of rate mechs was made up. Somehow my name got on it. After all I had done to get on this ship I didn't want to be left behind. So I talked to my division officer about it.

Well, they had to cut down the number of rated men and they didn't have any place for me. But on investigation it seemed there was a place on the master-at-arms force for a rated man. To stay with the ship I took that job although I didn't like it.

The master-at-arms is the sheriff of a ship. So I was a deputy sheriff. I was in charge of the mess cooks in one of the mess halls. My job was to oversee their work and to be responsible for the cleanliness of that mess hall. It is usually considered by other rates that if an "airdaile" goes into the M.A.A. force it is because he is not so good as an "airdaile."[30] So, because, I was a little bit ashamed of it I didn't write you about it.

However as of today I'm back with V-2 Division.[31] An M.A.A. does have added privileges, such as "dragging the gedunk line" (going to the head of the line at the soda fountain). Therefore some guys like the job. A second class A.M. [aviation mechanic] in V-2 division decided he would like it. So we got together, talked to the proper authorities, and arranged a swap.

Now my job is as a "plane handler." I am now in charge of a crew of 10 plane handlers. So the net result of the whole series of events is a sort of backhanded promotion.

While I say I didn't like the job of M.A.A., by no means do I regret the two months spent as such. Any experience in life is worthwhile if it broadens one's mind and adds to his future. I made some pleasant and worthwhile acquaintances, [and] learn[ed] many things about the ship's construction and organization I might not otherwise have known. . . .

Yours, Bill

Dear Pop, 2 December 1944

As of today, my nickname ceases to be "jimmy-legs."[32] I am an "airedale" again.

An AM2/c [aviation mechanic second class] in the metal shop decided he would like to be an M.A.A. There was an opening for me as a plane director on the hangar deck so we arranged a swap. I am now back in V-2 division.

I am one of the boys who wears a yellow jersey. There are ten guys in the plane handling crew under me. They are all seamen but one, who is a mech third. It looks to me like I'm getting a pretty good deal. What it amounts to is a promotion. When I first came aboard I was a plane handler myself. To avoid being transferred due to overcompliment I took this M.A.A. job. Now I'm back topside in charge of an outfit I used to be in.[33]

The time I spent as master-at-arms was by no means wasted. The experiences, while not in my line, were nevertheless interesting. I learned some things about the ship's organization, etc., I probably would not have otherwise. And I made some very pleasant and worthwhile acquaintances. I can't recall at the moment any experiences I've had in my life which are actually to be regretted. Even unpleasant things have added something to the future.

The bosun's mate who used to be in charge of the mess deck M.A.A.'s is now the leading P.O. [petty officer] in one of the deck divisions. He is the one I mentioned who quoted Shakespeare. We do a lot of light hearted kidding back and forth when we see each other.

It is the general opinion that when an "airedale" becomes an M.A.A. it is because he was not too hot at his aviation rate. (That is one reason I was glad to get back to V-2—to get out from under that stigma.) I kid this B.M. [boatswain's mate] about that, though, saying that even a no good airedale can do the regular job of a B.M.

Reading the biography of [Oliver Wendell] Holmes that you sent me I came across one part that made me think. It seems in one of the old Harvard buildings was an inscription on the wall saying: "Youth is the seed-time of life." It seems Holmes didn't like that. He meant to enjoy life as such at whatever age.

I am inclined to agree. Too many of my acquaintances here regard their Navy careers as merely a chunk taken out of their lives. To me that seems absurd. I am, like all of them, "striking for the rate of civilian." But I can see no point in wasting the experiences at hand.

Have you heard the story about the teacher who was endeavoring to instill proper manners into her pupils? She asked one little boy, "Jimmy, if I gave you a big apple and a little apple, which would you give to your brother?" Jimmy replied with a question, "Do you mean my big brother or my little brother?"
Yours, Bill

[Ulithi Atoll, Caroline Islands]
4 December 1944

Dear Pop,

I'm glad you wrote me as you did about the conscientious objector who talked with you. It's a subject on which I have strong opinions and in which I am deeply interested.

The man's sudden discovery of his conscientious objections at such a late stage in the game certainly does seem rather extraordinary. And as you said with such a well-chosen example, it is not a strict rule of his religion.

But I find it next to impossible to think of him as yellow. That is only partly because, as you put it, it is about the worst you can call a man. More, I think, is it because it is impossible to feel a characteristic of another man which is not part of one's own makeup. It's like trying to imagine a sixth sense, or a color outside the usual spectrum. I'm not trying to say that I've never been scared. I have. So has everybody who leads a normal life.

What I am trying to say is that nothing I can of my own imagination foresee in the future frightens me. It is entirely proper for a man to be *afraid* in the face of immediate danger. And it is good sense to be *cautious* about going near danger. But one should not be *afraid* of danger which has not yet presented itself.

If a man jumps instinctively at the bang of a gun it is a normal reaction. But if he were to spend his whole life in convulsions for fear he might someday hear a gun go off, it would be exceedingly abnormal. So much so, in fact, that it would be impossible to imagine the actual existence of such a case.

That is why I too would feel it right to give a suspicious C.O. [conscientious objector] every benefit of every doubt. It is like the maxim of American law: "Better a thousand guilty should go free than that one innocent should be convicted."

I do agree that the position of the conscientious objector is wrong. But I do not doubt the possibility of sincerity in such objections.

When your client objected conscientiously to taking typhoid shots for fear of "defiling the temple," I would have asked him if he drank or smoked. A positive answer would refute his stand although a negative answer would not necessarily prove it.

I am reminded by that quotation of a temperance speaker who came to St. John's High School that spring I was there. He said smoking and drinking were sinful because they defiled the temple. While I might have agreed with him in principle I hated him for what he said. He quoted from the Bible and then said, "Now this is what that quotation means." I thought, well who does he think he is to say arbitrarily what a Biblical quotation means. Had he said, "This is what it means to me," the matter would have been different.

To change the subject, I am better than half done with the Holmes biography. There are some very worthwhile things in it. I found myself this morning, after I had closed the book, thinking in "Holmes-ish" sentences. A sentence went through my mind which was similar in construction but diametrically opposed in meaning to the description of Holmes. My sentence was, "To him, life was merely a none too convenient means of existing." It sounded pretty good and I thought it could be applied to those short sighted guys in the Navy who think only of getting out as soon as possible and forget there is life to be enjoyed now.

Going back to your C.O., his case reminds me again of Shakespeare's "Cowards die many times before their death; the valiant taste of death but once."

Yours, Bill

[Ulithi Atoll, Caroline Islands]

Dear Mom, 6 December 1944

Your two letters dated 20 and 26 November came today. I wish I might be there to do my own Christmas shopping. That's much more fun than just sending a money order. And the fun of wrapping them up and putting the stickers on, I shall miss, too.

I'm surprised at you getting Butch a Chemistry set. Wasn't I a couple years older yet when you debated whether I should have one? As I recall it Grandma and Aunt Nellie came to my rescue with checks to you for the purpose. Or did one of them actually buy it?

We had another good movie last night and another one today. Last night's was "Frenchman's Creek." It was a color picture of pirates and old sailing vessels. This afternoon we had a matinee showing of "Kismet" with Ronald Colman and Marlene Dietrich. It, also, was in technicolor. Although it was nothing but fantasy it was a good escape picture. There was one extra good line in it which Ronald Colman got off in extra good manner: "I am trying to put you on a mountain top and you prefer to sit in the gutter." I'm going to send that to Dad as I think he can make a sermon of it.

For the last two evenings I've slept on the flight deck. It is wonderful up there at night. The cool breeze is invigorating. The moonlight, fresh air, and the sound of the sea remind me of those nights on the sleeping porch at Crystal Lake last summer. This morning, however, it rained before I could get dressed and get below. I was under the wing of a plane so I didn't get very wet.

This morning I accidentally dropped over the side my little black book in which I keep the muster-list of the men in my plane-handling crew. I didn't miss it that much though, as it was a loss easily replaced. But the notebook also served as a "catch-all" for odds and ends. The two things I regretted most to have lost were the address of a guy who owes me $3.45 and the typed copy of the blinker message they sent for me the night I spent on Dad's ship. The latter I had planned to send home as a souvenir. Oh well, that scrapbook of yours will be fat by the end of the war anyway.

They are having a Pearl Harbor day bond drive on the ship. Feeling as wealthy as anyone else I have signed up for a bond. They are to be made out for us at Pearl Harbor, with a special comemoration stamp and mailed home.

Yours, Bill

From Robert Catton to Bill:

[Eniwetok Atoll, Marshall Islands]
Dear Bill; 11 December 1944

. . . Do you know, I'm afraid if you don't look out you may find yourself deciding to be a preacher. When you keep getting ideas or germs of ideas that make you say to yourself "I believe there's a sermon in that," you have what is known as the homiletic mind. Not all preachers have it. Of course, there's more, or should be, to the profession than that. Perhaps the same habit will be useful to you if you turn writer or columnist. Instead of "a sermon in that," it would be, "I believe there's a column in that." . . .

I don't know who first said that ideals are like stars, though I have heard it before, too. By the way, sometime in your reveries on the flight deck of a starry night, you might remember one of the most notable of all words about the stars: Kant's "Two things fill the mind with ever new and increasing wonder and awe, the starry heavens above me and the moral law within me."

One thing you mentioned parenthetically has raised a question in my mind. You spoke of the chap who said you must know something about the Bible, having had it crammed into you etc. etc. referring, presumably, to your father's profession. I am wondering if you children have grown up being self-consciously minister's children. It wasn't altogether that remark, either, that made me think about it. I was talking Sunday after church, at some length, with a sailor off a D.E. [destroyer escort] that came to our church service. He proved to be from DeKalb, Illinois, and a member of the Congregational church. That is the church of which Mr. Caldwell was minister before he came to St. Johns, and so we were talking about him and St. Johns and that led to various personal matters. He had come to my room to see me, and so he saw the photos of you and the others on my desk. He asked about you, and among other things said, "I suppose he had the usual tough time trying to live down being a minister's son." I denied the soft impeachment; but then I reflected, I suppose the minister in the case never does understand how his children feel about it.

You mentioned being in charge one day of a bunch of fellows who were chipping paint or some such thing. This morning there was a terrible racket outside my port and I strolled out presently to see the same thing going on. There were four seamen on their knees on the deck chipping paint, and one M.A.A. [master-at-arms] standing by and watching them. Somehow it made me think of 1917 when the ships used to put in at Melville to coal ship. On some of those old timers they had to do that by hand, the boys carrying the coal on their backs in canvas baskets up over the side and down to the bunkers. To encourage them, I suppose the theory was, the marine band played martial music topside, which didn't exactly endear the marines to the sailors. Do you wonder that M.A.A.'s are something less than universally popular? You must have felt curious putting that 28-year-old on report. I am sure he doubly deserved it if he was lazy enough to get you worked up to putting him in report.

Dad

On 10 December Ticonderoga *sailed from Ulithi again in a huge armada of ninety warships. The fast carrier task force swept into position off Luzon, where it made repeated air strikes against Japanese airbases. Six days later Task Force 38 pulled back to refuel. On 17–18 December a typhoon struck the fleet without warning. While the big carriers rode it out with relative ease, the destroyers were perilously low on fuel when the storm struck, and some were unable to refuel in the heavy seas. Three destroyers,* Spence, Hull, *and* Moynahan, *eventually capsized and sank, with great loss of life.*

[Philippine Sea]
20 December 1944

Dear Mom,

We had a little spell of really rugged weather recently. Even this big tub bounced around enough so you couldn't ignore it.[34] . . .

Last night I dreamed we were in port along with Dad's ship. Soon after we dropped the hook, a boat came alongside and Dad came aboard accompanied by you and Jane!! Where you and she came from I don't know. It reminded me of the recruit who was asked at the induction center what he would do if he were out in the desert and met a German battleship. He said he'd submerge and sink it with a torpedo. The psychiatrist asked him where he got the torpedo, and he replied, "The same place you got the battlewagon!"

Anyhow, it was a wonderful dream. By special order of the skipper a swimming pool had just been rigged down on the second deck. After a short visit, you and Dad went up to the flight deck and Jane and I went for a swim. Then we sat out on the fantail watching the sunset. Then I woke up!

If I have been a little lax on writing letters lately, it's because I've been busy. My working hours as a plane spotter are longer than they were as an M.A.A. It's just about a solid day from reveille till the middle of the evening. Then by the time I've taken a shower, and perhaps washed a pair of dungarees, it's time to hit the sack. So, bear with me. I'll try to write as often as I have time. I'm still having fun.

Yours, Bill

[Ulithi Atoll, Caroline Islands]
Dear Mom, 22 December 1944

Last evening, I had quite an argument with another guy over a statement I made that the folks back home don't know what they're missing. He countered with the remark that they weren't missing a darn thing. What I said was apropos of the beautiful sunset we were watching from the rail. The ocean never seems to look the same two evenings in a row.

A lot of guys, especially those who were drafted into the service, seem to take for granted the beautiful things they are seeing, the fun they're having, and the friends they are meeting. They forget them entirely in their morbid reflections and think only of the things they don't like. To me that is looking for misery and finding it.

Whenever I talk about enjoying my Navy adventures some guy makes the remark, "He's a twenty-year-man," that being the term for one making a career of the Navy. When this business now at hand is over, I'll be just as glad as anyone else to get home. But right now I'm glad to be here, and I'm having fun.

Another argument I had yesterday was concerning the latest reports on the radio about German atrocities.[35] Some guy was quite upset over it. I said it didn't bother me much. War itself being the major atrocity one shouldn't worry about minor atrocities. I said that if he wasn't upset over the millions of Russians and Chinese killed in the whole war so far he had no right to be upset over a few hundred Americans involved in one incident.

When he said something about "the enemy should at least be a little humane," one of the other plane directors took up my side. He asked if there could be any such thing as a "humane war." To me it seems that war is a dirty business however you look at it.

I seem to look at things differently than others. And I do quite a bit of arguing.

Today I drew a small textbook on Navigation from the library and am making a leisurely study of the subject. It's interesting how logical it all is.

One of the guys asked me the other day who gets the job if a president dies. Thinking he was asking for information I poured it on thick. I told him the vice president by custom actually succeeded to the office, but that the constitution had never actually decreed thus, only saying "The vice pres. shall perform the duties of president in case of death or disability of the president." It turned out to be a gag, though. He told me that when the president dies, the undertaker gets the job.

Yours, Bill

[Ulithi Atoll, Caroline Islands]

Dear Mom, 24 December 1944

Your letters of 4, 7, and 10 December came today. I had been three weeks without any mail at all. . . .

According to your plans you are now in Benzonia. Needless to say I wish I might be with you. But Christmas is not by any means going unobserved out here. . . . Tomorrow there are to be services on the foc's'le in the morning. At noon we are scheduled to have ham and turkey, and all that goes with such, for dinner. In the evening we will have a community sing and band concert of Christmas carols on the hangar deck, followed by movies.

In my locker is a *vast* collection of Christmas packages to be opened tomorrow. It won't be like the old times. But the memory of those other years will be an inspiration. Dressing excitedly in the cold, while Dad built the furnace fire. Waiting till all were ready and going downstairs together with the Victrola playing "Joy To The World." The beautifully lighted tree and the array of colorful packages beneath. The gleeful smiles as each box disclosed its contents to expectant fingers. The reluctant departure from the tree in favor of the breakfast table. All morning to rejoice in the wealth of toys. And the family dinner at Grandmother's at noon. It has been a tradition well worth remembering.

And I think all of us out here especially, and those at home, too, will be rededicated in our hearts, this season, to the Christmas spirit in the future. For it is the principle of "Peace on earth, good will toward men," for which we fight.

Yours, Bill[36]

[Ulithi Atoll, Caroline Islands]

Dear Mom, Christmas Day 1944

This morning all of us awoke with a laugh. Instead of reveille they played "Jingle Bells." Following this musical rendition, the bosun's mate of the watch passed the word over the speaker system, "All hands, Merry Christmas, heave out and trice up!"

I got up, ate breakfast, and went out on the fantail to read my accumulation of letters. At 0800, church call sounded. They had a service of Christmas hymn singing. The Chaplain gave a brief sermon which was very good.

It was entitled "Three reasons I like Christmas." His reasons were: 1. It is the season when men's differences are laid aside and all are united in one spirit. 2. It is the season when men "fly their flags of faith." Religion begins to show through the surface instead of remaining hidden inside. 3. It is a season of hope, when all are filled with faith in the future.

At the service, which was held on the hangar deck, the movie screen was rigged as a background. Around it was colored cloth, red and white. Strung from the overhead was a series of signal flags spelling out Merry Christmas.

We had an almost unimaginable quantity of mail today, Christmas packages. And I broke out the ones I had stowed in my locker. Altogether there were three from you, I think, and one from Ruth, besides those from grandmothers, aunts, and uncles.

It was fun opening these gifts, reminiscent of the days of my childhood. But I wish all of you hadn't tried to outdo yourselves. I received so much stuff that it was difficult to find space for it all in my locker. Next year please make the boxes smaller. But, anyway, many thanks for everything. It has been a wonderful day.

We had a big dinner this noon and all were well filled. I'm enclosing both a menu and a copy of the greeting we all got from the skipper.[37] You will probably want to put them in your scrapbook.

In the afternoon, I spent a couple of hours up on the flight deck, tanning myself. The contrast between that and Michigan winter is strong.

I hope all of you had a very Merry Christmas even without Dad and me. It would have been nice to be home just for today, though. My thoughts were there.
Yours, Bill

In January 1945 Ticonderoga *and Task Force 38 steamed west of the Philippine Islands into the South China Sea, boldly cutting in two Japan's vital sea lane to the Dutch East Indies. While the Japanese stepped up their kamikaze attacks, the fast carrier fleet defiantly moved around the South China Sea sending its planes to destroy enemy shipping and airfields on Japanese-held Formosa and the Asian mainland. In one day, 12 January, the whole carrier group launched all its approximately 850 planes, and this mighty air fleet sank forty-four Japanese ships, totaling over 130,000 tons. For the Japanese merchant marine, this was the most catastrophic month of the war.*[38]

Air operations day after day, punctuated by spells of bad weather, kept the crew of Ticonderoga *very busy. Bill wrote home that he was working fourteen to seventeen hours a day—"But it's good, honest solid work, not scrubbing bulkheads, or swabbing decks, and it makes me feel as if I'm actually helping to accomplish something. . . . I wish I could tell you what kind of busy I am in addition to how busy."*[39]

Meanwhile, the kamikaze attacks increased, both in number and in effectiveness. On 21 January, when the task force was positioned about one hundred miles off the south coast of Formosa, four kamikazes with three escorts went after the US ships, stealthily trailing a group of American planes back to their carriers to escape radar detection. At 1210 a kamikaze dove on Ticonderoga *out of the sun and clouds and crashed through the flight deck abreast of the No. 2 5-inch gun turret. The plane and its 250-kilogram bomb exploded between the hangar deck and the gallery spaces forward of the bridge, touching off more explosions and fires among the closely packed and gassed planes. As black smoke rose hundreds of feet above the stricken carrier, more kamikazes homed in. Three attacking planes were downed by the ship's antiaircraft barrage while five others were shot down by the ship's own planes flying combat air patrol, but another kamikaze got through and hit the starboard side of the island structure. The two hits combined killed 144 men and wounded about 200 more. The air and gunnery officers were killed, and the skipper, Dixie Kiefer, was badly injured. An hour after the second hit, the fires were extinguished and the ship was saved from destruction. But the Big T was disabled for flight operations and would have to undergo extensive repairs.*[40]

Two days later a funeral service was held on the burned-out hangar deck. The dead were "buried at sea"—each body sewed up in a sailcloth bag with a 5-inch round to ensure sinking and cast over the side as a bugle sounded taps over the public-address system.[41]

Following protocol, Bill wrote nothing about the ship's calamity in the following days and weeks, nor did he write of the shrapnel wound in his shoulder or of having two mates in his plane-handling crew among the many dead. Instead, he wrote, as before, about much quieter elements of his shipboard experience.

[Ulithi Atoll, Caroline Islands]
24 January 1945

Dear Mom,

In the past three or four weeks, I think I have written a total of about half a dozen letters. Jane wrote me once that she had not heard from me for over two weeks and was beginning to worry. When you're very busy, two weeks passes rapidly. I hope any absence of letters from me over the past month hasn't caused you to worry.

I celebrated an uneventful birthday last week. About all that could be said for it was that on Sunday I was eighteen and on Monday I was nineteen. When some of the boys found out it was my birthday they took great delight in forcefully removing my pants, on the hangar deck. But such pastimes lose all their enjoyment in a purely masculine society.

I had a little visit with Chaplain Gilmore the other day. He returned the book of Dad's that I had lent him. As he is from Boston, I asked him what he thought of the advisability of me going to Harvard after the war. He suggested either Columbia or Minnesota for journalism.

William Robert Catton Jr. on the flight deck of the USS *Ticonderoga* (CV-14). He enlisted in the US Navy on his seventeenth birthday and joined the crew of the Big T in July 1944.

Bill was a senior in high school in Manistee, Michigan, when the United States entered World War II in December 1941. Many of his classmates signed up for military service the following year and, by 1944, were dispersed to battlefronts in western Europe, the North Atlantic, China, and the Pacific.

Bill and his parents, Helen Willard and William Robert Catton Sr., February 1944. They were a family of letter writers. Bill once teased his father, "Apparently the circulation of letters in the Catton family is pretty well organized: Uncle Bruce, to Grandma, to you, to Aunt Nellie." Helen saved all of Bill's letters home, a collection that came to number several hundred.

Bill with his brother, Edward; mother, Helen; and sister, Ruth, at Crystal Lake in northern Michigan, summer of 1944. His closeness to family and fond memories of his boyhood helped sustain him during the war.

Clockwise from top left: Bill's parents at the time of their engagement, 1918; Billy and big brother, John, in Grand Forks, North Dakota, 1928; Bill and Ruth in front of their home in Montrose, Colorado, about 1934; Ruth, Edward, and Bill in Manistee, Michigan, about 1937.

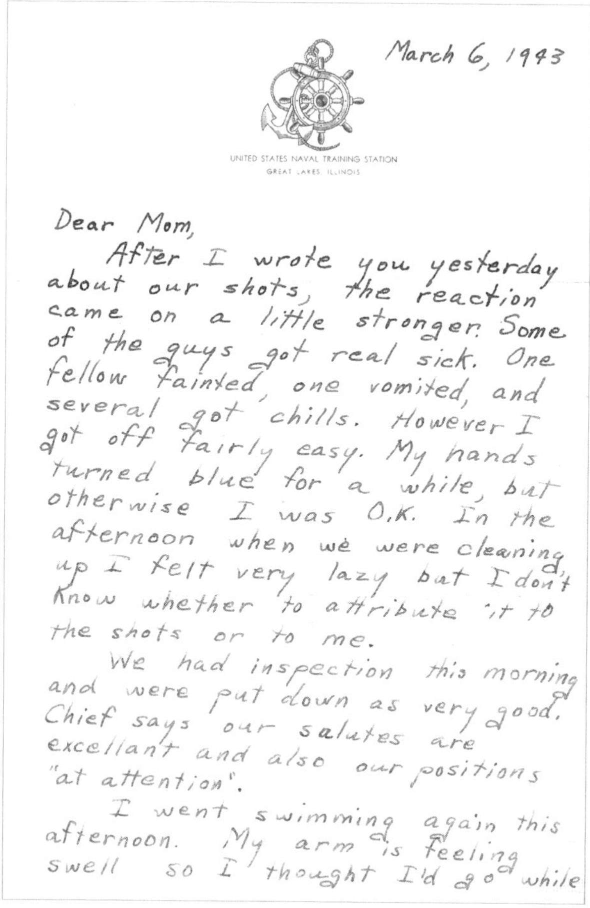

March 6, 1943

UNITED STATES NAVAL TRAINING STATION
GREAT LAKES, ILLINOIS

Dear Mom,

After I wrote you yesterday about our shots, the reaction came on a little stronger. Some of the guys got real sick. One fellow fainted, one vomited, and several got chills. However I got off fairly easy. My hands turned blue for a while, but otherwise I was O.K. In the afternoon when we were cleaning up I felt very lazy but I don't know whether to attribute it to the shots or to me.

We had inspection this morning and were put down as very good. Chief says our salutes are excellant and also our positions "at attention".

I went swimming again this afternoon. My arm is feeling swell so I thought I'd go while

Bill wrote to his mother and father nearly every day he was in boot camp. In this letter he writes about the dreaded vaccination shots that were administered to recruits over a period of several days soon after they began basic training.

Lt. William Robert Catton Sr., USNR. A World War I navy veteran and a minister in civilian life, Bill's father returned to military service as a navy chaplain and served in the Pacific aboard the USS *Oahu* (ARG-5).

Left: Father and son boarding the train at the end of their home leaves, February 1944.

Below: Bill and his best friend from high school, Tom Stege. On liberty in Chicago in November 1943, they went to a Bears-Packers pro football game at Wrigley Field and afterward had their picture taken at a cheap photo studio. Such studios as well as photo booths became ubiquitous around military bases, finding a ready market with young servicemen eager to send their images to loved ones back home.

Bill's photo of the Lake Michigan shoreline. The Pacific Ocean often reminded him of Lake Michigan, as in this passage from a letter to his mom: "The white foam kicked up by the ship could have been the ice on Lake Michigan in the early spring."

Bill joined the crew of USS *Ticonderoga* on 31 July 1944. "She's a big ship, a first-rate carrier of the Essex class," he wrote to his mom. "I paced the length of the flight deck and it's simply unbelievable." In this stern view the aft deck elevator is recessed and clearly visible amidships. During flight operations, the tall antenna towers folded out to starboard to be out of the way of airplane landings and takeoffs. *National Archives photo 80-G-234666.*

Grumman F6F Hellcats on the hangar deck of USS *Yorktown* (CV-10). Bill worked on the hangar deck of its sister ship *Ticonderoga.* In this view men in the foreground are preparing to load ordnance on the fighters' wing-mounted bomb racks while crewmembers seated in the background attend a presentation. *National Archives photo 80-G-419959.*

Grumman TBF Avenger torpedo bombers over the USS *Hornet* (CV-12), Philippine Sea, 1944. *US Navy National Naval Aviation Museum photo NNAM 1996.25.1089.*

Grumman F6F Hellcats fitted with centerline drop tanks on *Ticonderoga* preparing for takeoff. The bulge on the starboard wing of the first two aircraft contained a radar device to facilitate night-fighting missions. *National Archives photo 80-G-305244.*

Airmen on *Ticonderoga* at briefing prior to the launch of the ship's first air-strike, 5 November 1944. *National Archives photo 80-G-469512.*

A fast carrier task force heads for the Philippine Sea, 12 December 1944. The light aircraft carrier USS *Langley* (CVL-27) is on the left, *Ticonderoga* is on the right. In all, the giant armada comprised ninety ships. *National Archives photo 80-G-301351.*

Letter envelope postmarked by the Navy Mail Service and stamped "PASSED BY NAVAL CENSOR."

Above and facing page: This V-mail letter and envelope are shown actual size as received by Bill's mother after it was microfilmed, shipped, then photographically printed for delivery.

Print the complete address in plain letters in the panel below, and your return address in the space provided on the right. Use typewriter, dark ink, or dark pencil. Faint or small writing is not suitable for photographing.

PASSED BY NAVAL CENSOR

(CENSOR'S STAMP)

TO: Mrs. W. R. Catton,
404 S. Oakland,
St. Johns, Michigan

SEE INSTRUCTION NO. 2

FROM
W. R. Catton, Jr. AMM3/c
V-2 Div. CV14 USS Ticonderoga
FPO, San Francisco

(Sender's complete address above)

30 October, 1944

Dear Mom,

We had a mail call last night. I received your airmail letter of 17 October, a V-mail from Aunt Ione, and a V-mail from Jane.

There isn't much to write about. Or rather there isn't much we can write about. Having seen Dad last week I have formed a pretty good picture of what life has been like for him since July. Some of it may have been monotonous but it has some of it certainly been very interesting. I guess most of their repair work is done on small ships but he sees more than just that. Further than that, I guess we'll have to wait till after the war to talk about it.

Things certainly did work out well for us. We got together very quickly, had the maximum number of hours together and what with visiting each others ships and the conversation we had I guess we just about made up the five months since we were all together at Norfolk.

Yours,

Bill

HAVE YOU FILLED IN COMPLETE ADDRESS AT TOP?

REPLY BY V-MAIL

HAVE YOU FILLED IN COMPLETE ADDRESS AT TOP?

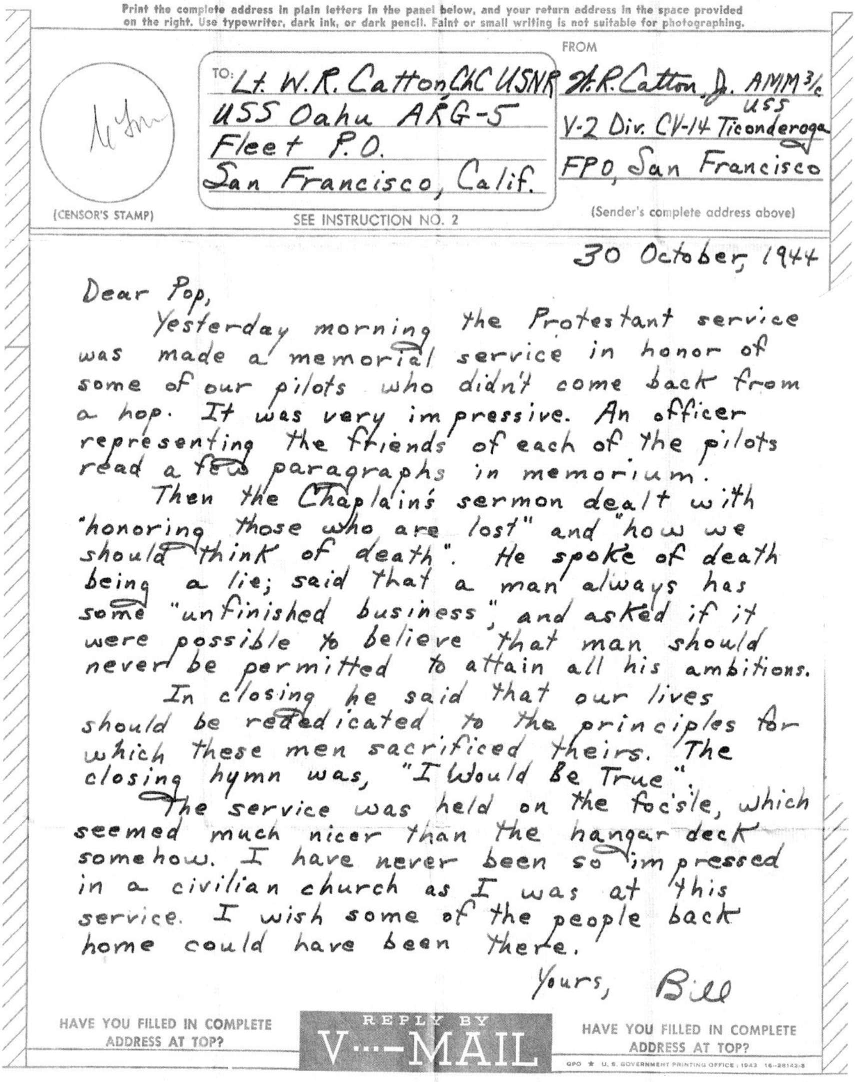

Print the complete address in plain letters in the panel below, and your return address in the space provided on the right. Use typewriter, dark ink, or dark pencil. Faint or small writing is not suitable for photographing.

TO: Lt. W. R. Catton ChC USNR
USS Oahu ARG-5
Fleet P.O.
San Francisco, Calif.

FROM
W. R. Catton Jr. AMM 3/c
V-2 Div. CV-14 USS Ticonderoga
FPO, San Francisco

(CENSOR'S STAMP) SEE INSTRUCTION NO. 2 (Sender's complete address above)

30 October, 1944

Dear Pop,

Yesterday morning the Protestant service was made a memorial service in honor of some of our pilots who didn't come back from a hop. It was very impressive. An officer representing the friends of each of the pilots read a few paragraphs in memorium.

Then the Chaplain's sermon dealt with "honoring those who are lost" and "how we should think of death". He spoke of death being a lie; said that a man always has some "unfinished business", and asked if it were possible to believe that man should never be permitted to attain all his ambitions.

In closing he said that our lives should be rededicated to the principles for which these men sacrificed theirs. The closing hymn was, "I Would Be True".

The service was held on the foc'sle, which seemed much nicer than the hangar deck somehow. I have never been so impressed in a civilian church as I was at this service. I wish some of the people back home could have been there.

Yours, Bill

HAVE YOU FILLED IN COMPLETE ADDRESS AT TOP? REPLY BY V···—MAIL HAVE YOU FILLED IN COMPLETE ADDRESS AT TOP?

GPO ★ U. S. GOVERNMENT PRINTING OFFICE : 1943 16-28143-5

Above and facing page: V-mail (front and back) that Bill sent to his father the same day as the V-mail letter to his mother. This one did not go through the microfilming process but was delivered in its original form on letter-size V-mail stationery. Note that the stationery folded up to form its own envelope. Usually, V-mail was microfilmed at a processing center for shipment by air, then printed off the microfilm reels onto 4¼ by 5-inch photo paper, folded once, and inserted in an envelope for delivery to the addressee. V-mail saved valuable cargo space for other uses.

FROM W. R. Catton, Jr. AMM3/c
V-2 Div. CV-14, USS Ticonderoga,
FPO, San Francisco, Cal.

Free

SEE INSTRUCTION NO. 5

U. S. OCT 31 1944 P.M. NAVY

V ···— MAIL

TO: Lt. W. R. Catton, ChC, USNR,
USS Oahu, ARG-5
Fleet P.O.
San Francisco, Calif.

CENSOR

FOLD HERE

FOLD HERE

V-Mail service provides a most rapid means of communication. If addressed to a place where photographing service is not available the original letter will be dispatched by the most expeditious means.

INSTRUCTIONS

(1) Write the entire message plainly on the other side within marginal lines.

(2) Print the name and address in the two spaces provided. Addresses of members of the Armed Forces should show full name, complete military or naval address, including grade or rank, serial number, unit to which assigned or attached and army post office in care of the appropriate postmaster or appropriate fleet post office.

(3) Fold, seal, and deposit in any post office letter drop or street letter box.

(4) Enclosures must not be placed in this envelope.

(5) V-Mail letters may be sent free of postage by members of the Armed Forces. When sent by others postage must be prepaid at domestic rates (3c ordinary mail, 6c if domestic air mail service is desired when mailed in the U. S.)

★ GPO 16-28143-4

Ticonderoga on fire after being hit by a kamikaze, 21 January 1945. While Bill was slightly wounded in the resulting explosion, scores of servicemen were killed. *National Archives photo 80-G-273437.*

Dixie Kiefer, captain of *Ticonderoga.* Trained as a naval aviator before the war, he welded the carrier's air unit and ship crew into an effective team. Severely wounded during the attack on 21 January 1945, he stayed in command on the bridge for eleven hours to see the ship to safety. Bill and his shipmates revered him; they mourned him after he was killed in a plane crash in November 1945. *National Archives photo 80-G-317386.*

Bill reading to Edward while home on leave, spring of 1945.

Bill posing with Jane while on leave in Michigan, spring of 1945.

A studio portrait of Bill taken in April 1945.

Bill took these wallet-size portraits of Helen, Ruth, and Edward with him during his second voyage on the *Ticonderoga*.

Left: Bill and Edward, 1945.

Below: Crew of the USS *Oahu* reacts to the announcement of Japan's surrender. On that day Bill wrote to his mom: "Now that we have peace a great weight is lifted from our minds out here. Till now it has always been a question of whether we would someday come home again. Now it is a question of when we are coming home." *National Archives photo 80-G-332796.*

Crew of the USS *Oahu* called on deck after the announcement of the Japanese surrender. At the captain's direction, Bill's father delivered a prayer over the public-address system. *National Archives photo 80-G-332794.*

Ticonderoga at Guiuan Roadstead, Samar, Philippine Islands, taking GIs on board for transport to the United States, November 1945. *National Archives photo 80-G-359982.*

Bill at Oberlin College, which he attended through the GI Bill.

Nancy Lewis of Greensburg, Indiana. Bill and Nancy met as students at Oberlin College in 1947. They married in 1949.

Nancy and Bill Catton in Yellowstone National Park, December 2000.

It's been about three weeks now since we've had any mail. I'm looking forward to a good-sized batch of letters next time. I don't know which I prefer, regular mail in dribbles, or irregular mail in torrents. Tell Butch to write. I'll try to write him when I get around to it.
Yours, Bill

[Ulithi Atoll, Caroline Islands]
25 January 1945

Dear Pop,

Your book, *A Time for Decision,* by Sumner Welles came today and your letter of 8 January.[42] The last paragraph of your letter interests me, wherein you refer to a possible change of duty soon. If it should come about I do hope you get carrier duty. As I look back on the last six months, since the time I came aboard this ship I think you would really enjoy it. There is so much to it, even routine carrier duty, that its seldom dull. And the strategy of modern sea war makes a carrier a ship you can be proud to be on.

However, don't try to come on the Big T. I don't want you censoring my mail!

I'm enclosing a birthday card I got today from the Blue Star mothers in St. Johns.[43] The letter on the back of it is a fine tribute to Mom, I think.

A belated Christmas package came today from the Church in Manistee. It like practically all my Christmas packages contained among other things a package of razor blades. I accumulated quite a wealth of said commodity. But I'm still using the same blade I used in boot camp.

One of Mom's letters last night enclosed some Christmas pictures. One was of Butch and his sled. The snow sure looked good. Do you remember the Christmas he got his tricycle?
Yours, Bill

Bill's ship anchored at Ulithi for one week until orders were received for Ticonderoga *to proceed to Bremerton Navy Yard in Washington State for repairs. Before leaving, Air Group 80 was transferred to the USS* Hancock *(CV-19).*

[Ulithi Atoll, Caroline Islands]
1 February 1945

Dear Mom,

Time does fly! Here it is, one twelfth of 1945 gone already.

Two of your letters, written the 14th and 15th of January came the other day. I was just re-reading the one dated the 14th. In it you reminisced over the Christmas season some nine years ago. One paragraph was very funny. It said: "You were really disappointed when we told you that Edward was the baby brother you would help take care of and we weren't expecting another (that was the disappointing part—not Edward)." That after-thought in parenthises sounds like something from a Stephen Leacock novel!

I have just finished reading the biography of Dewey that Grandfather sent me for Christmas and the pocket book of Lincoln that was in your box. There was as much contrast between the books as between their subjects, but both were interesting reading.

I spent some time on the flight deck today getting suntanned. There were so many others up there with the same intentions that it looked like Virginia Beach last summer.

News is beginning to sound more favorable the last few days.[44] However it still looks to me like a long war yet. In a sense we haven't made any progress since I joined the Navy. At that time I thought the war would last about two more years. Now, two years later, I still think it will last about two more years.[45] That can't be all my fault, though.

I had a letter from Bill Gillespie, my Gunnery school buddy, the other day. I think we may have been on some of the same operations, but of course there's no way either of us could check on it.

Yours, Bill

[Pacific Ocean]

Dear Pop, 5 February 1945

Yesterday at church they had a communion service with no sermon. The Chaplain announced, however, that next Sunday being the Sunday closest to Lincoln's birthday, he would preach a sermon appropriate to that occasion. Today I went up to his room and took him that biography of Lincoln I got for Christmas.

Last night there was another of those long bull sessions in the berthing compartment. It started off with somebody griping because the movie the night before was a "Limey picture." Another guy disagreed with his Anglophobic prejudice. About the time the discussion got around to the merits and demerits of lend lease, I got into it. The old question of why should we fight for Britain came up. To which I insisted, that the contrary was the case. We had actually tried to make the British fight by themselves a war which concerned both of us. The anti-Britons then said it wasn't our war. Our side countered with the question, "Why are we in it now, then?"

Well, it turned from one point to another as the evening went on, somebody disliking Russia, and then somebody else disliking Roosevelt, etc. Of course, neither side convinced the other but the letting off of steam was worthwhile.

I was reminded, when my opponents put themselves in the position of saying we could have stayed out of it even in 1941, of the sermon you preached in Manistee in 1939 the Sunday following the attack on Poland. You predicted that if the war lasted we would be in it before it was over. You said, now we are all praying, keep us out of war. But when we get in it, it won't be because England or France drags us in but because we have decided the issues concern us.

Even my opponents agreed with me that Mr. Roosevelt must have undergone a terrible strain in '39 and '40 when he was in the position of having to compromise not only what seemed prudent but what seemed necessary down to what the people would accept.

In the past I have frequently become terribly exasperated at the seeming short sightedness of my opponents in such bull sessions. But recently I have acquired among other attitudes one of tolerance, far greater than I'd ever had before. Someday I'll tell you why.[46]

News seems to be good from all fronts. The way the Russians are now driving to Berlin is very encouraging. In a way I'm almost glad the Americans were slowed up in Belgium. I think had they gotten to Berlin before the Soviets it would have been fuel for the fires of redbaiters. That is, men of such caliber as Fred Crawford would start yapping about us winning the Russians' war for them, etc. It still doesn't look to me like it's even close to the finish in either theater, yet, though.

Have you heard anything as to whether Bill Bruce is in service yet or not?

Yours, Bill

[Pacific Ocean]
10 February 1945

Dear Mom,

I received several letters from you the other day, the latest one dated 28 January. But I had none from Dad. I'm wondering if his "possible change of duty" has come through and he is now on the move.

Just now I was straightening out my locker sorting my collection of letters etc. I ran across several of your pre-Christmas letters. All that seems like ancient history now. It was good to read over again, though, the lines about snow, cold weather, etc.

You should see my sun tan now. I've been having more than usual opportunity lately to soak up tropical sunshine. I'm still not as brown as Dad was last fall when I saw him, though.

Today there was a flock of large graceful birds following the ship. They were bigger than gulls but equally beautiful. I'm not acquainted with what kind of bird is what but I thought these were albatrosses. They had a curious method of taking off from the water. A gull pulls himself out of the water by wing power alone. These birds, though, seemed to paddle furiously with their feet to get up flying speed before even spreading their wings.

I'm enclosing a cartoon I found in an old *Colliers* the other day. You may have seen it. I thought Butch would get a kick out of it. We had a Gene Autry movie aboard the other night. I thought of Butch as I was seeing it.
Yours, Bill

The Ticonderoga *entered the Strait of Juan de Fuca the morning of 15 February. Bill was on deck, his arm still in a sling, and enjoyed the view of the snowy Olympic Mountains beneath steely clouds as the ship made its way through Admiralty Inlet into Puget Sound.* Ticonderoga *anchored off Blake Island outside the port of Bremerton, then entered the navy yard the next day. As the ship was to be in dry dock for several weeks, half the ship's company was immediately given four weeks leave while the other half had to wait their turn. Bill was in the half that had to wait and was assigned duty as "fire watch," to stand with a fire extinguisher near a welder as the repair crews got to work on the twisted metal. Even now he could not disclose to his family that he was back on the US mainland since the hit on* Ticonderoga *remained a military secret. Impatient to share his adventures with his family, he also hoped to surprise them when he arrived home in Michigan four weeks hence.*[47]

[Puget Sound Navy Yard, Bremerton, Washington]
Dear Pop, 17 February 1945

. . . It is more exasperating than ever these days not to be able to write all my thoughts and adventures. But it will leave all the more fresh material for a good bull session after the war.

You seem surprised that in my letter of 15 January I made no mention of being conscious that it was my birthday. You were right that the business at hand distracted me from such thoughts. Along about noon one of my plane handlers asked me in conversation how old I was. I suddenly realized I was nineteen. Somehow the thought was unpleasant. It had always been fun, even a matter of egotistical pride, to be able to point out my youthful age. Perhaps it was because I felt anyone would know a kid of only eighteen didn't really have to be in the Navy. But anyone can be nineteen, I thought!

I had a letter from Stege yesterday. He is still at Navy Pier, but expects to leave there soon, and has applied for destroyer duty. His rate is now RT 3/c. I got some home town news from him. He mentioned several of the guys in the class of '42, including Kurt Illig (who was home with me last summer) who is now missing in Germany.

Stege said, "Everybody hopes and prays he is a prisoner. I know damn well he is, because you can't keep a good man down." While I share his sentiments, I disagree with his assumption. War is too real for that.

In the same mail yesterday, I had a letter from Ruth telling all about her participation in the Junior class play. It's hard to believe the kids are growing up. Mom writes that Butch is up to her shoulder now.

Well I'll knock off for now and write Mom.

Yours, Bill

[Bremerton, Washington]
24 February 1945

Dear Pop,

Two years ago today I left for Great Lakes, having been sworn in the night before in Detroit. Looking back, it seems longer, I think. That's not because the time has dragged at all but because it has been so full of experience and adventure.

That evening after we were sworn in, they put us up in a hotel. I called Mom, for 15¢ net—there was 65¢ in the coin return on the pay phone. You had gone down to the movies to see the *March of Time* or something. I wrote Mom last night that it was strange now to think of you having been a civilian then. A letter from Grandma Catton says she was startled to realize on looking through her snapshot albums that all the pictures she has of me in civilian clothes show me as "such a little boy."

Your letter enclosing the *New York Times* clipping came day before yesterday. I had previously read the same editorial in *Readers Digest,* which had gotten it from the *Times.*

It is true that even if we should fail completely in our efforts after the war, the war won't have been a failure. We shall, if only temporarily, at least have saved the country's neck. As Herbert Agar said,[48] wars are fought to determine only one thing: who shall have control in the immediate postwar period. If we don't use that control wisely we may waste our victory but we shall still have had the victory.

I don't know whether I wrote you about the guy who said to me awhile back that the U.S. ought to keep the territories we wrest from the enemy as our own possessions. When I asked him why, he replied, "Well, don't you think with all the fighting we're doing we ought to get something out of it?" That oversimplification of the issue is the kind of thing a demagogue will use to his own political ends.

It doesn't seem to me necessarily wrong to keep as our possessions the areas we liberate. But to assume that "getting something out of it" means material possessions is likely to blind one to the ideals for which we profess to be fighting. If we gain not one square inch of territory but do establish a United Nations federation we will have "gotten something out of it."

In that connection, guys like Bertie McCormick will holler after its over that the war cost us more than it did any other nation. He is assuming that "cost" can only mean money. I used to say *academically* that I was glad we were "paying for it" and having the war fought somewhere else instead of at home. Now I can say it with the conviction that only experience can bring.

Well, two more years and I'll have a hash mark.

Yours, Bill

[Bremerton, Washington]

Dear Pop,

27 February 1945

Today's mail brought a copy of *Time* magazine, and letters from Aunt Nellie, Mom, and you. Yours was dated 19 February. I wish it were possible to give you the straight dope on all the information you can only guess at in your letters. I am amused at the varying degrees of error in the "shrewd guesses" as to my whereabouts and activities in the letters of my various correspondents.

In a back number of *Time* magazine in the "miscellany" column I noticed a little anecdote I thought would amuse you. It seems a contest was held in a Navy Hospital to see who could identify from a number of photographs the legs of Betty Grable. The winner of the $50 first prize was the Chaplain!

Mom writes that they recently received a box of corals, stones, etc. from you as souvenirs of your present habitat. I have a collection of similar items in my locker which I've not gotten around to mailing yet. She mentioned having chicken for Sunday dinner. Apparently, they still consider that a treat at home.

In your letter you seemed surprised that I should have remembered a sermon you preached in 1939. Well, I only remembered one out of 52 from that year. So it's a tribute to the sermon and not to my memory. I hope others remembered it, too, although I imagine to some its memory would be distasteful. Of my own acquaintances, for instance, take Dewey Bucher. He used to say in those days that he thought Lindbergh was the only one in the public spotlight who knew what he was talking about. Dewey is now an Ensign in the Navy in spite of our "3000 miles of ocean," which was supposed to protect us.

News is good again from all fronts except that the Marines are having a rugged time of it, I guess. Do you remember that article about Swing in the *Reader's*

Digest? It said, "He takes the news personally." I hope that proves to be an asset. I'm getting that way, too.
Yours, Bill

[Bremerton, Washington]
8 March 1945

Dear Pop,

Last night I happened to be reading a copy of *Magazine Digest.* I read the following paragraph aloud: "A traveler on the road met a Russian peasant. 'What would you do,' he asked, 'if you knew you had only one more day to live?' The peasant answered, 'I would finish my plowing.'"

Two guys who were with me immediately expressed opinions as to what *they* would do. Both would promptly spend all their money getting drunk and then "paint the town red." To them I suppose that seemed logical in that they figured they wouldn't have to account for their actions.

But I disagreed. I asked the question, "If you really believe that the best way to enjoy 24 hours is to get roaring drunk, why aren't you out doing it now?" They replied that they could wait till some other time. Then I asked, "Why *waste* the present?"

The Russian, it seems to me had the right idea. My friends seemed to think that if death were coming on short notice they should do their utmost to pack as much into the intervening time. Whereas the Russian felt that you should be doing, all your life, something so worthwhile that you would be willing to continue it even in the face of death. His daily living was to him that important.

And, of course, there is always the point to be brought up that, for all any of us know, each tomorrow might be the last. That is similar to what Chaplain Gilmore meant in Bible class when he said, "every day is judgement day."

It's funny the thinking you can base on one of these "thumbnail philosophies."
Yours, Bill

In mid-March Bill received twenty-five days leave while his ship remained in dry dock at Puget Sound Navy Yard. He rode the train across the country to Michigan. He met Jane in Ann Arbor and brought her with him to St. Johns, arriving home on Saturday, 17 March.

[St. Johns, Michigan]

Dear Pop, 20 March 1945

Sunday, we slept a little later than I have been used to for some time. I did manage to get up in time to take a bath before breakfast. It feels funny to sit in a tub again; positively cramped. After breakfast, we all shoved off for church.

I was right in what I wrote you some time ago. A civilian church isn't quite what the fo'c'sle of the Big T is. Mr. Caldwell preached a good sermon but it didn't seem as vital as Chaplain Gilmore's. And the lack of the sunshine, breeze, and blue water seemed strange. However, the company was good. I guess Mom sent you a copy of the program. Mr. Caldwell remarked as did several others on the seeming error in the dedication, stating that I was "overseas." I told Mom I could have stayed home to avoid embarrassing her like that.

Jane had a pretty blue dress and red coat on and after we got home from church I took Ruth's camera and took a couple of Kodacolor shots of Jane. Ruth took one shot of the two of us.

We had a chicken for dinner Sunday. It was good but not as much of a treat for me as for the rest of them. We have even been known to serve turkey as a "substitute" when we ran out of chicken on the Big T. But it was a good Sunday dinner. After dinner Butch continued showing his things to Jane. He seems to like her. She and I looked over my collections of photographs, J-hop, football, various shots I made for the high school annual, etc. It was fun.

Jane had to be back that night in time to write a theme for Monday morning. So, we drove to Lansing in time to catch a 5:40 bus for Ann Arbor. I left the car in the parking lot and got it on the way back later at night. As we were pulling into the bus depot in Ann Arbor, Jane remarked that it seemed longer ago than just yesterday that we had left there. And yet we had both enjoyed the time immensely. I wish all my leave could pass as slowly and be as well spent.

I brought back with me from the ship a little model of the Big T carved from a piece of the flight deck planking. It is about two inches long. Monday, I spent most of the day painting that and mounting it in a cute little celluloid case for Mom. It is now sitting on the bookcase in the living room. I had whittled it while waiting for the starting day of my leave to roll around. Monday, I also finished a little model of a schooner in a bottle that I was making for Jane. It approximates the ship we were out in on Lake Michigan last summer. By the way, I got a glimpse or two of Lake Michigan coming up from Chicago last Friday. It looked just about like most of the places I've been. The China Sea was rougher but no prettier.

Today I went to [the] Rotary Club as the guest of Dr. Kraft. All the guys were standing around before dinner asking me many questions about my adventures. I was the only service man there today so I was getting all the attention. Mr. De-

Witt saw that everybody was interested in where I'd been and what I'd done so he had Mr. Ebert give me a spot on the program to tell what I could. I am glad I am home from the western Pacific and the China Sea instead of Fentress Field.

This afternoon I was downtown with Mom and we went into the bank to deposit your latest war bond. She got out the little deposit box and I "fingered my horded wealth." I felt like a miser. Mom remarked in the A and P store when she saw a lady buying beer that she wished we had the money we save by our non-indulgence. It occurred to me that my accumulation of war bonds is just that.

We played a few hands of rummy last night. Butch and I were partners against Ruth and Mom. Twice Butch got up to go to the kitchen for a plate of cookies and some glasses of water. It reminded me of last summer at Williams Court. That seems a long time ago.

I was listening on the radio tonight to a broadcast from the Chicago Service Men's center. It was amusing to hear some of the boots talking. I feel like a real old salt now.

Mom has been reading Ernie Pyle's column regularly.[49] Several of the people around here have remarked to me that they like it better than most columns. It is different than others. It is written from my point of view, say, rather than [Admiral] Nimitz's.[50] You can't get an impression of the news that way but you do get a feeling of the personal war. Today's column is about *my* duties. Mom bought three extra copies of the paper.

Reading through some of a collection of letters Mom has from you and me it occurred to me that all she would need to do would be to take the whole bunch, edit them a bit, write an explanatory preface, and she would have a saleable book. Don't you think so. I was surprised at how some of my letters sounded like Ernie Pyle's columns. I presume it would be permissible, they already having passed the ship's censors. The two contrasting points of view of the war, yours and mine, would really just about cover the whole Navy I guess.

Sunday I am driving down to Ann Arbor to spend the evening with Jane. I shall stay overnight in that town and Monday she and I are going into Detroit. I want her to meet Mr. Redman and see the studio, and also I want her to be photographed. I may look up Aunt Belle if I get the time, but I shall probably be preoccupied. Sunday seems a long way off. Usually when one is anticipating a pleasant occasion he wants the time to "go fast" till then. In this case though that would be wasting my leave.

Mom has arranged for me to speak at the Blue Star Mother's meeting next week. I'm not sure I like the idea. They didn't send me any poker chips. All they sent me was a useless package of razor blades, shaving cream, etc.

If a WAC is a girl soldier and a WAVE is a girl sailor, what is a WOCK?

A WOCK is a thing to throw at a wabbit!
Yours, Bill

[St. Johns, Michigan]
Dear Pop, 21 March 1945

Although I had sworn to myself that I would not waste my leave sleeping I woke up this morning at 10. It is a pleasant but expensive luxury, sleeping late.

Butch and I have been playing some checkers today. He is a little demon at it. At first I thought I'd be generous and spot him four men, then a game or so later I reduced it to two, and finally I had to play him even up before I could beat him. And even then I have to be really on the ball.

I heard Raymond Gram Swing tonight on the radio. He comes at 6:15 our time now. It was good to hear him again, the first time I guess since you and I were home last year.

We all went down to the movies tonight. The feature was "North Star," a picture of the start of the war in Russia. I had seen it, in Chicago I think. The audience reaction was what interested me most this time. Scenes of bloody battle they reacted to like a western melodrama. As the Russian guerillas came charging into the village on horseback, dashing through flames, and shooting up Nazis, the audience cheered. That's all right. I didn't resent it. But I just noticed that it was to them only a movie and not a record of reality. They also showed the newsreel shots of the Iwo [Jima] invasion.[51] Coming home we met Mrs. Kraft. She asked if the newsreel scenes were "hard to take."

Even though the movies may present an accurate and fairly realistic impression of the war, and people know from the news what war is like it isn't real to them. As Sumner Welles says in *A Time for Decision,* "On occasion, one has to undergo certain experiences personally in order to grasp fully what one may already know and tacitly admit to be the case."

How is the beer on Mog Mog?[52]
Yours, Bill

[Aboard the *Hiawatha* train, Washington State]
Dear Mom, 7 April 1945

The train was a bit late and I got into Spokane about midnight last night. I recognized Aunt Nellie right away and she seemed to know me. We got a taxi and went up to her house right away.

We visited for about an hour before turning in. One of the first things she asked me was whether I'd been hurt at all. She got out a map and had me show her a few of the places we'd been. She asked about you folks, and about my short visit with Grandma and Aunt Barbara.

When I told her about spending some of my time in Ann Arbor and why, I was surprised to learn that U. of M. was her Alma Mater. She said she knew where Jane's dorm was.

I had a bath this morning which I really needed after a day in Chicago and two on the train. We went downtown a little before 8 and had breakfast in a hotel coffee shop. Then I caught my train at 0845.

I shall be back aboard the ship by 10 tonight I think.

Yours, Bill

[Bremerton, Washington]

Dear Mom, 8 April 1945

I got back to the ship about 10 o'clock last night. Several of us stood around comparing notes on our 25 days. About midnight I finally got undressed and hit the sack without bothering to unpack.

Reveille was a stranger to me this morning. I had been dreaming that I was still at home and when the bugle woke me I lay there wondering how I'd gotten back to the ship.

I haven't got all my mail yet. I did get a handful last night though, including four letters from Dad. None of them was written, though, since he had heard of my leave. Also your letter written just before I got home was here.

Aunt Nellie asked me when I saw her how I felt this time about going back. I told her it was harder than ever before. She wanted to know if that was because I knew what I was going back to. After a moment's thought I replied that it was only partly that but mostly because I knew more clearly now what I was leaving behind. Home means more to you when you come to it out of the middle of war. And also I was thinking of Jane.

I bought you a roll of color film in Chicago which I asked Aunt Bobbie to mail. It fits the folding camera. Be sure to set it at f/11 or f/16 and 1/25 second when you use it. Otherwise it won't be sharp and you'll have a color fringe, with the lens fouled up as it is.

Be sure to send the pictures of Jane when they come. And when you get that black and white film finished you'd better get two or three reprints made of the one of Stege and me to send Mrs. Stege.

Yours, Bill

[Bremerton, Washington]

Dear Mom, 10 April 1945

I'm tired all over tonight but it feels swell. We've worked hard for twelve long hours today. It's the first honest sweat I've worked up since I got that hole in my arm. You should have seen my appetite tonight. Your ration points would dwindle badly if you still had to feed me!

Incidentally I found out today that my arm is definitely O.K. A guy came up behind me today and by way of friendly greeting slugged me on the shoulder, right over one of my scars. And it didn't bother me.

I went on liberty last night and had one of the best times I've had since being in the Navy, with the exception of my leaves. I called Jane up long distance. It took a couple hours to get the call through but it was worth it. She asked if I'd called for any special reason. I asked if *she* wasn't special enough.

By the time that I got through calling her it was too late to start the ball rolling on a call home, although I had had it in mind. I went out shopping for a birthday present for Jane. I found a nice bracelet that I think she will like and made a deposit on it. Tomorrow I shall pick it up.

My thoughts since I got back to the ship have all been about my leave. It really has been the best leave I've had. Those evenings in front of the radio, Butch beating you in checkers, our rummy games, the home cooking, sleeping late, wearing civilian clothes again, all have a fond place in my memory. And that weekend when Jane was up in St. Johns was wonderful, as were my evenings with her in Ann Arbor, and that day in Detroit. Thanks for making it possible.

Well, those memories will probably have to last quite a while. But someday I shall have even better experiences to remember. All the guys on the ship are talking now, not in terms of "our next leave," but when we "get home for good." That is really something to look forward to.[53]

Yours, Bill

[Bremerton, Washington]

Dear Mom, 12 April 1945

While we were working this afternoon, the skipper announced over the loudspeaker that President Roosevelt had died. Our flag was then lowered to half-mast.

It seems hard to believe. I don't know if it will affect the length of the war or not, but you can be sure it doesn't make the Japs and Germans very sad. And I'm afraid the loss will be a setback in our efforts toward permanent peace.

The death of such a person makes me feel very humble. Suppose last winter instead of slowing down a piece of shrapnel with my arm, I had stopped it with my head. The whole town of St. Johns would have regarded me as a hero.

In no less degree did Mr. Roosevelt die for his country. His death can only be considered as directly due to his extreme burden. And yet in his case, the people of St. Johns, as you will no doubt notice, will not be unanimous in acclaiming him as a hero. But how much greater is the loss to the country in his case than it would be in mine.

Your letter written last Sunday came today. It is the only up to date mail I've gotten so far since returning to the ship. Jane must have sent her letter by regular mail instead of air mail.

We worked from 0800 this morning till after 9 this evening. I'm tired, but I thought I'd better write before going to bed. I had steak and eggs and fresh milk when we finished work. My steak was about as big as each of those we had while I was home.

Yours, Bill

The nation mourned the death of the president. Bill's Aunt Barbara wanted to share the national mood with her brother Robert, who was still at Eniwetok Atoll 10,000 miles from home, so she wrote him this evocative letter, which Robert forwarded to Bill:

Dear Bob: 15 April 1945

This is three days after the death of Franklin Roosevelt, and exactly eighty years since Abraham Lincoln died. Certainly nothing between those two dates has affected the country so strongly.

For three days there has been such a genuine outpouring of grief and mourning as to leave no doubt about his place among the people. One radio commentator, in describing the reactions of various people, spoke of certain businessmen who had habitually complained of Roosevelt trying to be a dictator, and so on. "They had accused him," he said, "of being 'immortal'—and now they find that he is."

I hope they got plenty of the radio broadcasts across to you people. The radio stations did a staggering job pretty well. As soon as the news was received, all the regular programs (including, thank goodness, the commercials) went off the air, to leave room for news bulletins, appropriate music, prayers, and eulogistic speeches. Naturally, the whole thing had to be prepared quickly and there were some instances of sentimental bad taste mixed in with a lot of tremendously moving stuff. Occasionally you'd hear a bad soprano sing "Crossing the Bar"—but then there was the Chicago Symphony playing the second movement of Beethoven's *Eroica,* or Lawrence Tibbett and the "Battle Hymn of the Republic." There were descriptions of the funeral train on its various stops from Warm

Springs to Washington, and a really magnificent account of the procession from the Union Depot to the White House. For all the crowd, it was so quiet that you could even hear the singing of birds, there in the trees on Constitution Avenue. Curiously enough, one of the little instances that "got" me the most was the Marine Band playing, very softly, "Hail to the Chief" when the coffin was lifted from the train to the caisson on which it was drawn up the streets. . . .

Another thing that has been interesting: many, many times on the various programs they have quoted the sentence from Roosevelt's first inaugural: "The only thing we have to fear is fear itself." It's good for us to think of [that] now, I think. . . .
Love, Barbara

[Bremerton, Washington]
19 April 1945

Dear Pop,

Your letters of the 10th and 12th arrived last night. They seem to come as quickly as those from home.

I felt quite gratified at the proper display of envy in your letter regarding my leave. I'm willing to bet, though, that you'll get home again before I do. Between the two of us, anyway, it's certainly your turn next.

I'm sending your letter of 10 April on to Mom and I took the liberty of quoting parts of it to Jane in a letter last night.

One paragraph of yours was particularly meaningful. It was, "No doubt this leave meant vastly more to you than any previous leave you had, even your boot leave. You came directly from war and its experiences to home and its experiences. I'm glad you had that chance. And I think you had a chance to see that life's prizes are well worth life's difficulties."

Just about all of us feel that this is the best leave we've had. I would even go so far as to say it was the best 25 days of my life. And I certainly learned more than anything else that "life's prizes *are* well worth life's difficulties." I lay awake an hour or more last night just thinking of those words, and my leave; and feeling happy.

I had a letter this morning from Bob Mauzy (Ensign, USNR) who is now at Hollywood, Fla. He and his wife have an apartment there. It is funny somehow, to think of a high school classmate of mine as being both commissioned and married. His letters definitely make his life look rosy, but I think I prefer my own.

Kurt Illig, who had been reported missing, is now a prisoner in Germany. How long he will remain a prisoner is a subject for hopeful thought.

If you still have my letter expressing my reactions to President Roosevelt's death I wish you'd save it. Fifty years from now, when current politics are far enough back in history, and people begin to speak of Roosevelt with the same note of reverence they now feel for Lincoln, I should like to have that letter.
Yours, Bill

CHAPTER 6

USS *Ticonderoga*, the Second Voyage

On 21 April 1945 Ticonderoga *weighed anchor and slipped out of Puget Sound. Its first stop was Alameda Naval Air Station, San Francisco, where it embarked extra aircraft and passengers to take to Hawaii. Bill enjoyed two days shore liberty in Oakland and San Francisco before* Ticonderoga *set course for the western Pacific to engage in the final campaigns of World War II.*

[Naval Air Station, Alameda, California]

Dear Puddle Mush, 25 April 1945

While you folks were listening to the news broadcasts of the opening of the San Francisco conference,[1] I too was in this fair city.

I went through Chinatown tonight looking for souvenirs. I found a little knick-knack for Mom, and a Chinese newspaper for Butch. I guess this folder will have to do for you.

Well, it isn't long till I'll be saying so long to the states again for a while. I hope next time I come back it's to stay. Anyway, it's been nice being back and I'm going to miss the good old U.S. Write soon and same to Butch.

Bill

[Pacific Ocean en route to Hawaii]

Dear Mom, 26 April 1945

Your letter of the 22nd with the color photos came today. The pictures were certainly well worth waiting for. The colors aren't quite true but they are good pictures anyway. I don't know why you don't like the one with me in it. I'll admit it doesn't make me look nearly as handsome as I really am (I'm not conceited am I?) but I like it best of all. That's because it shows Jane and me together.

I like the background, too. The pictures are full of hometown atmosphere. These pictures not only are likenesses of Jane but they commemorate a place, an occasion, an experience, and bring back wonderful memories. If anyone ever again asks me what I am fighting for, I shall merely show him these pictures.

I also had a letter today from Grandma Catton. She gave me Bill Bruce's address at Camp Blanding. I do feel sorry for him not getting in the Navy. But I guess he'll make the best of it and personally I admire the Army. I'm going to write him now, and then Dad, so I'll knock off for the time being.

Yours, Bill

[Pearl Harbor, Hawaii]

Dear Ruth, 1 May 1945

Your letter came today together with ones from Mom, Dad, and Aunt Ione.

I'm glad to hear you enjoyed the J-hop. You told me all about the decorations, and about shopping in Lansing for a formal. Mom told me how nice you looked in it. But both of you neglected to mention whom you went with! Apparently, you don't consider that very important. But my curiosity is aroused.

I'm glad you folks saw that *Coronet* magazine with the carrier photos in it. I don't think any of the pictures are from this ship. Mom said Mrs. Scott had one guy in a picture all picked out as being me. You can tell her it isn't. So far, I don't think I've been published, so to speak.

When do you kids get out of school? The month of May always used to be the hardest month for me. By that time, my mind was on baseball and other outdoor sports. I was looking forward to swimming, picnics, etc., and classrooms seemed pretty stuffy. I wonder how it will be when I get back and start college.

Write again soon, and have Butch do the same.

Bill

[Pearl Harbor, Hawaii]

Dear Mom, 2 May 1945

I listened to a couple of news broadcasts on the radio this morning. The European war is certainly smoothing out at last. With a truce in Holland, and surrender in Italy and Austria, and with the Russians holding all of Berlin, there's not much left of Germany.

A great many people will be disappointed, I suppose, to know that Hitler is dead. It seems so easy for him after all that has happened. I think the best fate for him of any that I heard was the proposal to exhibit him as a sideshow monstrosity all over the world.

What was the reaction at home to the false alarm on European Victory the other day? We didn't hear about it till after it was reported a mistake. A lot of people who went wild with feigned joy probably felt pretty sheepish afterwards.

If the Japs would decide now that they'd be better off not to follow Germany's example all the way to devastation, we'd all be better off. But I don't look forward to it with more than a faint ray of hope, certainly no actual expectation. I don't think the Japs are capable of giving up. And it doesn't do any good to wonder why they can't see the light. After all, they undoubtedly wondered why we didn't quit after the ringing defeats we suffered at the start of the war.

Of course, it would certainly help if Russia were now to fight Japan. But if she doesn't, it may be the Americans who are partly to blame. Certainly, Russia is not palsy-walsy with Japan, and the language in which she has referred to Jap policy lately sounds like a prelude to hostilities.

But if the peace is to be lasting it is obvious that there must be solidarity between Russia and the U.S. among others. Unfortunately, there are many people in our country who are inflicted with an anti-Russian prejudice, as for instance William Randolph Hearst and Robert R. McCormick. If Russia declares war on Japan they may not say anything now but someday they will use that bit of history to brand Russia an aggressor. They already talk that way about her relations with Poland, yet if you will remember when Czechoslovakia was dismembered Poland was very anxious to have some of it.

Russia is between the devil and the deep blue sea. If she attacks Japan, our reactionary elements will call her an aggressor. If she doesn't, they will call her a slacker for not helping us as we helped her. It might be that what they are trying to do over there is to infuriate Japan enough to provoke a futile attack by the Japanese. Then it will look right in the history books. However, it's a good thing Japan hasn't attacked Russia yet. Suppose when the Nazis were fighting as deep into Russia as Stalingrad and we were still taking a beating in the Pacific that Japan had invaded Siberia then. It might very well have worked to our tragic disadvantage.

Anyway, you might say that the news of today makes it "two down and one more to go."[2] . . .
Yours, Bill

[Pearl Harbor, Hawaii]
Dear Pop,
6 May 1945

I had two letters from Mom today dated 27 and 29 April and one from Aunt Nellie. Mom sent me your snapshots taken of you aboard ship. You look in the pink, but had I taken them I could have posed you so that the light would have been more complimentary to your figure. That's one thing I've got to admit, you've got more guts than I have!

From the picture of you in whites I see you are wearing three ribbons now. I still haven't gotten around to getting mine yet. Mom was quite disappointed that I wouldn't wear any while I was home. I think she wanted to show me off in a little grander style.

Aunt Nellie's letter spoke of Mr. Roosevelt's death. She said that when it was announced that his health had been failing for sometime she thought it was wrong that he should have decided to run for re-election last fall.

I disagree. I'm afraid Mr. Truman may not be of much greater ability than Mr. Dewey would have been. But if the party dominates him as almost certainly would have been the case with Dewey, at least it won't be a party with an isolationist record.

Roosevelt must have known that he might not complete his term. But he had a conscience and it wouldn't permit him to risk the continuation of the policies he believed in to the opposition.

The skipper announced V-E day today. It is just eleven months since that day when I was mess cooking for the waves at Norfolk and heard the news of the invasion of France. My duties today were much more interesting.

They had church services twice today but I missed both of them. We've been pretty busy the last few days. My job involves a lot of yelling. I feel tonight like I used to after a good football game; hoarse!
Yours, Bill

[Pearl Harbor, Hawaii]
Dear Pop,
7 May 1945

Today, as I was spotting a plane on the hangar deck, I heard a voice behind me say, "That's fine. Now, if you'll bring the tail over the starboard it will be just the right angle." I looked over my shoulder to see who was trying to tell me how to do my job. It was a photographer's mate with a flash camera, waiting to get a shot of the pilot in the cockpit.

It so happened that as he spoke I was about to bring the tail to starboard anyway. Just as I got it as far around as I wanted it he said, "That's swell. Now, bring it straight ahead just a little." I had to do that too, to lock the tail wheel. So, I left him thinking I'd done him a special favor.

Your letter of the 30th amused me. I quoted the paragraph about the pictures to Jane. You said you thought she was the better looking of the two of us. I added, "What a triumph of understatement." . . .

Yours, Bill

[Pacific Ocean]

Dear Mom, 13 May 1945

It's been several days I guess since I wrote you. We've been pretty busy. Today we were working and I missed church again. We did get a little time off this afternoon. After reading for a while I decided to hit the sack, I was so sleepy. First I made sure I wouldn't oversleep by asking one of my plane handlers to wake me if flight quarters sounded. Then just as I was lowering my bunk to crawl in the bugle blew flight quarters. We airdales despise that call even more than reveille.

A year ago on Mother's day we were in Washington, D.C. You had stopped at Uncle Bruce's and Aunt Hazel's on your way back from Norfolk. I had unexpected weekend liberty and surprised you all at 8 or so Sunday morning. Remember how I rang the bell three times before Bill Bruce in his pajamas sleepily opened the door and said, "Whadda you want?" To which I replied, "I want to come in."

After breakfast we all went to church together and spent the day visiting. Ruth and Bill saw me off on the Bus that evening.

Remember how I wondered then if I was going to get any sea duty before the war ended! That seems funny to look back on now.

I suppose you've heard of the Army's point system for discharging veterans. The Navy announced today that a small portion of its men would get inactive duty on a similar basis. All the guys here have been wishfully computing their point ratings. Needless to say I am very low on the scale. Now if I had three dependents or a couple more years sea duty I might have my hopes up. As it is I'm expecting to finish out my hitch and I probably won't be disappointed.

Yours, Bill

Robert Catton to his wife Helen:

[Eniwetok Atoll, Marshall Islands]

My Dearest: 17 May 1945

Today completes two years in the Navy for me, during this war. I think it was May 18 that I took the oath, before Lew Wolf in the bank. You were in Grand Rapids at the time. It was not until May 24 that I started for Williamsburg, but I learned that I was considered as "in" the Navy from the moment I took the oath, as would naturally be the case. I have now been in the Navy longer in this war than I was in the other, even if you count the weeks I was waiting in 1917 for orders to Boston Tech for aviation duty. It is also a day more than one year now since our ship left Norfolk for the Pacific. That was, I believe, May 16. I surely trust that another May will find me back in the States somewhere, if not at home. . . .

All my love, Robert

[Ulithi Atoll, Caroline Islands]

Dear Mom, 22 May 1945

How long has it been since I've written you? I've lost track of whom I've written to, when. Every night since I started back from leave I've written Jane. And my intentions have been good towards other correspondents. But by the time I finish Jane's letter each evening I've worked up such a sweat that writing is difficult. So I usually give it up and hit the sack.

We had a mail call today. It was rather disappointing. All I had was one little V-mail. But that was from Jane so I was naturally glad to get it. The address was printed. Her printing is almost identical to yours. So until I opened it I wasn't sure which of you the letter was from.

I guess I'm not going to see Dad right away unless his ship moves again. It would have been nice to be able to tell him personally all about my leave. But as I used to say while I was at home, I guess we'll win the war anyway.

Sunday morning I went to church for the first time in three weeks. My duties had prevented it the two previous Sundays. This week services were held on the hangar deck. The altar was set up by the forward elevator. There was a row of planes down each side close to the bulkhead and the seats were set up in the space between. It was a very nice lay out.

After church I went up and asked the chaplain if it would be possible to have a picture taken of the service in that arrangement some time and have it printed

in the *Big T.* He said he had almost been on the point of sending for a photographer's mate before church and hadn't gotten around to it.
Yours, Bill

[Western Pacific Ocean]
25 May 1945

Dear Mom,

I'm back at my old pastime again: writing letters by the moonlight. The moon is almost full and the sky is very clear tonight. The white wake of the ship is visible a long way back and the ocean sparkles in the light.

Yesterday morning I hit the jackpot at mail call. Six letters and a *Time* magazine. Your letters of the 11th and 13th came, Ruth's letter, one from Dad, one from Bill Bruce, and one from Eleanor.[3]

Bill is apparently having a pretty rugged time of it in the Army, but seems to like it. He still envies me and I guess I am one to be envied. My luck has certainly been good all my life.

Eleanor wrote something about finding it hard to imagine my interest in girls (referring to Jane) being anything more than platonic. She reminded me of how I used to stick ice cubes down her neck.

Ruth's letter was exasperating. In reply to my question about who took her to the J-Hop she said, "Don't you wish you knew!" I'm bursting with curiosity.

I liked the worship program for V-E day that you sent. How did people in St. Johns react that day?

There are patchy clouds in the sky which keep hiding the moon momentarily. So, I guess I'll knock off writing for tonight.
Yours, Bill

[Western Pacific Ocean]
26 May 1945

Dear Pop,

We are now permitted to tell of our experiences in San Francisco.

I had two evenings liberty there. The first night I went out with a Bob Reed of Eugene, Oregon, one of my plane handlers. The other evening my buddy was John R. Gregory of Stephens City, Virginia, another plane director.

We had a very good view of the Bay area, and surrounding municipalities from the Oakland Bay Bridge. I rode across it once on the bus and once in a car, hitch hiking.

I went down to the waterfront, to fisherman's wharf, rode a cable car to the top of one of the hills, visited Chinatown, etc.

You are right that Frisco is a city in a class by itself. It has a distinctive atmosphere. It is typically American, and yet more than that every bit of it is typically San Francisco.

As you said, there is something to the slogan, "Join the Navy and see the world." I enjoy all the new places I see. But I mourn the lost opportunities that accompanied the gained opportunities. Everywhere I go I wish repeatedly that I could have a good camera with me, a big supply of film, and unlimited leisure time. Someday, as a civilian I'm going to revisit many of these places with the proper companion, the time, a camera, and the freedom of a civilian.

To change the subject, whether you know it or not, I'm beginning to appreciate what you mean when you say you're starved for some good music. My tastes aren't identical to yours, but you'd be surprised at the change in me. When I was home I spent a good deal of my time at the radio listening to music. It wasn't what you'd call classical, but it was the slow kind where the melody and harmony are what count more than the rhythm.

Yours, Bill

[Western Pacific Ocean]

Dear Mom, 30 May 1945

I am certainly getting the breaks this time. We have a swell hangar deck officer. His name is Lt. MacMurray. He's a pilot, but he doesn't fly from this ship. The assistant hangar deck officer is a good egg, too, except that he worries too much. And the hangar deck chief is easy to get along with.

Also, my crew of plane handlers are all good guys. They work hard and they don't gripe much about the work even though it is hard. When you have a good crew under you, spotting planes is a fairly good job.

Between all those factors my luck has added up to another stripe on my sleeve. From June first on my rate is ABM 2/c. That ABM stands for Aviation Bosun's Mate. It's a new rate for the special job of plane handling. That and several other jobs on a carrier do not fall strictly under any of the old rates, so the Navy put out a new rate to cover them.[4]

Being a new rate, openings for advancement are available. So, by changing from AMM to ABM they were able to give me another stripe.[5] My friend Gregory made it, too.

Remember when I was home and I was describing the duties of a plane director to you. I said we sometimes have to put planes where you wouldn't think there was nearly enough room. The other day the assistant hangar deck officer asked me if I thought we could get nine planes into a certain place. He didn't think we could. We wound up putting ten in with room left over for another.

A year ago now I was mess cooking for the WAVES at Norfolk. Two years ago, I had just entered Navy Pier in Chicago. Where do you suppose I'll be next year at this time? I wish it would be home.

Yours, Bill

By this time, Ticonderoga *had cleared Ulithi and was operating in Japanese home waters, having rejoined the fast carrier task force. In the last four days of May, it took part in the final stage of the battle for Okinawa. On 2 and 3 June its aircraft hit enemy airfields on the Japanese home island of Kyushu.*[6] *Bill worked sixteen- to eighteen-hour days on the hangar deck, moving planes to and from the flight deck via the ship's elevators. Per usual, in letters home he could not reveal anything about his ship's military operations.*

[Western Pacific Ocean]

3 June 1945

Dear Mom,

This ship will soon be a regular menagerie if things keep up as they are. You've heard of "deck-apes" and "bilge-rats," and I've told you about the butterflies we had aboard a while back. Today we had another visitor. It would have been hard to believe had I not seen it with my own eyes. One of the flight deck plane directors came down as we were working earlier this morning and clutched in one hand was a little owl about six inches tall.

It was the cutest little thing you ever saw. No bigger than a ball of yarn, it was just as fuzzy. Its eyes were like those of a teddy bear, big, round, and glassy. When we offered it the tip of a gloved finger or something similar it would snap at it viciously.

Where it came from nobody knows. It was found calmly perched on the wing of a plane sitting on the flight deck as dawn broke this morning. Little things like that make life interesting out here.

I have been up since 0330. It is just after breakfast now. Last winter, when the days were shorter, we didn't usually have to get up so early. We have to be up at dawn, so we don't get too much sleep. When you get used to it, it isn't bad, though.

Church services are scheduled for both morning and afternoon today. I hope I get a chance to go. Last Sunday, I had to leave in the middle of the sermon when flight quarters sounded.

The subject most under discussion nowadays on the ship is when the war will end. One guy said, this August. I wish he were right, but I'm afraid he is much too optimistic. The longest anyone except me seems to think it will last is another year. In my opinion, it could end any day if the Japs would use their heads. Otherwise, there's no telling how long it may continue.
Yours, Bill

On 4 June Admiral Halsey's Task Force 38 ran into its second typhoon in six months. Ticonderoga *came through this storm unscathed, and all ships stayed afloat, but a heavy cruiser had its bow ripped away. Altogether, the carriers lost seventy-six planes, some swept overboard, others smashed up beyond repair when they broke their lashings and collided. One officer and five enlisted men were killed or lost overboard.*[7]

[Western Pacific Ocean]
Dear Mom, 9 June 1945

Mail call today brought me two letters from you, one from Dad, a *Time* magazine, and a letter from Mrs. Bill Gillespie. He apparently has duty in the states now. The letter was postmarked Norman, Oklahoma. He must be an instructor there or something. . . .

Dad's letter was optimistic. He said he has been feeling lately that there is a reasonable chance of the Japs surprising us and surrendering before they are beat-up as badly as Germany. I hope so. I have had the feeling, too, but have suppressed it, thinking it overoptimism.

Standing in chow line sometimes without moving for half an hour or so you get pretty restless. You feel it's got to move pretty soon. Then when it does move pretty soon it seems as though your feeling must have had something to do with it. Of course sometimes you go on standing there another half hour anyway, in spite of yourself.

I think we are at that "restless" stage in the war. I keep talking in terms of being away from home a long time yet. But somehow there's a subconscious urge that says I *can't* be away that long, that something will end the war soon. This time I hope intuition is right and reason wrong.
Yours, Bill

After three weeks of continuous offensive operations, Task Force 38 retired to San Pedro Bay in the Philippines to refit and replenish. The men were permitted shore leave on Leyte, but Bill could only write to his mother vaguely about swimming on a beach somewhere. Censorship rules were starting to ease, however, so he could now write about places he had recently been.

[San Pedro Bay, Philippine Islands]
Dear Mom, 21 June 1945

Today, theoretically, is the beginning of summer. Are you have real summer weather yet at home? We are, definitely. I went swimming the other day. The water felt good, it being my first swim since last December. But it was not like good old Lake Michigan or Crystal Lake.

I haven't got much of a tan yet. During sunny hours of the day I am usually working below decks. When I do get some time off there's always letter writing to do, or a book to be read, or if nothing else, a little nap is always desirable. When I do get into the sun I tan without burning. Remember how I used to get sunburned at Butch's age?

It has been more than a month now since we were making liberty in Hawaii. So, I guess I can tell you a little bit about it now.

When we were there last fall my impression of Honolulu was very "Norfolkish." I made the mistake of spending my time mostly in the commercialized parts of town, downtown and at Waikiki beach. This time it was different.

I went out with one of the plane handlers in my crew, a Jewish fellow. We rode into town on the narrow-gauge railroad. Our first stop was at a swell U.S.O., where we ate and got information on a sightseeing tour.[8] The tour was simply a ride on a couple of the regular city buses, but it was a beautiful trip. We went way up on a high hill into a residential part of town called Maunalani Heights. The view from there is absolutely breathtaking. Its grandeur was indescribable. All I can say is that it was like a combination of a Colorado autumn from Grand Mesa, and the scene from Crystal Downs out over Lake Michigan. I longed for a camera and some color film.

Both the people and the homes up in that part of town were very nice. Yards were beautifully landscaped. There were flowers of all imaginable shapes, sizes, and colors both in the gardens and all over everywhere.

After our stopover up on the hill we took the bus back down again, transferred, rode out around Diamond Head, came into Waikiki from the far side, and on back downtown. We stopped at Waikiki long enough to drink a quart of milk apiece.

Downtown, we happened to pass a music store. I stopped in and bought an ocarina (sweet-potato) thinking I'd learn to play it in my spare time. So far it hasn't been out of my locker since.

The sales slip from that purchase, and the note of directions from the lady at the U.S.O., I'm enclosing for your scrap-book.

I wrote Jane a letter on the flight deck last night, but they turned off my moonlight before I could start one to you.

Yours, Bill

[San Pedro Bay, Philippine Islands]

Dear Mom, 25 June 1945

The book *Black Boy* came in the mail today.[9] How long ago did you send it? It was interesting to notice the fact that it had only four cents postage on it. Considering the distance it had to come, that's pretty good testimony to the generosity of Uncle Sam.

Yesterday I had four letters. There was yours of the tenth, Ruth's of the same date, one from Jane, also of the tenth, and one dated June 13 from Bill Bruce. Jane's letter had a clipping from the Ann Arbor paper with an article about and a picture of Jack Brennan. He is home on leave after a stretch of duty out this way. I wish I had his address. I think he is on a CV [fleet carrier].

How does Grandmother like the apartment? How long were she and Grandfather and Lizzie with you?

At church, yesterday morning, a photographer's mate busied himself during the service making some pictures of the congregation, band, and chaplain. He used flash bulbs, which were noticeable but not annoying. I hope some of the shots will be printed in the ship's paper so we can send them home.

The chaplain has started two regular weekly meetings. On Wednesday evenings, he holds a Bible class in the library. And on Sunday evenings, we have a discussion group in the same place about whatever subjects the men bring up. Last evening, we discussed race prejudice. It is very worthwhile, and the men enter into the discussion with real interest.

Well, I've got to write Dad and Bill Bruce yet before chow, so I'll close for now.

Yours, Bill

[San Pedro Bay, Philippine Islands]

Dear Pop, 25 June 1945

Chaplain Gilmore has started two regular weekly meetings. On Wednesday nights there is a Bible class in the library. On Sunday nights there is an open discussion on any subject we wish to bring up. Last evening, we talked about racial prejudice. The week before we discussed several subjects, one of which I brought up. That was the professed belief in fatalism that seems to prevail among men at war.

It is natural for a guy to try to comfort himself in danger by saying something like this: If my time's up they'll get me whatever I do; if it isn't I've got nothing to worry about. Men speak in terms of a bullet "with your number on it." I don't believe in this philosophy myself and I doubt if many of those who talk that way actually believe it. If they did, they wouldn't bother with medical aid. If their "time was up" it would be useless, if not it would be unnecessary.

But I got to thinking of something very much like fatalism along another angle the other night. We had the movie "The Clock," with Judy Garland and Robert Walker the other evening. Have you seen it? I liked it in spite of the reviewer in *Time* magazine who described it as "a very improbable series of events."

Isn't *life,* after all, a very improbable series of events? It is one crossroads after another; each new choice depending on the decision made at the last one. That word choice refutes fatalism—and yet does it. Sometimes a thing happens that seems absolutely to have been inevitable. And yet it always depends on thousands of factors, in fact on everything that ever happened before.

When two people's lives cross, the crossing depends on the entirety of each life separately. And this is truer than ever when it becomes more than just a crossing.

In "The Clock," the hero and heroine become separated in New York City, each with seemingly only one chance in seven million of finding the other. And yet they did meet again. That was one of the "improbable events." As you used to say referring to the heroes of radio soap-operas, "They had the script writer with them." Sometimes life writes a pretty good script, too.

I wrote some of this to Jane, with perhaps a little different flavor to it. Anyway, it's something one can think about endlessly.

Something else I thought of today was in regard to a letter I had yesterday from Bill Bruce. He was protesting against my thinking that he was anxious to see combat. He said he had talked to too many guys back from overseas not "to know the score." I used to think I knew the score, too. But it was only second hand. No matter how accurately one can visualize war, the vision hasn't the same effect as the reality. Grant's [*sic,* Gen. William Tecumseh Sherman's] line, "War is hell," has no meaning to one who has never seen either.

Fortunately, this works both ways. The reality of anything good and beautiful is much greater than its anticipation. It was pleasant this winter to look forward, while the first leave party was away, to my own forthcoming leave. When I got home, I found that war had taught me to appreciate home, and love, as such things ought to be appreciated. And the realities of my leave proved to be far more wonderful than my anticipation could ever have conceived.

It occurred to me that you might be able to make a sermon out of this. I made two pages of it in a letter to Jane.

Yours, Bill

[San Pedro Bay, Philippine Islands]

Dear Mom, 30 June 1945

I had letters yesterday from Dad and Grandmother Catton congratulating me on my new rate. Grandmother has some stationery just like yours, with the world map on the inside of the envelope. The day before, I had a letter from Grandmother Willard also with congratulations. She made the statement that she was sure I deserved the rate. I'm glad she thinks highly of me but she is certainly in no position to judge my abilities as a plane director.

According to the news the other night, Secretary Stettinius has resigned and is to be the American representative on the United Nations security council.[10] Such prompt action on the part of the president in making the appointment is encouraging.

As for the results at San Francisco, they're definitely not perfect. In my opinion the biggest mistake is the veto power of the big nations. It is as if the Senators from the big states, New York, Pennsylvania, Illinois, Ohio, had the same veto power in our government as the president. But we will do better to accept the charter with its defects, get it working, and then gradually correct the defects, than to reject it altogether as we did last time.

Do you remember Ernie Pyle telling in his column about the rivalry between general service and air department personnel on a carrier? Today a Chief Bosun's Mate asked me if "airedales get that way being airedales or get to be airedales because they're that way."

Yours, Bill

On 1 July Task Force 38 departed San Pedro Bay and headed north to resume raids on Japan. Two days later Ticonderoga *had to break away and set a course for Guam for repair of a damaged reduction gear in its propeller system.*[11]

[Western Pacific Ocean]

Dear Pop, 3 July 1945

Do you remember those cartoon "sympathy chits" you gave me last fall when we met? If you have any more could you send me a few. Our hangar deck chief was in a grumpy mood one day a while back about something or other. Somebody jokingly said, "We ought to give him a sympathy chit." It just happened that I had one of these in my pocket, so I walked over and handed it to him. He got a great kick out of it. A little later he had occasion to use it similarly on the hangar deck officer. Each has now asked me if I can get them two or three more to use on their friends in CPO [chief petty officer] quarters and the wardroom respectively.

A school of porpoises swam past the ship today, (going the other way—we're not that slow!) jumping and frisking about. They were arching gracefully through the air and splashing back into the water. It looked like great fun.

Somebody was offering to bet that we'd be back in the states for Christmas. . . . I doubt if the war will be over by then.

Yours, Bill

[Western Pacific Ocean]

Dear Mom, 4 July 1945

I think we are to have a special dinner this noon, but other than that, there's nothing special to mark this as a holiday. . . .

News is good these days. I especially like something I heard a day or so ago about some press association taking a poll of the Senate on ratification of the United Nations Charter. The results of the poll were very gratifying. More than the necessary two thirds favored ratification. Some few wanted modifications first. Some were undecided. But no senator has yet openly opposed ratification.

I should like to have heard President Truman's speech when he presented the charter to the Senate. I don't know what he said, but I would have said something like this:

"We had our chance to build a world of peace last time and the Senate threw it away. Now our fighting men are giving us another chance. So far, we think we have done better this time than last time. As you consider this charter, realize that by your decision you can either help this country to repeat its mistakes, or help to correct them. On you at this moment depends the success or failure of civilization."

I think maybe similar thoughts are in the minds of many of the senators. So there is good reason to hope for the best.

Yours, Bill

On 5 July Ticonderoga *moored in Apra Harbor, Guam. The men were given shore liberty while the ship underwent repairs. During the two-week break from action, Bill had an exchange of letters with his dad in which they shared thoughts about Western civilization, fascism, and the changing world order.*

[Guam, Marianas Islands]

Dear Pop, 6 July 1945

Yesterday was payday and I collected a sum of 75 dollars, which is the biggest pay I've drawn since I went home on leave. We had no mid-month payday in June, so this was a full months pay and my first one as second class.

Tomorrow I'm going down to the disbursing office and raise my allotment again. It is now sixty dollars; I think I'll increase it to eighty. Mom can then buy a $75 bond each month and put the other 5 in my bank account. That will still leave me more than enough to get along on. They had a war bond table set up next to the pay line in honor of Independence Day.[12] I bought an $18.75 bond, feeling more wealthy at the time than I thought necessary.

Another guy and I got into a very good argument the other night. It was over the definition of the word civilization. We tried to settle it by consulting the dictionary. But that only led to arguing over what the dictionary's definition meant.

The other fellow said civilization meant culture, refinement, and appreciation of good things. I said that those were characteristics usually accompanying civilization, but that civilization to me was similar in meaning to organization. He thought I meant that civilization and government were the same thing. So I explained with this illustration. Take a hundred people interested in photography. They are unorganized. But they get together and form a camera club. Now the whole club is in the organization, its officers such as Pres., vice pres., sec-treas., etc. are its government. Likewise all the people living in a certain area such as this nation are a civilization but the government is merely the body of officials who direct the affairs of that civilization.

My opponent said that Germany and Japan were not civilized because they aligned themselves against the civilization of the world. I made two contrary points then. (1) that in and of themselves Germany, before defeat, and Japan were more civilized than we. That is the individual was more completely a part of the state. (2) I said that that civilization had been directed toward the wrong purposes, perhaps had less of his "culture and refinement," but that you could not say it was against the civilization of the world because there was no such thing. There is no *international* civilization. There is a material for one, a body of nations with common purposes, but we are only now in the process of building an actual civilization of nations.

It was a healthy discussion because neither of us was trying to prove a point. We both realized that it was a matter of definition that we were arguing about. We were merely expressing opinions based on our differing definitions.

My assertion, that the axis nations were more civilized than we, needed this qualification: that they were more civilized politically but completely lacking in morals. Their entire civilization was aimed in the wrong direction. Without morals civilization is worthless, like a good automobile sitting out in the sahara desert doing nobody any service.

Yours, Bill

From Robert Catton to Bill:

[Eniwetok Atoll, Marshall Islands]

Dear Bill: 13 July 1945

. . . To your discussion of the meaning of civilization I would add this suggestion: consider the Latin roots of the word. Not that words in modern usage necessarily are confined in their meaning to their derivations, but the derivations are frequently suggestive. The word civilization comes from the same group of words from which citizen, state, etc. come. I would feel that a civilization implied that people had learned to live as citizens, enjoying the rights of citizenship and acknowledging its obligations. It implies some sort of group organization to secure those rights and enforce the obligations, but the "higher" the civilization or the more civilization there is, the more do the rights come freely and the more are the obligations freely acknowledged. The wider the spread of civilization the more people or groups there are who may claim its privileges and who acknowledge its responsibilities.

I would feel that the Germans, or any fascist type of society, had a distorted or corrupted form of civilization. Rights, in Germany, were not freely enjoyed, but were the possession of too few people. Indeed, it was a part of their credo that these rights were only for the few. The responsibilities of belonging to the group in Germany were not based on free acknowledgement but were enforced by an authoritarian government, and it was a part of the official credo that force and authority were a necessary basis for society, largely to the exclusion of any other social cement. In fact, that is chiefly what fascism means, the use of force by those who can get it to compel the obedience of whomever they can. In the American idiom a fascist is one whose philosophy is "I am entitled to whatever I can get away with." As opposed to a fascist, a democrat or a liberal or anyone who believes in freedom says that the mere ability to "get away with it" confers no title at all. Your title to enjoy the benefits of civilization is conferred upon you by your fellows and must be consistent with your free acknowledgement of their title to similar benefits.

Sometime at home, to a civilian congregation, I am going to preach a sermon on fascism and democracy. I have found my text. It is in the 62nd Psalm, and its presence there would indicate that the issue is at least that old, if the terminology has been more recently evolved. The words are, "Trust not in oppression, and become not vain in robbery: if riches increase set not your heart thereon. . . . Power belongeth unto God. Also unto Thee, O God, belongeth loving kindness; for thou renderest to every man according to his work."

We read that psalm in church a few Sundays ago, and even as I read those words the ideas for a sermon on that theme crowded upon me and I was at some difficulty to keep my mind on what I was doing the rest of the service, for the sermon that day was on something quite other. Those first three phrases seem to me to express quite pungently the ideas of fascism, which corrupt civilization. Power is based on oppression and robbery, and its end is riches or the aggrandizement of the powerful. There seems to be no end other than that. Those at the top can arrogate to themselves power to exploit the others. The object of their exploitation is to increase their own power so that they can exploit the more. Religion is directly opposed to any such idea. For religion is committed to the faith that "power belongeth unto God." You are not entitled to whatever you can get away with but to what is *right* for you to have. Your civil "rights" must be morally "right" and just, and the principles of justice and righteousness are eternal and in the mind of God. If power "belongeth unto God" then as among men all are equal, in the meaning that Jefferson gave the word in the Declaration.

I think civilization must evolve along this free or democratic line and that fascism is ultimately the enemy of civilization. I see what you meant in suggesting that the Germans were more civilized than many others: you meant they had more group self-consciousness, more statism, if there is such a word. But the principle of fascism would none the less ultimately destroy civilization. I think it would ultimately destroy itself and that a fascist state could not permanently survive. It is an anachronism. For by destroying justice and the consent of the governed as a social cement and placing its sole reliance on force it continually *increases* the necessity for using force. It destroys loyalty in favor of fear and you can't build anything that way.

And, of course, the point of the sermon would be that these fascist tendencies can be recognized in all of us and must be subordinated in all of us. We were faced with an extreme and concentrated form of fascism in the Axis powers that had to be gotten out of the way if civilization could continue and develop, but the enemy is also within as well as without. In each one of us there is more or less of the feeling that we are entitled to whatever we can get away with, and we must recognize that feeling and try to rise above it. In each one of us also is something of a recognition of the rights of others, something of a feeling of neighborliness, or tolerance, of mutual forbearance. In each one of us something of a feeling that we all are created equal and that real power belongeth unto God. That feeling must be developed and strengthened.

I think it will be a never-ending struggle of which even this war is but an episode.
Dad

On 19 July Ticonderoga *left Guam and rejoined Task Force 38 for continued strikes against the Japanese home islands. By now, the remnant Imperial Japanese Navy was hopelessly penned up in harbor; the US Pacific Fleet steamed about Japanese home waters with little to fear but submarines, mines, and a dwindling number of kamikazes. Indeed,* Ticonderoga's *airmen found the skies over Japan eerily deserted of enemy planes.* Ticonderoga's *antiaircraft guns had not opened fire on another kamikaze since 6 June during the Battle of Okinawa.*[13]

[Western Pacific Ocean]
Dear Mom, 21 July 1945

Today was payday and we had mail call besides. So it was a happy day. The mail isn't all sorted yet but so far your two letters of 24 and 26 June, enclosing the notes by Butch, and a letter from Grandma Catton, have found their way to my bunk. They have taken quite a while getting here and I have already had some more recent mail. But even old letters are always welcome. I understand some parcel post came aboard today, too, so maybe my watch and Jane's picture will show up soon.

Last night before they darkened ship I stood at the side and watched a very beautiful sunset. There were all sorts of both brilliant and delicate colors in the sky. The water was smooth and looked very swimmable. Staring at the colored sky my perspective suddenly reversed. You know what I mean—like this drawing [stairsteps] an optical illusion that can be made to seem to slant either way. Instead of arching up overhead, the sky suddenly seemed to be slanting away from the horizon off into the distance. And its color looked like the sands of a parched desert. It was the kind of a scene which, if accurately color-photographed, would lead you to believe the color film was defective. . . .

It's getting late and I have to be up early tomorrow so I'll sign off.
Yours, Bill

On 21 July the navy released information to the US news media telling of the kamikaze hits on Ticonderoga *the previous January, the heroism of the men in saving the ship, and the triumph of getting the ship back to the battlefront in four months' time. Although the news of the attack was six months old, the story made newspaper headlines and got reported on the radio all over the nation. Several of Bill's relatives sent him newspaper clippings from their local papers. His mother heard it over the radio. The next letter, from Helen to Bill, is the only surviving letter from her. It is included here as a record of her concern for her son. This document (and the two after it from Bill's Uncle Tubby and Aunt Nellie) turned up not with the hundreds of letters Helen saved but rather in a box of mementos that Bill saved.*

[Benzonia, Michigan]

Dear Bill, 21 July 1945

Our letter writing I am afraid has been somewhat irregular. We don't get to town everyday and added to that they have taken off the P.M. train so mail comes and goes once a day now. . . .

Thursday a.m. I was very much startled when I turned on the 8 o'clock news to hear them telling about the U.S.S. *Ticonderoga.* The first broadcast didn't mention the attack took place in January but it did mention Captain Dixie Kiefer as the skipper. Ruth pointed out they were telling what happened to the skipper in January. Turning to another station we heard the story again, in that broadcast they said Jap suicide planes did this on January 21st off Formosa. We heard the broadcast six times in the morning.

In the afternoon we drove up to Traverse City with Edna.[14] Before we came home I got a Grand Rapids *Press* that had a picture of the Big T and Dixie. I'm putting one in your scrapbook. I thought you might like to see it too. I haven't gotten my *Time* magazine or *New York Times* yet. Perhaps they will have pictures too. This is the first time we have seen the name [of the ship] in print. For most of the morning I felt pretty shaky. The story was so real and sudden it was quite a shock. . . .
Much love son—Mom

From Thurber Catton (Bill's uncle):

Dear Bill, 22 July 1945

I thought maybe you'd be interested in seeing what your skipper had to say about the little unpleasantness you were in. The news was finally released here at

this late date; I presume that indicates that the ship is back in action now. Have you seen the Jap coast yet?
Good luck, Tubby

From Nellie Catton (Bill's aunt):

Dear Bill, 28 July 1945

"Now it can be told!" That is what I thought when a couple of days ago radio and newspapers began broadcasting the "news" of the attack on the big "T" last January. How you could sit in my room and talk commonplaces, with such heroic exploits in your recent experience, I cannot conceive. Surely the navy draws heavily on the loyalty of its (her?) men!

I'm wondering, as always, just what particular page of history you are helping to write these days. My guess is that your carrier has either been sending out planes to Borneo or to Japan itself. At any rate, I'm sure your days are full of stirring action. I only hope that the rumors of peace talks may materialize into the real thing one of these times. . . .
Love, Aunt Nellie

On 24 and 28 July the Ticonderoga's *air group joined in the Third Fleet's bombing attack on Kure Naval Base near the southern end of the Japanese island of Honshu, which resulted in the sinking of nine capital ships and the final destruction of the Japanese Imperial Navy. On 30 July* Ticonderoga *launched bombing attacks on industrial areas in central Honshu. Following the atomic bombings of Hiroshima and Nagasaki on 6 and 9 August, the carrier launched air attacks on military installations in northern Japan on 9 and 10 August. It made attacks on the Tokyo area on 13 and 14 August. Its planes were called back from still another attack on 16 August when word came of the Japanese surrender. Bill expressed surprise and a profound sense of relief over the war's swift end—notwithstanding the ominous dawn of the atomic age—sentiments widely shared by American servicemen at the time.*

[Western Pacific Ocean]
Dear Mom, 7 August 1945

This afternoon, as I was working, somebody started telling me a fantastic tale about a new bomb that had just been tried out on Japan. He told me about how it had completely devastated a certain city and a lot of other stuff that sounded like something out of a Superman comic strip. I laughed at him and went on about my work.

But similar scuttlebutt kept drifting around and as I gathered more and more details from various people I began to think there might be something to it, though I was still extremely skeptical. When I got a slack moment, I hunted up a radio and waited for a news broadcast. One had just started with only a brief mention of the essentials when flight quarters sounded again and I had to leave. But I was able to listen to all of the chaplain's newscasts tonight and finally got the dope.

Many of the guys are speaking now in terms of an early end to the war. The stock greeting on the ship now is: "Have you got your blues pressed?" But I think that is going too far. However, I'm not making any more bets on a long war. The Japs will have to be very foolish indeed not to quit now.

One is naturally appalled at the destructive possibilities of this new weapon. But I think the moral viewpoint was correctly expressed by the president when he said that the Japanese could avoid it by surrendering and otherwise the responsibility for their own destruction rests with them, not with us.

Personally, I'm highly enthusiastic over the peace time possibilities of this thing. Some time ago, before the war, I think, I read some figures on the potentialities of atomic energy. It was said that there was enough atomic energy in a lump of coal the size of a bean to heat an average American home for a whole year, *if* that energy could be released. Apparently, that "if" is now on its way out. That's just one example.

Anyway, there could be only one better piece of news and that would be the actual ending of the war. I imagine when that news comes I shall be as skeptical about it at first as I was about this.

Let us be extremely thankful that this good fortune has come to us and not to the enemy. And more than ever we must realize the responsibility that rests with us to make war unnecessary in the future. The handwriting is on the wall not only for the Japanese, but for us as well.
Yours, Bill

From Robert Catton to Bill:

[Eniwetok Atoll, Marshall Islands]

Dear Bill: 8 August 1945

I wonder what you are hearing or reading about this new atomic bomb. It sounds a fearful thing to me. I'm glad that it is on our side, certainly, but I am sort of afraid of it's even being in existence. I suppose that is because it is new. After all, if you are going to kill the enemy I don't suppose it much matters how you do it and perhaps it would be more "humane" to kill a million men the first afternoon of a war and get it over with than to kill a million over a period of a year or two. I wonder how long we will be able to keep exclusive possession of the secret. At any rate it makes organizing the world for peace even more urgent, if that could be possible, than it was before. A strange coincidence: Senator Hiram Johnson, whose name almost epitomizes isolationism, died just as this new weapon was being announced. "The old order changeth," "Time makes ancient good uncouth," etc. etc.

I thought for a couple of minutes yesterday afternoon I might be seeing your ship come in, but it proved to be another. I take it you are still a good ways west and north of here. I'm afraid I shall not get to see you before I go back, though I am keeping my fingers crossed. I should like very much to hear your personal account of the events of the last month or so.

Everyone hereabouts is speculating now whether the Japs can be frightened or compelled into an early surrender. It seems to me reasonable that they might. If that atomic bomb is what they have announced it is it would seem to me merely a question of nerve. We would have the ability to destroy their cities, almost completely and literally, if we have the nerve to do so. It seems to me we would more likely have the nerve to do it than they would have the nerve to wait and take it. There would presumably have to a be a demonstration that it could be done and the "secret weapon" were not just propaganda, but once such a demonstration had been made I should think they would be in a mood to yield.

But there won't be a mass movement home for everyone, even if the war should end tomorrow. There will be a lot of work for a lot of Navy out this way for a long time. Incidentally, I should think ships like yours might get home before ships like this. If I come out again at all, I hope it will be on a carrier, though not for that reason only.[15]

Dad

[Western Pacific Ocean]

Dear Mom, 11 August 1945

Back in the days when I was beginning to study history in grade school I used to have a feeling of envy toward the people of former times. I used to wish I had lived in a time when something important was happening, when history was being made. My wish seems to have come true. More history has been made in the past week than used to be made in years.

After the news of the first atomic bomb had come, somebody asked me what I thought would happen in the near future. I predicted "interesting developments" within the next few days. But I had no idea how much that ambiguous term was going to cover.

We were busy pushing planes on the hangar deck when the captain announced the news that Russia had declared war on Japan. A heartfelt cheer immediately drowned all other sounds. For the next few minutes trying to get the men to push aircraft was like trying to get some work done on Christmas Eve. One boy, whose feelings I asked, replied with a triumph of understatement. He said he was "slightly elated."

Last night we were awakened by the bosun's pipe sounding attention and then his clear, resonant voice saying, "Now radio San Francisco has just announced that Japan has indicated a desire to surrender." Another cheer filled the ship. Guys jumped out of their bunks and ran around from one compartment to another yelling and shouting. Somebody went into the band compartment, woke up some of the musicians and made them play "California, here I come."

I got up and went to the nearest radio to see what news I could get. Twice I heard the same report again, that Japan had communicated with the Swiss and Swedish governments that they are willing to accept the Allied ultimatum provided they can keep their emperor.

If they get this thing settled and peace is declared before the first of September, I stand to lose two dollars. But it will be the happiest bet I ever lost. Everybody here feels it's just about wound up.

However, the Jap emperor presents a problem. The fact that he is not only the ruler of the nation but also a religious figure puts him in the spotlight. When the war is ended, we are going to have to convince the Japanese that they were wrong in their whole concept of the war. Since their leaders have linked and interwoven the war and their religion, this will involve a change of that religion. Emperor worship must go. If they can maintain their emperor as a head-of-state but remove his religious significance, all well and good. But otherwise it will be a mistake to allow Japan this concession. That is the problem that now faces the allied leaders. Solving it may hold up the conclusion of hostilities longer than we hope. To accept the enemy's offer to surrender with that concession now would save many lives. But it might be detrimental to the future. The allies must calculate those two factors against each other in making their decision. I'm glad it's not up to me to decide.

A couple of weeks ago the chaplain's daily newscast was just an event in the daily routine. But recently all hands have been waiting impatiently all day to hear the news. It is now the most important event in the day. And we have the satisfaction of knowing that the whole world is waiting as anxiously for the same news we are hoping to hear.

Optimistically yours, Bill

From Robert Catton to Bill:

[Eniwetok Atoll, Marshall Islands]

Dear Bill: 12 August 1945

Long before you get this, I suppose, we will know whether this is the end of the war or a false alarm. I rather anticipate that it is the end. As I write we have the news up to the point where the Japs have received Secretary [of State James F.] Byrne's answer to their surrender proposal and we are waiting for the Japs to make up their minds whether they can afford to surrender on Byrnes' terms. I should think they would decide they could. Having already decided they can better let the Americans occupy Japan, surrender all their outlying possessions, pull their troops out of China, Manchuria, Korea, etc., they could hardly be expected to boggle at what little difference there may appear to be between what they said they understood would happen to their emperor and what Mr. Byrnes said. It must be that they really don't like the bombing we have given them. I don't know how much of it may be their alarm at the prospects of the atomic bomb, and how much of it is what they already knew could be done by regular bombing. I think the atomic bomb and the Russian entry had a cumulative effect upon everything else that was happening to them. . . .

I shall be anxious to hear from you, a letter postdated after V-J day. I believe you must have been in the task force which has been in or near Japanese waters so much lately. We hear every day, nearly, what has been done by "carrier based planes," and I always take it that is likely to mean your outfit. I haven't heard anything about any material damage to any of the said carriers, and I am hoping the reason for not hearing is that there wasn't any. . . .

Dad

The announcement of Japan's surrender occurred in the United States on the evening of 14 August and in the western Pacific on the morning of 15 August.

[Western Pacific Ocean]

Dear Mom, 16 August 1945

I should like to have been able to have seen the reactions at home to yesterday's news. And yet under the circumstances I'm glad I was out here when it came.

Ever since the first atomic bomb was dropped, we've all taken a keener interest in the news. And since the report of the first message from Tokyo to Washington, we've all been anxiously waiting for the word to come that peace has finally been obtained.

Yesterday, as we were re-spotting planes, the loudspeaker clicked on and a voice said, "This is the captain talking." I was busy at the time and don't remember the actual words of his statement. But the meaning of what he was saying was unmistakable. This was the long-awaited moment. The Big T was a happy ship.

A little later in the morning, after things had quieted down a bit, the captain said he considered this an appropriate time for a word of prayer. Chaplain Gilmore gave a very fine prayer of thanksgiving and then the skipper said carry on. We were bringing a plane off the elevator at the time. I gave the plane captain the word to hold his brakes as it was halfway off. Everybody bowed their heads, and at the signal carry on, we went ahead and parked the aircraft.

It will be some time yet, undoubtedly, before many of us return to civilian life. Everyone is hoping he may be among the first ones. I was thinking about that last night out on the fantail. The moon was up, the sea calm, and the stars brightly twinkling. War is terrible. I know that from first hand. But I have had experiences in the Navy that have been very much worthwhile. I found myself saying last night as I looked at that Pacific moonlight, "Bill, you're actually going to miss this."

But the thing that has made my experiences in the Navy valuable to me is their relationship to the deeper roots of home. That is why, though I have enjoyed my Navy career, I have always looked forward to the day it ends.

Now that we have peace, a great weight is lifted from our minds out here. Till now it has always been a question of *whether* we would someday come home again. Now it is a question of *when* we are coming home. That is no easier to answer, but remaining unanswered still, it is not nearly so ominous.

Yours, Bill

From Robert Catton to Bill:

[Eniwetok Atoll, Marshall Islands]

Dear Bill, 15 August 1945

Well, I seem to be still out here at the end of the war. Our radio, as I suppose yours did, gave us the news this morning at 1100 that President Truman had announced he had received Japan's unconditional surrender. There was a good deal of shouting and presently blowing of whistles etc. etc. Last night, after dark, there had been some firing of rockets and star shells when the news had come that the Japanese radio had already announced the surrender. There would have been a great deal more except that orders against firing of guns were rather explicit. There had been some casualties at Okinawa, you know, in a similar situation a day or two ago.

After the exuberance and shouting had subsided a little, the Ex. [executive officer] called the ship to attention over the P.A. system and then called on me for a prayer appropriate to the occasion, a copy of which I enclose. I admit there is one significant omission: the enemy. I should have managed to incorporate a phrase or two there, but did not for two reasons: one, that the thing was too long anyway, and I didn't wish to omit any of the other items; the other: I wasn't sure the men were in a mood to receive any such prayer for the enemy with anything except derision. This, you remember, was to be spoken in the hearing of all the personnel, not just the church group. If I am here Sunday, in the Sunday service there will be a somewhat more comprehensive prayer and it will incorporate something about "those who have been moved to be our enemies."

I am ready now for my relief and to go back any time. To be frank, I was rather loath to go as long as you were still out here. Now that the fighting part of the war is over I shall not have the same reluctance at all.

I think it is possible that I may be able to leave the service sometime this fall. There has been, of course, nothing official about it yet. But I surmise that presently reductions in the Navy will be authorized that will include chaplains. Hitherto, chaplains and medical corps officers have not been included in any directive permitting resignations as there is a shortage of those officers. I should think that as soon as any chaplains at all are permitted to resign I would be included in the permitted categories. But I shall probably be home, have my leave, whatever that comes to, and report for the next duty and then see what is what. I suspect it may be longer for you, but I should think you could begin counting on getting to college for the beginning of the 1946 year if not sooner. You and Ruth can go together. What if the whole family should decide to go to college together?

I trust that all is well with you and that I may hear from you soon. I think it would be futile, however, to reply to this letter by addressing the *Oahu*.

Dad

[Enclosure]

A PRAYER offered by the Chaplain, Lieut. W. R. Catton, on the U.S.S. *Oahu* (ARG-5) upon the announcement of the Japanese unconditional surrender, 15 August 1945.

Almighty God, whose providence has been manifest in the long history of our country, and who dost rule and direct in the affairs of men, we thank thee for this hour in which we are permitted to observe the dawn of peace upon this weary and bewildered world. Consecrate and bless this moment in our hearts and in our memories, we pray thee.

Our thoughts go out to our comrades in the armies and navies of the United Nations. Especially do we remember, with solemn pride, the sacrifices of those who have given their lives, on sea, on land and in the air, that this day might come. Make us who live today worthy of their sacrifice.

Direct our nation in the days ahead, that it may move wisely and steadfastly in the building of a just and lasting peace. Hasten the day, we beseech thee, when righteousness and justice may be established, when the world may be rebuilt after the bitter ravages of war, when broken homes may be reunited. And may we, who have worn the uniform of our country and fought its battles against a foreign foe in time of war, be even more zealous and devoted in the ways of peace, that our land may be an example to all the world of a nation whose ways are the ways of peace and whose foundations are laid on righteousness and truth.

Amen.

At the first news of Japan's surrender, war-weary US seamen naturally began to wonder how soon they would get to go home. But they also stayed on task. In the days immediately following the surrender, Ticonderoga *stood by to airlift emergency supplies to POW camps. On 28 August US forces began the occupation of Japan, and on 6 September* Ticonderoga *entered Tokyo Bay with other warships to enforce the surrender.*

[Western Pacific Ocean]
19 August 1945

Dear Mom,

We've been having movies again on the hangar deck the last few nights. The night before last, I went for the first time in about a month. The name of the picture was "Wilson." It was the story of President Woodrow Wilson and the misfortunes of his efforts for the League of Nations. The movie was rather long but it held your interest all through. It was in color and all parts were well played.[16]

There were one or two points in it that I thought didn't quite agree with history but that's a pretty good average. All in all, I would recommend it as a good picture for the whole family to see.

I was particularly interested in the audience reaction to it here on the ship. At one point, President Wilson was explaining to some soldiers preparing to go overseas what they would be fighting for. He used the expression, "war to end all future wars." There was a general hooting noise from various parts of the audience and I could hear cries of "What are *we* doing then?" Apparently, a lot of people don't yet understand a lot of things. The whole theme of the movie was to show how Wilson's efforts were undermined by certain senators. It is historical record that the war last time was a success but the peace a failure. We won the war. But we didn't make full and proper use of that victory in the peace.

The Senate has corrected its biggest mistake. It is to be hoped that public opinion has also thus improved over its shortcomings in 1919. The slogan "war to end war" has not been used this time. In fact, there seems to be a sort of feeling of revulsion toward it as a slogan. But essentially that hope has certainly been on our minds throughout the conflict. We have won our war, now. But *war* to end war is not enough. We must have *peace* to end war, too. Winning the war is like an appendectomy. Once the operation is over, it's done. But winning the peace is like breathing. You never say to yourself, "Well, now I've breathed enough air for a while, I'm tired, I guess I'll stop." You have to keep on breathing as long as you live. We shall have to keep on *building* peace as long as we *want* peace.[17]

We had a good big meal last night with steak as the main course. It was the kind that is referred to as "shipping-over chow," an inducement (imagined to be such, at least) to re-enlist. Every time I load up my tray with a big pile of good food and sit down to enjoy it, somebody remarks, "There's a twenty-year-man." Their logic seems in error to me. Just because I enjoy Navy life doesn't mean I want to stay in. I enjoy home life more.

Somebody asked me once how it was possible for me to enjoy Navy life. I told him I enjoyed Navy life simply because I enjoy life. I explained that as long as I had to be in the Navy I might as well make the best of it.

Several people have told me that they are *glad* they don't get along well in this outfit. They say that if they did, they'd probably make a career of it and they don't want to have anything to do with such a career. That simply reminds me of Dad's old story of the man who was glad he didn't like succotash. He reasoned that if he liked it he'd probably eat it, and he hated the stuff.

Human beings are the funniest people.

Yours, Bill

[Western Pacific Ocean]

Dear Mom, 24 August 1945

It was over a month since our last mail came aboard until early this week we got a little dribble of it. Then, yesterday, the accumulation caught up with us. Several hundred bags of mail were brought aboard. All day yesterday and today they've been giving it out as fast as it is sorted.

You seem to have spent a good deal of your time at Crystal Lake writing letters to me. I have a whole pocketful of them now. Also, letters from Dad, Grandma Catton, Aunt Nellie, Ruth, Uncle Tubby, and Jane.

Everybody has been sending me clippings of the newspaper accounts of our action last January. Aunt Nellie said, "How you could sit in my room and talk commonplaces, with such heroic exploits in your recent experience, I cannot conceive." I think that is an overstatement. Uncle Tubby's letter was just the opposite: "Thought maybe you'd like to see what your skipper had to say about the little unpleasantness you were in."

The newspapers seem to have written up our story pretty well. *Time* magazine has a very good account of it.[18] To read about it, though, was not like going through the experience itself.

Dad's last letter brought the news that his relief had arrived and that he had only to check out and await transportation back to the States. By now I suppose he is on his way. He said he had been reluctant to go, leaving me out here, but not so much so now that hostilities have ceased. I appreciate the sentiment, but can't see his reluctance. When I was going home on leave, I wished he could be there too, but I was certainly not reluctant.

Grandma Catton says Paul Brown is out this way again. I hope I may get a chance to see him some time. The last time I saw him was as a civilian that fall in Detroit.

The snapshots Ruth sent were very good. The one of Butch casually draped over the inner tube floating in Crystal Lake sure looked inviting. I have it in my billfold to look at whenever sweat runs into my eyes. How is Ruth coming at learning to drive? Remember as kids how we used to argue over who should get priority on the radio for such things as Tom Mix, Captain Midnight, etc.? When I get home again we'll be arguing over who gets to use the car. . . .

Yours, Bill

[Western Pacific Ocean]

Dear Mom, 30 August 1945

Well, my wristwatch finally came today. Rather it came about a week ago, and I just got it today. About a week ago, we had several hundred bags of mail come aboard. They sorted all the letters first, then the newspapers and magazines, and finally they're working on packages. The watch seems to be in good shape and running O.K. Jane's picture was mailed about the same time, the middle of May. I'm hoping I may have it by the time they finish sorting these packages.

I have been having quite a little heat rash on my face and neck lately. The salve they put on it at sick bay is more of a nuisance than the rash itself. I've been putting off getting a haircut till my skin cleared up a bit. I finally went into the barber shop today. They've been getting strict on regulation haircuts lately and the barbers have been having a swell time butchering some of the guys' flowing locks. The guy that cut mine today complained that my hair was too short; he couldn't have any fun with it.

We've all been figuring up our points for discharge lately and wishing there were some way we could stretch them. The talk of the ship is how much longer we'll have to "sweat it out." Our first eligible men have already started home. They were cheered on their way with a bunch of envious good-byes.

In case you're interested, I have 25 points (10 for age, 15 for time in service) out of 44 needed for release. So, it will be a little while yet before I start buying my civilian clothes. Much as I would like to be leaving for home now, I wouldn't want the other 19 points to be for either age or time in the Navy. I'm glad I'm as young as I am, and I'm glad I have had the experiences I have in the past.

I presume Dad is on his way to the States now and I suppose it is possible he will get home about the time this does. It's been over a month since I've written him, knowing that he might leave his ship before a letter would reach him and it would have to chase him a long way. If you've been saving any of my recent letters lately, consider them addressed to both of you. . . .

Yours, Bill

[Western Pacific Ocean]

Dear Mom, 1 September 1945

Last night it was announced that censorship regulations are now relaxed so that we may tell where we have been, where we are, but not where we expect to be next. I don't know where we expect to be next, anyway, so that's beside the point. As to where we are now, I think you've heard it in the news.

Where we've been is another matter. I've been having adventures since I left home. Coming out here this time we stopped only briefly in Ulithi, not long enough to arrange for liberty parties. That's really nothing to regret, except that us old salts who pitched liberty there last winter had been filling the newer members of the crew with tales about Mogmog. We had thus acquired sort of a sense of "proprietorship" toward the place like one feels when telling a stranger about his hometown.

After a period of operations with the fleet, we anchored for some time in San Pedro Bay in the Philippines between the islands of Leyte and Samar. You may recall my writing you about going swimming a couple of times back in June. That was the place.

The towns and villages on Leyte and Samar are restricted. But the Navy has established several Fleet Recreation Areas on Samar, so we had liberty regularly while we were there. It was an hour and a half ride standing up in an LCM [Landing Craft–Mechanized] to the beach that we went to the first time and the recreation facilities were not worth the trip.

But the Filipinos had established a trading post just outside the area and that was well worth the trouble. It was a wet, muddy plot of ground with little bamboo huts for shops. They had handmade straw hats, shoes, mats, pocketbooks, grass skirts, necklaces, etc. for sale as souvenirs. But their best-selling commodity was worthless Jap invasion money. Little kids half as big as Butch would approach a sailor, hold up a fist with two ten-peso notes in it, and chatter, "Jap money—one dolla!!" They have little conception of change and even less idea of the value of money. Ask the price of anything and the answer is invariably, "One dolla," or maybe "Thlee dolla."

It is cheaper to barter. The thing they need most is clothing. A sailor's skivvy shirt makes a good dress for a little child. And the adults were clad in G. I. dungarees, or made-over mattress covers.

The second time we went ashore was a twenty minutes' ride. It was a nicer place, better swimming, and with Filipino kids playing around in the same area with the sailors. There I saw a very amusing sight. Four little tykes who looked to be from four to eight years old were playing poker. They had an American deck of cards, and each one had a bag of U.S. money hung around his neck. Other kids were watching and making side bets on the games. One squirt, only about knee high to me, lost a bet, and reached a little brown hand into his bag three times before he could find anything smaller than a ten-dollar bill to pay it with.

Swimming seems to come naturally to them. Youngsters from two years old on up were splashing in a stream and making great sport of diving for coins tossed to them.

They're little people, from four to five feet tall when grown, brown skinned, with dark eyes and black hair. They all have fine teeth and show them often in warm smiles and hearty laughter. They live very poorly, in bamboo thatched huts. I didn't see any fat people, but on the whole, they didn't seem undernourished either.

This, of course, was all in the back woods part of the Philippines. Someday I hope I get to see the more civilized parts and the modern cities. I felt a real sympathy for these people living in poverty and ignorance. But when the benefits of civilization come to them, I hope they may still retain their simple, unaffected happiness.

We didn't really get around much, but from what I did see of the geography of the place I'm more glad than ever that I'm in the Navy and not the Army.

It's almost inconceivable to me how soldiers can stand the rain, the fudge-like mud, the jungles and mountains, and actually defeat a well-established enemy. We gripe because we have to keep our bunks triced up during the day, when we should be grateful for the mere fact that we have bunks.

Our next liberty port was Guam. But it's time for chow now so I'll tell you about that later.

Yours, Bill

[Western Pacific Ocean]

Dear Mom, 4 September 1945

This morning the skipper announced that personal mail will no longer be censored.

In my last letter, I told you all about our liberties in the Philippines. Now I'll say a little about what we did at Guam. We had left San Pedro Bay for some ten days of gunnery practice and flight operations before striking Japan again. During that time, we burned out some important bearing in one of the engines and had to leave the rest of the fleet. We put in at Apra Harbor on Guam and were there when the Third Fleet began to be in the news again.

Being there for the purpose of getting that bearing fixed we weren't bothered with loading provisions, the usual in-port routine. We kept busy chipping paint, scraping rust, etc. Every fourth day, we had liberty. The beach wasn't swimmable, but with the Red Cross Canteen, good ball fields, and an open-air theater, we had fun. Also, they had bottled Coca-Cola for those who didn't drink beer. It tasted like a bit of home.

One day, Lt. Brooks, the flight deck officer, an old regular Navy pilot, got up a special liberty party of all the flight deck plane directors and two of us from the hangar deck. We got a boat over to the beach and hiked a couple of miles around to the Navy airstrip. Mr. Brooks' original intention had been to check out a transport and fly us up to Saipan for the afternoon. There were no big planes available, though, so he had to be content with a TBM. He took us for a half-hour hop around Guam, four at a time. That's more people than a TBM normally carries, but when you consider that it's built to carry a 2000-pound torpedo, it was hardly what you'd call overloaded.

It was a very pleasant excursion. I rode in the turret, which seemed like "old times." We really got a good view of the various air strips, the B-29 bases, a village, the mountainous parts of the island, etc. Parts of it looked a lot like places I flew over in Florida and Virginia. There were good two- and four-lane highways all over it. We passed over the ship again before landing. All our planes were on the flight deck; we always clear the hangar deck when in port. They were spotted beautifully in even, straight rows, like marching men keeping perfect formation. Big T is a pretty sight from the air.

After all of us had had a turn in the air, Mr. Brooks took us down to the recreation area and checked out two cases of beer for the gang. There were three of us who didn't drink it but our thirst was satisfied with water. Then he shoved off for the officers' club and left us to get back to the ship on the regular liberty boat.

It was also at Guam that we had the USO show aboard with Eddie Bracken and Peggy Ryan. I wrote you all about that already so I won't go into further detail.[19]

When we finally did get under way, we joined the fleet in time to make several strikes on Hokkaido and northern Honshu before the war began to end. We were thus occupied when the news of the atomic bomb and of Russia's entry into the war came. We had retired to refuel when the first announcement was made that Japan wanted to quit. All of us hoped that it could be squared away before we had to do any more striking. But such things just don't work that fast. So, we made some more attacks in the Tokyo area to hurry them up. On the day the Japs finally accepted our ultimatum, we had already sent out one strike which was over the target and another wave was on its way. It was recalled. We watched the explosions on the horizon as pilots jettisoned their bombs, and then we landed everything that was in the air. Taxiing planes off the elevators, we filled an almost empty hangar deck in 14 minutes. The skipper gave the hangar deck crews a well done.

Since then we have been flying patrol hops mostly off Kyushu. The end of hostilities leaves things in such an unsettled state that we can't take any time out for a while.

Now that we're not dodging kamikazes anymore, we work most of the time with our shirts off. If we keep it up I may have a good tan before I get home. I would like to get back to a cooler climate though. Our compartment gets pretty hot at night. It will seem good when I do get home to sleep under blankets again next to an open window.

Yours, Bill

[Western Pacific Ocean]

Dear Mom, 5 September 1945

Today was payday but I let mine ride on the books. I've got enough on hand to take care of expenses for several months yet and the easiest way to save money is not to draw it. I'm enclosing a money order to pay the bill on my wristwatch, which I believe you said was 18 dollars.

It's a little cooler today, we've been heading somewhat north. I slept on the fantail last night. The temperature was much more comfortable there than in the compartment and I'm able to adapt myself to the hardest of decks. But it's right over the screws and you can really feel some vibration. With my mouth partly open it made my teeth chatter. It felt somewhat like driving in the car over a "wash-board" road.

I forgot to mention in my letter last night that after we left Guam we had some very distinguished passengers aboard. There was a vice admiral and a couple of rear admirals. Also, a Mr. H. S. Hensel, assistant secretary of Halsey's staff.[20] We transferred them to the *Missouri* when we rejoined the Third Fleet.

Commander Stassen had just returned from the San Francisco Conference.[21] One night at the movies our skipper introduced him and had him give us a talk on the World Security Charter. His manner of speaking is pleasant. He held his audience very well and gave me the feeling that I was indeed listening to one of our future great men. His speech was mostly in general terms but he used one metaphor that is very noteworthy. He said that by forming this world organization we have "won a beachhead" on lasting peace. The implication of that statement and the rest of what he said was that this is only a beginning, that we must keep on working to realize our hopes, just as in war we have to keep on fighting for more or lose what we have already gained.

I am glad I had the opportunity to hear him speak. I should like to meet him personally someday.

Yours, Bill

Tokyo Bay

Dear Mom, 6 September 1945

Back in the states when two servicemen go their separate ways the standard farewell is, or was, "See you in Tokyo." Well, here I am.

I slept on the fantail again last night. We don't have general quarters at dawn anymore, so reveille was at 0515. It was cool, and I woke up a little early in time to see a beautiful sunrise. We were just pulling into the outermost part of the bay at the time. Land was visible on both sides. A misty atmosphere made it a mystic scene.

The ship made a slight turn and there, off our port bow, was Fujiyama. As the sun rose higher the top of the mountain became tinged with pink which gradually spread downward like brush-strokes of rouge. The sea was glassy smooth. There was a belt of low hanging clouds around the horizon with this volcano thrusting its head majestically above them.

We anchored about 9 o'clock. There are a lot of other ships in here, too, though only a few carriers. Several British cruisers and destroyers are anchored near us. We have spent most of the morning sending all our planes to the flight deck. With the hangar deck cleared, we will probably be loading supplies. There are a good many supply ships, etc., in here. We've been at sea since July 18, so it seems good to see land around us again.

In a way, it all seems like a dream, though. Suppose someone had told me at Easter time, when I was home, that before the middle of September my ship would be anchored within sight of Yokohama! I'd have thought the person was nuts. But here we are. As we were pushing planes this morning, I thought of the difference between a month ago and the present. Then those planes were flying over this area with engines roaring and guns blazing. Now the engines are silent, the guns empty, and the aircraft are simply an object to be pushed by men who wish they were home. As long as we can't be at home, though, we might as well make an adventure out of this.

Yours, Bill

P.S. I can almost hear Butch now, telling his classmates at school, wide-eyed with excitement: "My big brother is in Tokyo Bay!!!"

[Tokyo Bay]

Dear Mom, 7 September 1945

The fun I had today was from an experience that shows what kind of a war this is. I made an acquaintance this afternoon with a very nice fellow who is as far from his home as I am from mine, and our two homes are about that far apart, too. He is English.

The British carrier that is anchored near us is the H.M.S. *Indefatigable.*[22] Today, a large party of sailors and some officers from that ship paid us a visit. Once they got aboard, all formalities ceased and friendships began. A couple of our guys would meet a couple of them and proudly show them around the ship. A sailor may gripe about the faults of his ship, but he is always willing to show a visitor around and takes pride in doing so. That pride is doubled when the visitor is from another country.

Our living conditions are much better than theirs, it seems. They were amazed at our mess hall and the spaciousness of our berthing spaces. They don't have bunks like we do, but still sleep in hammocks. They have no laundry and no "gyp joint." And the gap between officer and enlisted man is apparently wider with them.

We told sea stories to each other, stories of our adventures both similar and dissimilar. It was a good old bull session such as we have every day whenever several fellows get together. Only this one had men of two nationalities in it.

The fellow I got to know was an aircraft mechanic. He has been in the navy a little over three years. He gave me his name and address and I gave him mine. We're going to write to each other.[23]

After they had left, an American sailor said to me, "They sure talk funny, don't they?" I said, "What do you mean, *they* talk funny? It's *their* language."

British and American friendship was strengthened by the experience, I think. One guy said, "You know, I used to hate the Limeys, but now that I've met some, I think they're awfully nice fellows." Lots of us swapped addresses and there was a lot of exchanging of cigarettes and coins as souvenirs. Their last liberty port last winter was in Australia, so they had Australian money with them. I got a shilling and a penny from one guy and gave him a half dollar, a dime, and a U.S. penny.

They wore white shorts cut just above the knees, skivvy shirts with a little blue neckband, and white flat hats. The enlisted men had black shoes and blue socks. The officers had white shoes and socks. Their socks reach almost to the knees. They look odd when you're used to dungarees, but they were clean and looked pretty sharp at that.

Their ship was hit by a kamikaze a couple of months ago, but was not badly damaged. Only a couple of dozen casualties. They carry Sea Fires, Fireflies,[24] and U.S.-made Avengers. Their ship is smaller than ours but somewhat heavier and faster. It's got beautiful smooth lines.

I'm afraid we won't be able to return the visit, though I certainly would enjoy it. They are supposed to leave tomorrow for Sydney, Australia. Some of them are hoping to be back in England by Christmas.

We had a little mail call last night. I had a letter from you written 20 August, one from Grandmother Willard and a V-mail from Aunt Ione.

You are mistaken in thinking we were hit again off Okinawa. We did take part in some raids on that island in June, but we have come through this cruise unscarred. The newsreel scenes you saw were of our episode in January.

Your tale of the mice in the apartment and Butch trying to persuade you to acquire a cat was amusing. I was particularly tickled by the thought of trying to catch mice with flypaper.

The best news in your letter was the word that gas rationing has ceased. I am looking forward now with even greater anticipation to my next homecoming. This morning, I was talking to my Chief Bosun's Mate friend. He said kiddingly that he wouldn't be surprised if I were to ship over. I said no, I was looking forward to the day when I could wake up on a Friday morning and say to myself, "This is not Field Day, it's just Friday," turn over, and go back to sleep.

Yours, Bill

[Tokyo Bay]

Dear Mom, 10 September 1945

This evening after chow I watched two very exciting basketball games. Some British ship, a cruiser I think, sent over an officers' team and a men's team. The officers played our officers first and then the enlisted men played our aircrewmen. Both games were more fun than a circus. The British boys were rather clumsy in handling the ball and their shooting was so vigorous that the ball frequently rebounded half the length of the court. But they were fast and furious in getting the ball into scoring position. Both games were rough but nobody got mad. There was excellent sportsmanship on both sides. Every time our side scored we would boo, and every time they scored we cheered loudly.

I had intended to stay for the movies after the game but changed my mind when the title was announced. It was "Song of Nevada" with Roy Rogers, more Butch's speed than mine.

When I went back down below I found a letter from Jane on my bunk. It was written the 15th of August and told all about the reaction in Manistee to the surrender of Japan. That is one of the few occasions I should like to have been several places at once. I'm glad I was on the Big T at the time. It was the right place for me. But I should also like to have been in Manistee, St. Johns, and Tokyo simultaneously. That's an odd combination perhaps, but I'd like to have seen the enemy's reactions to the news and I'd like to have celebrated it in both my home towns.

Scuttlebutt, by the way, has it that we may some of us get liberty in Tokyo or Yokohama before long. That scuttlebutt is backed up by the fact that the skipper said this noon he would try to fix it so we all "get at least one foot on Japan" before we leave here. He said we will probably be here till around the 20th. Then what, we're not sure.

Most of our working time now is spent chipping paint and painting. One kid in my crew was wielding a brush rather awkwardly. (Perhaps I told you about this.) I started to bawl him out for doing such a poor job. He said, "Well, what do you expect—Rembrandt?" When he gets to be about 70, I think he'll be a second Monty Woolley.[25]

The *Roosevelt Memorial Pocket Book* came the other night with this much wrapping and no string left on it. How I ever actually got it, I don't know. I'm about a third of the way through it. It's very well done. Thanks for sending it.

How do I stand now on war bonds and bank account?[26] I've been thinking it over and it seems to me maybe I ought to build up that bank account while I can. So, perhaps it would be a good idea for you to continue buying only a $37.50 and an $18.75 bond a month as before and with my increased allotment you can then put $23.75 a month in the bank. I guess I'm still behind on what I drew out for my leave. It was worth it though, many times over.

I hope Dad has as swell a time as I did. He'll probably be home when you get this. Yours, Bill

[Tokyo Bay]

Dear Mom, 15 September 1945

Be eternally grateful that you were born an American and not a Japanese. I saw parts of Yokohama today on liberty that were a good example of the results of war.

We went ashore in whites. It felt good to be dressed up again. An LSM [Landing Ship–Medium] took us over. It took perhaps an hour from the ship to the dock getting there at noon. On the dock, the liberty party split up into groups of 20 or 25 with one officer, one shore patrol man, and one hospital corpsman in each group. Our officer was a torpedo pilot, Lt. Hendrickson. He told us we were supposed to stay somewhat together but that he wasn't going to make us hold hands or anything. At times, we were as far as six blocks apart, but we always managed to stay "somewhat together."

We had two objectives in mind: exploring and obtaining souvenirs. I had sufficient of both. All our traveling was done on foot. There were streetcars running now and then, a few charcoal-burning buses, and hardly any automobiles. Lots of U.S. Army jeeps and trucks were on the road, though.

There seemed to be no stores open in the part of town where we were. Japs carried little knapsacks of articles for sale, and here and there they had their wares spread out on the sidewalk for display.

We did our purchasing with Jap currency. Some Japs would take it. But most of them preferred to barter. The money is valid but there is nothing they can buy with it. We were issued K-Rations for our lunch. I carried mine under my arm. Whenever I'd stop a moment I'd be immediately surrounded by 20 or 30 Japs wanting to buy my lunch from me. Candy, chewing gum, and cigarettes, especially the latter, were more valuable than money in obtaining souvenirs. One Jap wanted 50 yen (about 3⅓ dollars) for a pack of some 40 picture postcards. I gave a nickel pack of cigarettes instead and he was very happy.

We found a few who spoke good English. It was fun trading with them. Almost all of them can speak a few essential words of English, more of our language than we speak of theirs, anyhow.

The part of town we saw was badly devastated. Areas of several blocks at a stretch were leveled. Other large areas had been very badly burned. In one vacant lot that had recently been a building we saw the stabilizer of a B-29, evidence of about a dozen guys who aren't coming home. Looking at the ruins, I kept thinking over and over, "I'm glad this isn't my home town." The other boys said they thought the same thing.

We saw a theater building that was nothing now but four walls on the outside and heaps of second-hand building material on the inside. A large girder from one wall to the other was all that remained of the balcony. I wondered if the place was full of people when it was hit.

Farther up the street, there were a couple of other theaters, damaged, but still showing movies. Through all the scars you could see that they were modern buildings, just like ours back home. Kids were lined up on the sidewalk waiting to buy tickets, just like a Saturday afternoon in the States.

The Japanese seem to be taking the surrender in good faith. They are very polite. They gave us the right of way on sidewalks although the streets were crowded. They seem now to be anxious to get along with us. But I'm glad we didn't have to invade Japan.

If anyone tells you we should never have used the atomic bomb, tell them to think of it this way. Today, several thousand sailors went peacefully ashore armed only with Japanese currency, a canteen-full of water, and a box of K-rations. Would it have been better for them to have been several thousand soldiers instead, armed with rifles, bazookas, and flame throwers, backed by big guns of the Navy and covered by hundreds of combat aircraft? Invasion by gangplank is infinitely preferable to invasion by landing barge.

And if the people of St. Johns complain about unemployment, food shortages, and so called "inflation," tell them I said it's much worse in Yokohama. That is an understatement.

Yours, Bill

[Tokyo Bay]

Dear Mom, 19 September 1945

It was announced this afternoon that the ship will get underway at 1300 tomorrow. We have a big load of passengers sleeping all over the hangar deck. Scuttlebutt says we are to pick up some more at Okinawa. Whether that's true or not I don't know. Indications are that we are to be in the States by Navy Day. We are all keeping our fingers crossed, but don't get your hopes up too high. There is still a chance of some transfers at Pearl Harbor. However, some scuttlebutt says we may not even stop there. I hope we do though. I'd like to make one more liberty there.

We had an interesting thing happen this morning. The flight deck is full of planes all but for the space forward of number one elevator. An army helicopter came along about 10 o'clock and landed in that space. He bummed some gasoline from the ship and then took Admiral Sprague,[27] the captain on his staff, our skipper, and the flight deck chief, by turns, up for short hops. It was interesting watching the darn thing perform. It reminds you of a huge dragon fly.

Outgoing mail will close at 1700 so I better get this in the box.

Yours, Bill

Ticonderoga *got underway and stood out of the anchorage in Tokyo Bay at 1:04 P.M. the next day according to schedule. It would now take part in Operation Magic Carpet, transporting American soldiers back to the United States for discharge.*

[Pacific Ocean]

Dear Mom and Pop, 20 September 1945

As I walked from the shower back to my locker tonight I was conscious again of that barely perceptible rolling motion the ship makes in a calm sea. Also, the vibration of the engines tickles my feet as I stand on the deck in my wooden shower shoes. It's good to get back to sea again, especially since we are heading east. We are scheduled to be in Pearl Harbor in about nine days.

We pulled up the anchor promptly at 1300 this afternoon. After threading our way out from among the other ships anchored in the bay we brought up the rear of a long column of capital ships. Six battlewagons and a couple of cruisers were ahead of us plus our escorting tin cans [destroyers]. As Tokyo Bay widened into Sagami Bay the battleships and cruisers began to bear farther to the west. They are going to Okinawa first; we are heading direct to Hawaii. When I went below for supper, land was still visible off our port quarter.

The skipper says we may not have much liberty in Pearl Harbor. As it stands now we should hit the west coast about October 7 or 8. Of course, we're still sweating out the transfer situation at Pearl, but I doubt if many will leave the ship. I'm not worrying much about it. There are a lot of guys with less sea time and less time in the Navy than I have. But on the other hand, they haven't my rate. We don't know yet what west coast port we'll make, but the general opinion seems to be San Francisco.

When we get there, I don't know if we'll go into a yard or just unload and come back out for more passengers. We are supposed to be due for overhaul. That would include drydocking and probably considerable time in a navy yard.

In that case, it would be reasonable to anticipate a leave just as we had last time we were in a navy yard. Anyway, we're all hoping it works out that way.

We had a final mail call this afternoon soon after getting underway. I had a letter from Ruth and Butch's letter on the Hotel Chippewa stationery. Ruth told of Dad's arrival, her final adventures at Ann Arbor, and the family's excursion to Lansing, including dinner at the Olds Hotel. Butch's letter was his usual brief, to-the-point style: "We are now in Manistee. Tomorrow we will go to Benzonia for the weekend. Then we will go back to St. Johns." It would probably take me a page and a half to say the same thing.

A letter from Jane the other day asked me whether I had enlisted for four years or the duration and six months. I devoted several paragraphs to an explanation of the difference between USN and USNR [US Navy and US Navy Reserve], the point system, etc. She may not understand it. There are many who don't. I asked if mere curiosity prompted her question or whether she was concerned about when I'd be getting out.

It may seem foolish writing this letter just after starting for the states. It can't leave the ship till we reach Pearl. But with all these passengers aboard it's too much work going to the movies. You have to get there an hour early to get a seat. So this is a better way to spend an evening.

Yours, Bill

[Pacific Ocean]
23 September 1945

Dear Mom and Pop,

I don't know whether this will reach you before Pop's leave is up.[28] It won't leave the ship till we get to Pearl Harbor.

We have been at sea three days now. We are steering a straight course, no zig zagging.[29] Reveille is at 0600, no morning G.Q. [General Quarters, or battle stations] anymore. And we don't darken ship at night anymore, either. I guess the war is really over.

Our planes are mostly on the flight deck, leaving plenty of space on the hangar deck for passengers. So far, we haven't been doing any flying since before we entered Tokyo Bay. Our working hours are spent according to Navy tradition, keeping the ship clean. That's one thing the Navy overdoes.

On account of the extra men aboard, we are now having two movies a day. The first show begins at 1630. By going to that and then to chow, I still have a whole evening to myself. After a leisurely shower, I can read a while or write letters and still get to bed early.

Today we had holiday routine in honor of it being Sunday. It was the first time we had enjoyed that privilege at sea. I slept till 0730, got up and went to chow, and reported for sweepdown at 0800. Then I read a magazine till church time. After church, I went to chow. We swept down again at 1300 and at 1330 I attended a lecture on the hangar deck by one of the ship's officers. His topic: the G.I. bill of rights.[30] He began with: "Those of you who have served more than 90 days. . . ." That got a good laugh. After the lecture, I went back to bed again, getting up just in time for the movies. We service men sure lead a hard life!

Last spring, when I called on Dr. Merrill in Mt. Pleasant, he asked me my post-war plans. He seemed surprised when I told him I intended to make a career of writing rather than in science. I explained that we had advanced far enough in the physical sciences so that lack of further advancement would not be a great tragedy. But, I said, we need to advance much farther in the social sciences to avoid tragedy.

The chaplain said much the same thing in his sermon this morning. He said our moral advancement needed to catch up to our scientific advancement. He described the discrepancy as a disease of humanity, characterizing the war as a symptom of that disease. We must cure the disease, he said, or the symptoms will again plague us.

Somewhere in his sermon he used the story in which the prophet told David "Thou art the man." I don't know now what the connection was because my mind wandered. Dr. Parr in Ann Arbor used that as a text once. So, for a moment this morning I was going to church with Jane in Ann Arbor.

Going through the snapshots in my locker last night I found one of little Billy and Ruthie having a picnic with Mommy by a lake in the mountains in Colorado. Chronologically, that must have been during the Depression. "These are hard times," people said then. But the little Jap kids who wanted to buy my K-rations the other day would not have thought so.

Who was it who said, "Crisis is another word for now."? I would also add, "'Hard times' is another word for now."

Yours, Bill

[Pacific Ocean]

Dear Mom and Pop, 25 September 1945

Yesterday we had an inspection in whites. We lined up on the hangar deck and were looked over by the air officer. It was a very easy affair, not like the ones we used to have every Saturday at Navy Pier. The Admiral's pantry happens to be located directly above where we were, on the gallery deck. While we stood at attention the delicious aroma of freshly baked cherry pie teased our noses. This was the first dress inspection I had stood since coming aboard the ship. Afterwards we had to stand by our lockers while the Air Officer nosed into them. It was a nuisance but no more so than chipping paint.

Today we had flight quarters right after reveille. It was quite a show for our passengers! Also, it involved quite an adventure for me. Somebody "big-dealed" hops for three of us from the hangar deck: myself, Gregory, J. R., ABM2/c, and a guy named Brock from Detroit. At 0700 we reported to Ready Room 4. There, we were loaned flight gear and assigned to planes, TBM's. Mine was 302. About 0740 we went up on the flight deck and crawled into the turrets of our respective aircraft. When I got squared away in mine, I got out a note book and pencil and started to make a record of my experience. The following paragraphs are written from those notes:

I've climbed into the turret, latched up the armor plate under my feet, and plugged in my head phones. The radio man tunes up his gear and says to me over the intercom, "Radio to Gunner, how do you hear me? Over." I answer, "Gunner to Radio, I hear you loud and clear, out." Then Radio checks with pilot and pilot with me and we're all set.

The planes are turning up now. There are two fighters on the catapults, but I can't see them from here. We are the next plane following them. We will be launched from the deck, however.

It's crowded in this turret. My parachute harness is tight around my waist. We wait.

Now we taxi out to position. I can't see the flight deck officer, Mr. Brooks, but I know he is about to give us the go signal. Our wings are spread. We rev up, release the brakes and start down the deck. It's smoother by far than any runway I've taken off from. I can't feel when we're airborne; the fo'c'sle 40s suddenly pass under us and there's the ocean below. The ship is sure pretty from this angle.

We make a right turn to clear our slipstream from the launching area. Then we turn parallel to the ship again. Now we're over the AA cruiser, about half a mile off the Big T's starboard bow. We climb a little. I watch the ship and see the next plane come off. The launch is slow today, a long interval.

We are flying smoothly now so I let down the armor plate and give myself more room. It's just a little misty up here.

Another plane is off now. The second TBM is coming up to rendezvous. The air is a bit bumpy but not bad. T-301 is now off our port wing. We're circling slowly so that we head back over the ship. 305 is on our starboard wing.

Now there are a few fighters above us. We are circling continuously to the left. Four of us are in a smooth close formation, as if mounted firmly on an invisible frame. It's getting cool.

305 passes under us and takes position to port. We have turned through 360° now. Ships are dead astern. Continue turning. The sea is calm with little, white foam specks. More TBM's are joining up. I guess the deck load is all launched. Another 360° turn complete.

308 is aft and below, 305, 304 and 307 approaching us. There are a few bombers below us now, too. I hear some chatter on the radio. Some fighter is having engine trouble, intends to land, wants to know about jettisoning belly tank. To drop or not to drop, that is the question. We're over the AA cruiser again. Her deck from the bridge forward has a bright new coat of red paint.

The launch is complete, there is an angle in their wakes, so the ships must be changing course. Our pilots seem to be in a rut; we're still circling to the left. This makes the fourth time around. There are fighters above and around us now and bombers below.

I close the armor plate again. A little more cozy now. The Big T is turning to Starboard. I can count 15 fighters overhead. We head west. The water to the east is silvery in the morning sun with gray shadows from the clouds.

There are 22 fighters in sight. Radio man just came into the tunnel compartment from the second cockpit. While his phones were unplugged the pilot called him. He has borrowed my cord. The one in the tunnel doesn't work.

Bearing a shade north of east. The Radioman is starting to operate our radar gear. We have climbed somewhat higher. Circling again. 305 is sending us a blinker message. Wish I could read it. Clouds below. Chilly.

Tunnel wire is working again, so I have mine back. Have turned another 360°, heading east once more. There is a bit of static in the headset caused by our radar. It sounds like a bowl of Rice Krispies in cream. (umm)

The weather strip on the gun slot in this turret is missing. So, it's getting very noticeably cool in here. A left and then a right turn of 90° each. Why, I don't know. The fighters aft of us turn and head the other way; presently, we follow.

There is a ghostly looking half-moon in the sky just above 307 off our port quarter. Bearing N.E., I think we're to make a simulated attack on the ship. Turn complete, bearing west. We're flying in three formations of four planes each. Radioman is blinking an answer to 305. Five bombers below us.

Slow turn to port—180°—now bearing east by a little north. Radioman has task group on radar scope, one mile ahead.

This head set is tight on my ears. But it keeps them warm. Like earmuffs. Radioman is puttering with some T-shaped antenna that sticks up aft of the turret.

Task group must be way behind now. We've been cruising east for some time. I just ate a chocolate bar I had in my pocket. It tasted good. Took my mind off the temperature. Getting rid of the wrapper was no problem. Held it in the slipstream and—fft, it's gone.

I don't know our altitude, but it's high enough to be cold. I'm shivering. I pity the fighter pilots; they're still higher. Chatter over intercom between radioman and pilot about how to drop our practice bombs.

Turn to starboard, bearing south by southeast. The clouds below us are broken. Shadows on sea look like islands. Turning again. Bearing southwest. Bearing west.

For a minute, I didn't know what that little flash of light in 309's turret was. I guess the gunner lit a cigarette. The radioman is returning to his cockpit now. I'm going down in the tunnel to see if it's any warmer there.

Much better. There's a clock down here. Time is 0955. About two hours since we took off. Altimeter shows 9500 feet. No wonder it's chilly. Besides, I'm wearing no skivvy shirt. Temperature is 15° C. or 59° F. It feels cooler. The view isn't so good down here but I have more room.

The radioman has come back in the tunnel with me. He's fiddling with radar again. We hit some more bumpy air. Not enough to make it interesting.

Back in the turret again. Chilly. Circling slowly to left and descending a little. Between clouds below, the air seems clear. Yet there is apparently a little mist down there because our shadow is flying several thousand feet above the water.

Bearing north, now. Continue circling slowly and descending. Fighters and bombers closing in. Task force sighted. The ships are hard to distinguish, but their white wakes are plainly visible. A small white wake follows in the middle of the biggest one. Apparently, the Big T is towing a spar. That's our target.

Chatter over intercom. Pilot can't receive from the ship. He wants radioman to check the trouble. Whatever it was, it's quickly remedied. Bearing south over T.F. Circling to starboard now. Peeling off to port and commencing 45° dive. Warmer almost immediately. Somebody splashed a couple of rockets near the spar. It wasn't us, though. For some reason, we weren't carrying any.

We level off and circle to port just under the misty layer. It must be three or four thousand feet above the water. The task force is off our port wing, with more splashes near the spar. Other planes are rejoining us as we continue to circle. Bearing northeast. Bearing north. Up through the clouds. Cooler. Bearing west. T.F. still off port wing. It's the center of our wide circle.

Turning toward target again. Over task force. Pilot waggles his wings, peels off and commences second dive. These dives aren't very steep and the pullout isn't too fast. We level off right over the Big T. Flight deck is empty. All planes not in the air must be on the hangar deck.

Bearing east, closing up again. It's warm right up to the mist layer. Circling to port, and descending slowly. Bearing west, still circling. Bearing east again, over task force, still circling. Tail hook down.

Radio chatter with the ship. 304 is going to land with one rocket still aboard, which it can't fire. Over task force, still circling starboard destroyer is going over to follow the Big T as plane guard. Fighters have started to land.

I let down the armor plate again to give my legs a final stretch before landing. A fighter has been waved off and is pulling away from the ship to go around again. We're still acting like a horse on a merry-go-round. Circling and descending.

Armor plate back in position, feet up in turret. Thirteen fighters have landed.— Over the ship again, 19 fighters now aboard. Circling tighter, lower. Lead plane peels off, we're next. Bank to left, wheels and flaps down.

We're in the landing circle. First TBM has landed. Taxis forward. We're approaching. We're in the groove. I crane my neck for a glimpse of the landing signal officer. Can't even see the ship. We bank a little one way, then the other, apparently in response to L.S.O. Cut signal, we nose down a little.

Uhh [wavy line]. We're down. The cable pulls us to a stop.

We taxi forward, stop. Fold wings and taxi on. One of my colleagues is doing his stuff, but I can't see him. Our wing is in the way. We're spotted now, chocked up. The pilot cuts the engine. I climb out. 1130.

That's the end of my notes. I went back to the ready room, took off my gear, and compared my experience with the others. Brock thought the diving was pretty rugged. It was his first hop. Imagine starting your flying career off of a carrier. Then we went to chow.

This afternoon, we re-spotted for tomorrow's hop. All the planes on the hangar deck went topside and those that flew today came below. I wish I could fly again tomorrow. It was fun. I'm glad the target wasn't shooting back at us, though.

We cross the date line tonight. Tomorrow is Tuesday the 25th all over again. We'll work an eight-day week this week. Too bad they didn't contrive to have two Sundays, instead, so we could have two days of holiday routine. Oh, well!!

Yours, Bill

[Pacific Ocean]

Dear Mom and Pop, 27 September 1945

We are supposed to pull into Pearl Harbor tomorrow afternoon. The skipper said today that our orders so far are very indefinite. We are to leave Hawaii "by the 19th of October." With all these passengers aboard he doubts if we'll be there all that time. He thinks probably we'll get the word tomorrow to go on to Frisco or some such place within a couple of days. Eventually we are to wind up in Seattle for Navy Day. . . .

This afternoon all Air Group and Air Department personnel had to fall in for quarters on the hangar deck, while a bunch of pilots and air crewmen received awards. We had had a similar affair for ship's company a while back. The guys who were hit last January received their purple hearts at that time. Myself and some other egg from one of the deck divisions missed out then on account of some mix-up in our medical records. We got ours today with the Air Group.

Men receiving awards had to be in whites. Everyone else was in dungarees. There were two ranks of officers in front and two more of enlisted men behind. As our names were called out we marched up individually and received our awards. Most of the air group people were getting D.F.C.'s [Distinguished Flying Crosses] or Air Medals. Rear Admiral Sprague,[31] ComCarDiv 2, was the one who presented the medals. I was next to the last on the list. I saluted the Admiral, he returned the salute, handed me the purple heart, shook hands, I saluted again and walked back to my place in ranks. It was very simple, with altogether too much to-do about it.

The Purple Heart is a heavy, gold, heart shaped medal on a purple and white ribbon. On the gold is a smaller heart of some purple stuff like pearl or something. On that is a small gold head of Washington. The whole thing is done up in a neat purple box, in which it stays. On my uniform I wear only a bit of purple and white ribbon. . . .

Yours, Bill

[Pearl Harbor, Hawaii]

Dear Butch, 29 September 1945

We pulled in last night and had mail waiting for us. Your letter of the 23rd was in the bunch. You type well. . . .

When we came in yesterday, there was a Navy Band on the dock to greet us, together with a chorus of waves. It was just a little over a year ago that we docked here for the first time. A reception by some chirping cherubs of the women's reserve wasn't even imagined then. . . .

Your pal, Bill

[Naval Air Station, Alameda, California]

Dear Mom, 5 October 1945

We docked at noon today at the air station pier, Alameda, California. The ship is to be here about four days and then we'll go back to Pearl Harbor for our air group. That means we'll probably pull out Tuesday.

I was on a detail to handle one of the mooring lines, so I only got a glimpse of the two bridges as we came in. Our flight deck has a fresh paint job and most of the crew were lined up at quarters up there, so the ship probably presented a very pretty sight to spectators over our heads. It was a nice sunny day with just a little mist in the air.

Sections one, two, and three are all on liberty now. I am in section four. After our 2000 passengers disembarked and three-fourths of our own men had left the ship for liberty, those of us who were left cleaned up the hangar deck. There was five days' accumulation of trash from our 2000 passengers to be swept up and taken onto the dock. It was quite a job.

With the contrast between the crowd we've had aboard recently and the single section on duty now, the ship seems quite deserted.

There is an extension public phone on the hangar deck. I tried to call you up a little while ago but the operator said there'd be a two- to three-hour delay so I gave it up. I may try again tomorrow. If I get through, you'll hear from me that way before you get this letter.

We had a little mail this afternoon when we got in. I got a letter from Dad written September 11 telling about getting home and describing the trip in the car up to Manistee, up M-22, around Crystal Lake, and that region. It really sounded nice. Hope I can be making the same trip soon.

It's nice and quiet in the compartment now, so I guess I'll get into my bunk and read a while.

Yours, Bill

[Alameda, California]

Dear Mom, 8 October 1945

Our section was granted weekend liberty from 1300 Saturday till 0900 today, Monday. I made good use of that time.

Just after I came down the gangway on Saturday afternoon a car started with a couple of officers in it. One of them yelled, "Anyone going to Berkeley?" So, I bummed a ride over to the university campus. I bought a ticket and went into the stadium to see University of California play University of Washington. It was a good game and I enjoyed it.

But more than the game itself, I enjoyed the audience. It was good to sit there eating a hot dog, drinking Coca-Cola, and listening to the cheering of enthusiastic spectators. The scene was good to look at: people in all different colors of clothes, kids, old people, young guys and girls together. Altogether I thought it was a pretty good way to spend my first afternoon back in the States.

After the game, I thumbed back into Oakland, ate, and hitchhiked on across the bridge to Frisco. There I found a tailor shop where I could buy an ABM2/c rating badge. Then, I looked around for a hotel room. Everything was filled up. At one place, though, I just happened to be at the desk when a party checked out of a double room. So I took it, together with an ensign who happened to be there, too. More good luck.

Then I went out, ate again, and went to a movie. It was about midnight when I came in and hit the sack.

My intention was to get up at the good, respectable hour of 8:30 or 9:00, eat a leisurely breakfast, and go to church somewhere. But when I woke up it was 11:30 already.

When I went out to eat, I decided it would be breakfast in spite of the hour. So I ordered waffles. After chow, I took the streetcar out to the Cliff House and browsed around a bit.[32] One could certainly spend a lot of money there if he chose to. I spent 35¢ for a hot dog and a milkshake.

Then I hitchhiked across the Golden Gate Bridge. At first I thought I would just go across and back for the view. But there is no end to the scenery on the other side and it's a very pleasant drive. So, I rode on as far as the little town of Petaluma, about 30 miles.

By the time I got back to Frisco it was dark. So, I ate and then thumbed across the other bridge to Oakland. There, I met a marine from the ship, the captain's orderly. He and I went to a movie together. It was "Song of the Islands," in technicolor, one of those typical Hollywood misconceptions of South Seas life. After it had run about ten minutes, the star, Betty Grable, came into the picture. I exclaimed loudly enough so that several people nearby heard me, "Hey, that's Betty Grable." The marine said, "Who'd you expect it to be?" I replied, "I was looking for Dorothy Lamour." That apparently struck him as funny and he almost got the hiccups from laughing so hard.

We got back to the ship about midnight, first stopping at a little restaurant where I drank three glasses of orange juice.

I'm going out again today at 1300 to do some more hitchhiking. We leave for Pearl Harbor again tomorrow.

Yours, Bill

[Pearl Harbor, Hawaii]

Dear Mom and Pop, 14 October 1945

This morning, prior to entering Pearl Harbor, we had gunnery exercises, which interfered with having church. The chaplain was pretty annoyed about it, but couldn't do anything as it was the bright idea of some bigshot over on the beach.

We pulled in about 10:00 and got the gangways rigged about 11:00. It was almost noon before the liberty party got off. I was in it.

I spent the afternoon sightseeing. I went up to that place called Maunalani Heights again. It's a thrilling ride on the bus. The bus takes a winding route up the hill. Each time it turns around another cutback, you see an increasingly gorgeous view. At every turn, you say to yourself, "Well this must be nearly the top. It would be hard to beat this scenery." And then you make another turn, the view is even better, and you say it all over again. One thing that impresses me is the fact that houses on the low side of the street face away from the street. Remember your pet peeve in Colorado used to be houses that faced a road with their backs turned to the view.

According to our hangar deck officer, we can now have cameras aboard. So, if you can mail mine to me I'd appreciate it. Enclose the portrait lens and the exposure meter.

Which brings up another subject. Our plans have been changed. We are to be converted into a troop transport. The conversion will consist merely of welding bunks in on the hangar deck. Most of the air department will be transferred. Only enough of the airedales will stay aboard to maintain our respective parts of the ship.

I have volunteered to stay aboard. There are to be ten men and two P.O.'s [petty officers] on the hangar deck. We'll sail between Pearl Harbor and the west coast so it will involve fairly frequent liberty. All in all, it looks like good duty.

This is all to take place after our Navy Day appearance in Seattle. My reasons for volunteering to stay aboard are these: We haven't enough sea time to be sure of a leave when being transferred. We're not even sure of *shore* duty. And chances of shore duty *near home* for me are very remote. Rather than be stuck at a coastal port with duty like I had at Norfolk, I'd rather stay on the ship.

Also 5% of ship's company is to be on leave at all times. So, I might be in the lucky bunch. And if we do transport duty for a few months and then decommission the ship it is exceedingly unlikely that I'd go to sea again and quite likely that I'd rate a leave.

But there's still one other possibility looming on the horizon. Something is wrong with the reduction gear in one of our engines. It doesn't reduce our effectiveness as a troop carrier but it does mean we're not in A-1 shape. The dope is that our skipper has applied for a major overhaul in a navy yard before conversion. If that comes through, we might get a leave out of that.

At any rate, my address will still be CV-14 for some time yet.

On the way back to the base this afternoon, I stopped at the navy hospital and looked up Donald Norton PhM3/c of Manistee, who is stationed there. We had

a good bull session and he walked down to fleet landing with me where I caught the ferry to Ford Island. He has just been here a month. He was home when I was on leave a year ago last July. It seemed funny to think I hadn't seen him in that length of time.
Yours, Bill

[Pacific Ocean]
Dear Puddlemush, 18 October 1945

Mail has been a little scarce of late. I had only one letter from Mom, this time at Pearl. Your letter of September 27 came just before we left Alameda.

How come you're trying to talk me into going to Oberlin [College]? Have you actually decided to go there yourself? That might well be a college worth considering but I'm not making up my mind till it's time to enroll. I want to pick a place I can stay four years without getting the urge to see new scenes.

We have a hangar deck full of soldiers aboard now. Many are air force men, but some are infantry, coast artillery, etc. They are all favorably impressed with our chow. I overheard one guy in the mess hall tonight saying he had half a notion to join the Navy when he gets out of the Army. I trust it was *only* half a notion.

We hit Seattle next Monday the 22nd. This letter won't leave the ship till then so it'll be stale when you get it. But the movie's a corny one tonight, so I thought I'd write instead.
Yours, Bill

[Puget Sound, Washington]
Dear Mom, 22 October 1945

We are now at anchor again just off Tacoma. At about noon we dropped the hook off Seattle, an LCI [landing craft, infantry] came alongside, and some of our men being transferred got off. Some civilians from a local radio station came aboard and set up their gear for a special broadcast. Then we upped anchor and went on to Tacoma. Tomorrow we go in and tie up to a dock and will have three section liberty in the evening.

This morning we launched about 40 aircraft while passing through the Strait of Juan de Fuca. The re-spot was made early and they began launching about 0730. It was quite cold, and with the ship headed into the wind, which was augmented over the deck by the propeller slipstreams, the flight deck crews were definitely conscious that we'd left the tropics. The catwalks were lined with our soldier-passengers watching the performance. Unfortunately, we catapulted all the planes. Deck launching makes a much better show.

All day yesterday we had very rough weather. The ship bounced and shivered all over. The sea was beautiful, though. It was a deep grey, streaked with brilliant white foam that glistened in the bright sun. In the evening, a big wave smashed in one of the steal roller-curtains on the side of the hangar deck. A lot of our passengers got wet, but nobody was hurt. Soldiers' shoes could be seen floating here and there about the deck.

While the repair party mended the leak in the dike the hangar deck crew got rid of the water. We opened the curtains on the lee side and pushed the water out with squilgees. I began by taking off my shoes. The idea proved quite popular and we had a gang of barefoot swabbies wading in cold salt water, having the time of their lives. It was fun.

At Church yesterday morning, we had communion service. It was Chaplain Gilmore's last service. He is to be discharged presently. As the band began the music for a hymn the chaplain said, "Shall we stand." Seemingly in reply the ship lurched furiously and we all sat down again involuntarily.

In addition to my intention of hitchhiking around the country a ship mate and I have thought of another idea which seems quite adventurous. It involves getting a couple of motorcycles and riding them from the northern end of the Alcan highway to the southern end of the Pan American highway. Want to come along?

Yours, Bill

[Pacific Ocean]

Dear Mom and Pop, 15 November 1945

. . . Day before yesterday our morning's work was interrupted by the captain announcing over the loudspeaker that he'd just gotten the word over the radio that Dixie Kiefer had been killed in an airplane crash. He didn't give many details except that it seems to have occurred in an attempted landing at Quonset Point in a fog.[33]

Our skipper is a southerner with a very strong accent and a poor microphone voice. It's always hard to understand him. So, he was halfway through his announcement before most of us realized that the words "Dixie Kiefer" and "killed" were part of the same sentence. When the meaning dawned on us we were shocked just as we were that day back in April when a similar unbelievable announcement was made.

To many of those who heard the news, Dixie was just a legend. But to those of us who began our seagoing careers under him, he was an irreplaceable part of the ship itself. Even the replacements who had come aboard in Bremerton know how we felt. It was a personal loss. I kept thinking of his last words as he left the ship in a stretcher at Ulithi: "Remember, you're still Dixie's kids."

Captain Sinton radioed an order for flowers for the funeral to be paid for from the ship's welfare fund. We were unanimous in favor of it. It seems like our flag ought to be at half mast, but I guess the rules don't say so.
Yours, Bill

At Sea
Dear Pop, 18 November 1945

This afternoon I got permission from the O.O.D. [officer of the day] and broke out my camera and took some snapshots on the flight deck. It was a beautiful day for it. The sun was brighter, according to my exposure meter, than it has been for any previous picture taking excursion of mine. I shot up the roll of black and white film I got in Hawaii just taking pictures of various eggs.

The flight deck today was like Jackson Park Beach in Chicago on a Sunday afternoon in July. There were two volleyball courts in use, a badminton court on the flight deck, and a basketball court on the No. 1 elevator. Also, several games of so-called football were in progress on the flight deck, and many individuals were tossing baseballs around. In addition, most of ship's company were scattered about in various degrees of nudity becoming tan. One group of four was having a picnic. They had a blanket spread out on the deck and were eating cheese and crackers and drinking pineapple juice. Beyond them was a portable radio making a noise resembling music.

I'll try to send to you the roll of film I took today plus the Kodacolor roll I used in Honolulu by airmail from Samar. Please have the color roll sent in to Eastman's for processing and have the black and white one done locally. Have one print of each made in both cases. Some of the guys whose pictures I took today will want prints. When they see them, and tell me how many of each, I can send those negatives to you for reprints. Keep track of the cost and sometime when it's convenient I'll reimburse you. Thank you.
Yours, Bill

At Sea
Dear Mom and Pop, 29 November 1945

Last week we were leaving Samar and our passengers were just getting settled so we postponed Thanksgiving Day. This week we crossed the dateline on Thursday, November 29, yesterday. So that makes this the 6th Thursday in November and we are having Holiday routine, Church, and Turkey. . . .

This is my third Thanksgiving in the Navy and I guess I've got more now to be thankful for than ever before. It's like you used to say about moving to another town. All the old friendships still existed and new ones were to be made. All the blessings recounted at previous Thanksgivings are still there and more have accumulated. The thing everybody undoubtedly has in mind above all else this year is the end of the war. What must it have been like in 1918 when Thanksgiving followed only a couple of weeks behind Armistice Day?

While now I am wishing I were out of the Navy, I am constantly and consciously thankful simply that I'm still alive.

Yours, Bill

At Sea

Dear Mom and Pop, 5 December 1945

We dock at Alameda tomorrow noon. The Captain announced today that we were scheduled to be there seven days, leaving again on the 13th. He didn't tell us where we're going next; I guess he doesn't know yet himself. Scuttlebutt says: China, India, Suez, Gibraltar and Brooklyn. But Scuttlebutt said that when we were in Tokyo Bay, too.

Undoubtedly we will be quite busy reprovisioning this coming week. I hope that doesn't cut down on our liberty too much, though. I want to do some Christmas shopping. It looks like we'll be having Christmas at sea again this year. . . .

Yours, Bill

[San Francisco]

Dear Mom and Pop, 10 December 1945

There is a radio in the room where I'm writing which is now playing Christmas carols. It is a very pleasant sound to be hearing and a good ending to a fine liberty.

We were granted liberty yesterday noon expiring tomorrow morning. I spent the afternoon Christmas shopping, in what few places were open on Sunday. In the evening I went to a movie, "Lady on a Train" starring Deanna Durbin. It was kind of a far fetched story but it was worth the price of admission just to hear her sing "Silent Night."

I stayed overnight in the King George Hotel, Room and bath $1.50. It was a very pleasant place and to me the privacy seemed elegant. I soaked for an hour in the bathtub this morning, running in more water as fast as it became cool. That's something you can't do on the ship.

After breakfast I set out via thumb for Sacramento. Hitch hiking was good and I got there before noon, making it in five jumps. First I went up to the Capitol grounds and nosed around. It is a very beautiful setting comparable to the lay out at Olympia. One building is inscribed "Bring me men to match my mountains."

In front of the legislative building I met a middle aged negro. We got to talking and the conversation lasted an hour. He was very intelligent and a pleasant conversational partner. Among other things we talked about race prejudice. It was the first time I'd ever discussed that subject with a colored person and I was deeply impressed. His viewpoint was so similar to mine that I was actually startled several times when I "re-noticed" the color of his skin. He never seemed resentful, only bewildered.

When we parted I went downtown and shopped for film. I succeeded in getting a roll of Verichrome and one of Kodacolor. Then I ate lunch at a dime store.

Next I went to a U.S.O. and called up Jane. From the time I dialed the operator till Jane said hello was scarcely five minutes. It cost me more because it was mid-afternoon but it was well worth it.

When I'd finished that brief three minutes I started back to Frisco. Made it in three jumps. I ate here at the service center and then went to see "Spell bound" starring Ingrid Bergman and Gregory Peck.

My hand is getting tired so I guess I'll stop and listen to the music on the radio.
Yours, Bill

511 AM 12 12
REV W R COTTON
BOX 26 ST. JOHNS MICH
YOU ARE INFORMED THAT YOUR SON WILLIAM R COTTON IS CONSIDERED SERIOUSLY ILL THIS HOSPITAL WITH DIAGNOSIS FRACTURE PELVIS WILL KEEP YOU INFORMED OF ANY CHANGE IN CONDITION.
MOINC US NAVAL HOSP OAKLAND CALIF

1 32PM 12 12
REV W R CATTON
BOX 26 ST. JOHNS MICH
YOU ARE INFORMED THAT YOUR SON WILLIAM R CATTON IS SERIOUSLY ILL THIS HOSPITAL WITH DIAGNOSIS FRACTURE PELVIS X. WILL KEEP YOU INFORMED OF ANY CHANGE IN CONDITION
MEDICAL OFFICER IN CHARGE
US NAVAL HOSP.
OAKLAND CALIF.

605 PM DEC 12 45
REV WILLIAM CATTON
CONGREGATIONAL CHURCH
ST. JOHNS MICHIGAN
ACCIDENT SERIOUS BUT NOT CRITICAL TRIPLE FRACTURE PELVIS 5 MONTHS HOSPITALIZATION LETTER DETAILS FOLLOWS.

REV LOPER

Dec 12 –45
Clement M. Pung
St. Johns, Michigan

Retel William R. Catton ABM 2/c injured accident aboard ship father informed by navy son seriously ill doctor states severe fracture pelvis some bladder injury general condition good fine spirits telephoning father today family presence not indicated further report follows

Oakland USNL
Red Cross

From Reverend Loper to Robert Catton:

[Oakland, California]
12 December 1945

Dear Catton:

I have just returned from calling on your son. I discovered that he has had a very serious accident but that no fear of his life is anticipated whatsoever. He is in for a period of at least five months of hospitalization. The lowest figure given to me was three months.

At the end of that time they have every confidence that he will be able to walk. He will not be able to participate in such athletics as football. He will probably have some weakness there which might evidence itself in such a thing as arthritis. A further operation might be necessary. There seems to be no possibility, however, that he will be crippled in any permanent way, whatsoever.

The injuries, the terms which the doctors used and which you will probably want to refer to your own doctor are as follows. I might also say that I saw the X-ray plate showing his condition. There is a fracture of the pelvis—left superior and inferior rami of the pubis and a fracture of the pelvis. There is also a fracture of the right sacrum—5th lumbar vertebrae. In the right leg the sympathetic nerve has been disrupted. The latter will take some months to recover but will come along in good shape.

Fortunately, I was there at the time the consulting physician came in to examine him together with the house physician. I talked with both of them and neither of them felt there were any internal conditions which need to cause any anxiety. There is, however, some internal hemorrhaging which is not considered serious. Both doctors felt there need to be no occasion for worry on your part in regard to his recovery but that you must all brace yourselves for a long period of hospitalization.

William realizes this as he was told it by the doctor in my presence. He seems to be taking it all in excellent spirits, was cheerful, seemed happy to visit with me and was looking forward to a long-distance call which he was expecting to receive shortly from you.

The hospital is about a half hour's ride from the church so it will not be possible for me to call often but I will keep in touch with him as frequently as is possible. I left a note for the chaplain stating his condition and relationship to you and asked him to keep an eye on the boy.

He was obviously receiving the very best of care. He had the picture of his girl fastened in the frame so he could look up at it while lying on his bed. He has various contraptions holding up his limbs. He is obviously a very fine boy and in good spirits in spite of his mishap. I did not get the exact nature of his accident but it happened on board ship. Part of a truck which was being loaded on an elevator went down and threw the machine on which he was riding on him. In general, this was the nature of the accident which occurred.

If there is anything that you feel I might do that would help in the situation other than I have suggested, please know that I am at your service. I was very happy to get acquainted with your boy. He certainly is an excellent lad.

With my cordial personal greetings, I am

Sincerely yours, Reverend Loper

[Oakland, California]

Dear Mom and Pop, 19 December 1945

I've been here over a week now and this is the first letter I've written.[34] I'm sorry not to have kept you better informed but it's so much easier not to write than to get around to making the effort that I've just let it go.

They have me in a room by myself although there is another bed in it. On my bed is a steel frame over me with pulleys and weighted on the other end. It seems my right pelvic bone is what got fouled up the most. It's broken and twisted. This traction is to pull it back into place before they put a cast on me. That will probably take some time.

My legs are O.K. except that being all tied up they get tired and numb. And my insides don't seem to have been damaged.

I can't complain of the kind of care they're taking of me. There is a hospital corpsman assigned to me alone. And about three or four doctors work on me together, although technically I'm assigned to just one of them. And, of course, there are scads of nurses flitting about the place. A hospital wouldn't be bad at all if one didn't have to be sick to be in it.

My room has been pretty bright. The flowers from the church came the other day. And there is also a pine branch with two huge cones and a piece of red ribbon tacked up on the wall. Directly above my head on the bed-frame is Jane's portrait.

It was certainly good to talk to you over the phone that first day here. Hearing your voices did more to soothe me and make me rest than anything else. I don't know whether I gave you a very good description of the accident then or not. I'll try to make it a little clearer on paper.

To begin with, I was on the flight deck forward. We were loading provisions to cart them around. We had one of those little trucks, a forklift. The forks that stick out in front can be raised and lowered to lift equipment. We were carrying some heavy stuff and instead of lifting the forks the control would cause the back end to rise. So, I was sitting on it to hold it down. We were running empty across the number one elevator. Just as the front wheels were on the deck proper and the rear wheels were on the elevator, it started down. The truck tilted backwards and I jumped off but couldn't get clear in time. It came down sideways and landed on top of me.

I wasn't knocked out or even winded so all I could do was lie there and yell while they tried to lift it off of me. My first thought, though, while I was pinned there was, "Thank God it didn't kill me."

Mail is coming to me regularly now. Had a letter yesterday from Aunt Nellie who had gotten the news from Aunt Ione. She has connected it with your trip and thinks you're out here with me. The letter was even addressed to W. R. Catton, Sr.

I'm using an unfamiliar pen and I'm lying on my back so this tires my hand pretty quickly. So, for now I'll stop.

Yours, Bill

[Oakland, California]

Dear Pop, 2 March 1946

Mom's train was only a few minutes late this morning. She was met at the station by Joe Gauger, whom she apparently recognized easily from description. And she got out to the Sprague's home O.K. They brought her out here shortly after one this afternoon and came back for her at four.

She was apparently very glad to see me and naturally I was glad to see her. She brought the typewriter, a box of cookies, some candy, and those snapshots with her. I immediately proceeded to test out the typewriter by writing Butch a letter. Then we looked at snapshots, ate candy, and generally shot the breeze.

I beg to differ with your analysis of the defects in the last batch of snapshots. They don't seem to me so much underexposed as underdeveloped. There is a difference. Underexposure would give loss of detail. Underdevelopment causes a muddy appearance. If she had some intensifier solution Ruth could fix up those negatives so that they would give fairly respectable prints. I like the composition of one of them very well. That is the scene of Ruth and Butch on the bridge.

Mom noticed my moustache right away this afternoon. I forget just what she said about it. She asked if I were going to keep it as a permanent fixture. I told her it was just an experiment. She also noticed I had more hair than usual. That too is only temporary. My moustache, by the way, is still not yet trimmable.

This little clipping is from an old *Coronet* magazine. I thought you'd get a kick out of it. I'm also enclosing a letter from my English friend. Mom read it this afternoon. I think you will enjoy particularly his story about the American plane that tried to land on his ship. Please save the letter for me.

As of today, I have points enough for inactive duty. In a manner of speaking I guess you could say that's exactly the kind of duty I've got, at that.

Yours, Bill

[Oakland, California]

Dear Mom and Pop, 11 April 1946

Four months ago tonight I came in the main gate in an ambulance. This afternoon I went out the same gate in a station wagon. The Red Cross took seven of us from this ward for a ride this afternoon. We were out about an hour and a half or so. We went here and there and elsewhere, including mostly the University of California campus in Berkeley. It was most enjoyable seeing houses and trees and people and dogs and cars and grass, etc., again. On the campus, we circled around a couple of blocks slowly just as some classes were letting out. There were girls galore flitting to and from and many whistles rent the air accordingly.

In one more or less secluded place that was nicely shaded by trees we saw a couple walking along. They had a friend with them who happened to be a great dane. I leaned out the window and barked at him. He wasn't sure where the sound was coming from and assumed a very perplexed expression. All hands including the Red Cross woman who was driving were moderately amused.

Yesterday afternoon I spent about half the afternoon outside the ward on the lawn. It was a very nice bright sunny day and I really sweated for the first time since my sea duty ended. Besides, the muscle builder was out there giving me a workout.

While I was out there, I was walking around on both feet. I still supported most of my weight with the crutches when the right foot was on the ground. But I can stand easily with both feet down and without the crutches. It was no trouble at all walking down the slanting ramp. This afternoon, after the auto ride, I came into the ward at the sunporch and where there are about ten steps to ascend. I made them without any difficulty.

We had a show in the ward this afternoon just before I went out. It was sponsored by the Red Cross and consisted of piano music, singing, and dancing. There was a colored fellow who played the piano and sang. He had a very good voice and his fingers tickled the ivories quite skillfully, too. Another guy played the piano while a little girl danced and sang. The small female was about Butch's age, I should judge. She had a cute little costume on and did some acrobatic dancing. All of us wished we could do the same, of course. It was the best show of that kind that we've had in several weeks.

I am anxious to see those two books about the Atomic Age when they come. Mr. Swing's book especially should be interesting. I wish I could have heard the broadcasts originally. It has occurred to me that it might be worthwhile for me to write a book sometime. I don't know when I may get around to trying. But what I have in mind is a little off the beaten path. Instead of showing the *necessity* of preventing war in order to save the world, I would like to show the *desirability* of saving the world. In other words, I'd show the many ways in which the world is worth saving. Some of those ways are the things I saw this afternoon: the dogs and children, college students, trees, nice homes, lawns, people here and there just living life as it comes along. Some guy once asked me on the ship how I could actually enjoy navy life. I told him that I simply enjoyed life. The theme of the book could be something like the little rhyme by Stevenson, wasn't it, that goes: "The World is so full of a number of things / That we should all be as happy as kings."

It all comes back to that tired out expression about "hard times" and a "cruel world." In spite of the many troubles, real and imagined, which beset the human race, I think it's a pretty darn good world. Anyhow I think it deserves a chance to survive.

Yours, Bill

Epilogue

What became of Bill Catton after the war, and how did his World War II experience shape the rest of his life? And, to address a question that may be on the minds of readers who are interested in William R. Catton Jr. the sociologist, how did the war experience come to influence his seminal thought on human ecology?

He was discharged from the US Navy in August 1946 on the recommendation of a medical board after doctors determined that they had done all they could for him in hospital. He was left with paralysis of his right peroneal nerve, which, in the perfunctory language of the medical report, made him "unfit for military service in any capacity." In practical terms this meant he would never be a fast runner but was otherwise in shipshape for a return to civilian life.

The serious accident on the ship and long recovery in hospital prolonged his time in the navy by several months. During the protracted hospitalization, his and Jane Hanson's ardor cooled, and they went their separate ways.

Returning home to the Midwest, the young veteran availed himself of the GI Bill, which provided him full tuition and living expenses to go to college. He first enrolled at Millikin University in Decatur, Illinois, where the family had moved in January 1946. Bill then transferred the credits earned there and completed his undergraduate degree at Oberlin College in the small town of Oberlin, Ohio. Since he did not have to get a summer job to defray living expenses, he attended a summer session at the University of New Hampshire between his sophomore and junior years. The GI Bill may not have been critical to his getting a college education, but it saved him expense and gave him more choices, for which he remained forever thankful. Bill was among some 2.2 million World War II veterans who attended college through the program in the decade after the war.

During his senior year of college, he switched his major from history to sociology. I suspect the decision had something to do with his epiphany aboard USS *Ticonderoga*—when the kamikaze gave him his first profound encounter with the Other. Exposed to rampant racism in the navy, Bill had frequently argued with his peers and challenged them to embrace a more tolerant, less ethnocentric view of the great human family. The first book he ever reviewed in a professional journal was Morton Grodzins's *Americans Betrayed: Politics and the Japanese Evacuation*. One lesson Bill drew from the Grodzins book was that US military officials, in treating all Japanese Americans as suspicious aliens, had ignored sociological studies that might have headed off such a racist and unjust policy if only they had duly consulted those sociological studies.[1]

At Oberlin College Bill met the love of his life, Nancy Lewis of Greensburg, Indiana. He was twenty-one, she was eighteen. They were introduced to each other in debate club. For the first debate, two teams were to address the proposition, "There should be a world government." He was on the affirmative team, while she was on the rebutting team. Before the debate they went on a library date together. Sitting across a table from her in the college library, he kept stealing looks at her as she studiously prepared her rebuttals, a book propped open in her slender hands. He thought she looked lovely. This led to a courtship—with their debate about world government happily mooted—and then an engagement. They were married by Bill's father on 3 September 1949.[2]

The newlyweds loaded all their possessions into a 1933 Pontiac and drove across the country to Seattle, Washington. The city would be their home for most of the next twenty years. Bill entered graduate school at the University of Washington, earned a PhD in sociology, and, after a spell of teaching at other schools, became a professor in the University of Washington's Department of Sociology. Nancy, meanwhile, completed her bachelor's degree in sociology and worked as a welfare agent. Then, consistent with the temper of the times, she quit her job to have children and become a full-time homemaker, setting aside professional career aspirations in favor of being a faculty wife. The couple secured a mortgage on a nice house in a good neighborhood near the University of Washington. Over the next decade and a half, Bill flourished in his academic career, aided by his unheralded stay-at-home helpmate as well as the boom times in American higher education. Thus, Bill and Nancy rode the wave of general prosperity that washed over the United States after World War II. Contributing their bit to the postwar baby boom, they produced four sons during the years 1954 to 1964.[3]

As native midwesterners living in the West, Bill and Nancy found they were hardly alone; many of their new friends in Seattle hailed from the Midwest as well. They were all part of a huge migration to the Pacific coastal states precipitated by the war.[4] Even more than past American conflicts, World War II resulted in a vast uprooting and transplanting of people to new homes in different parts of the country. Millions of young Americans were put on the move—to factory jobs in cities or to training camps and battle fronts—and they returned home with broadened horizons. Some went home from the war with definite ideas about relocating when the time was right. Bill and Nancy were among the countless Americans affected. When Bill saw the Seattle area for the first time in 1945, he thought it was a place he would like to move after the war. He was on deck when *Ticonderoga* cruised into Puget Sound. The area's shining mountains and dark forests enthralled him. The sight of Mount Rainier seemingly floating on the sunlit haze beyond the Seattle skyline, as viewed from across the sound in the port of Bremerton, made an especially strong impression.[5]

Soon after their arrival in Seattle, Bill and Nancy began to enjoy weekend trips to Mount Rainier National Park. They took up outdoor recreation as their favorite pastime. Eventually, they made backpack trips and national-park vacations a central feature in raising their family. Love of mountains entered the family's bloodstream. But Bill's mountain adventures were not all just for fun. As the years passed, those frequent visits to national parks afforded him insights into the human condition that changed his theory of sociology. He wanted sociology to move in the direction of the natural sciences without giving up its important focus on the human species' singular ability to cherish *values*. He probed this theoretical problem in his first book, *From Animistic to Naturalistic Sociology.*[6]

In my view, my father's newfound interest in wilderness recreation now worked in tandem with his earlier experiences in World War II to lead him down the path to his major intellectual achievement. He began to focus his academic research on wildlands recreation. He surveyed campground users and studied other facets of public use of national parks. He analyzed the burgeoning problem of overuse of these resources. At the same time, drawing on his World War II experiences, he began to think in strikingly original ways about some of the big-picture issues of the day: the population bomb, pollution, and social decay. Key to his emerging thought was the concept of *carrying capacity.*[7]

Carrying capacity was not originally a sociological concept. It first appeared in animal husbandry to describe, for example, how many sheep could be grazed in a paddock without spoiling the grounds. Later, it came to be used in wildlife management to understand, for example, the effects of a deer population within a given natural range. Finally, carrying capacity came into use by sociologists working within the field of recreation management. How many river rafters at a time could go down the Grand Canyon before that delicate riverine environment, and the aesthetic experience of the visitors, became degraded? Or, how many backpackers at a time could tent out in a subalpine meadow in Mount Rainier National Park before the meadow began to get denuded? Bill's original idea—the thought that drove all the rest of his intellectual output—was to apply the concept of carrying capacity to the entire human population on a planetary scale. Becoming a human ecologist, he would insist that *Homo sapiens* has the same basic interchange with the environment as every other living organism: it takes substances from the environment in the process of living and puts substances back into it in the form of waste. But because humans employed technology, their relationship to the environment was unique in scale, far outstripping the effects of any other species. In this regard the human species is effectively a man-tool system, with the energy consumption and waste product of manmade machines being an extension of the human organism. In its ecological connection, he declared, *Homo sapiens* had become *Homo colossus.*[8]

First engaged with this idea when he worked on recreational-carrying-capacity studies for the National Park Service in the 1960s, his micro- and macro-level thinking about carrying capacity went hand in hand because Mount Rainier National Park literally bore scars from the excessive numbers of recreationists crowding into it while the greater Puget Sound region simmered in growing levels of air pollution and traffic congestion. Indeed, much to Bill's dismay, he found the drive from Seattle to Mount Rainier had transformed from a pleasurable weekend jaunt into a depressing slog as urban sprawl came to engulf much of the intervening countryside. Although I was just a youngster, I well remember my father's aggravation each time we fought our way in and out of the city to enjoy a weekend of hiking and camping.

As my dad became discouraged over the environmental problems in the Pacific Northwest, he found it harder and harder to bear the political and social turmoil in the nation too. What was there to believe in? A liberal Democrat, he loathed Lyndon B. Johnson. An internationalist, he opposed US involvement in the Vietnam conflict. A humanist, he found himself out of step with the women's liberation movement. He abhorred the rise of Richard Nixon. He disparaged the counterculture. He regretted the radicalization of students and the polarization of the University of Washington faculty. By the late 1960s, he was very glum about the state of the nation, not to say the fate of the world.[9] The optimism that had once carried him through World War II was gone. Indeed, he thought he might be headed for a crackup. He proposed to Nancy that they pull up stakes and move to New Zealand. Largely for his sake, she agreed to it.

The transition to a new life in the South Pacific restored Bill (and invigorated the whole family) as both he and Nancy had hoped. Bill taught at the University of Canterbury in Christchurch, New Zealand, for three years, from 1970 to 1972. There, in a burst of creative energy, he accomplished most of the writing of his major work, *Overshoot: The Ecological Basis of Revolutionary Change* (1980).

Overshoot is a very dark book. Insofar as the work shows traces of the "homiletic mind" that Bill's preacher-father had once recognized in his son's letters, the book is not a sermon but a jeremiad. It is a dark, sober, clear-eyed lamentation on the human fate. There is no God in it, for Bill had long since become an atheist. Yet it does intone the moral voice of the preacher's son–cum–sociologist, as well as carry an echo of the earnest young sailor in World War II, in the exhortation to readers "to cherish rather than to disparage the concept of human dignity."[10] While it was not a book for a mass audience, it did turn a lot of thoughtful minds. The ideas Bill developed in *Overshoot* have stood the test of time. Even today, forty years after the book was published, its interpretation of a world civilization run amok remains vital to an appreciative, if limited, readership. It is considered by some scholars and environmentalists to be among the most important books ever written.[11]

Overshoot's canary-yellow cover displays a glossary of key ideas that frame the book's dire message:

carrying capacity:	maximum permanently sustainable load.
cornucopian myth:	euphoric belief in limitless resources.
drawdown:	stealing resources from the future.
cargoism:	delusion that technology will always save us from
overshoot:	growth beyond an area's carrying capacity, leading to
crash:	die-off.

Perhaps it was that prediction of die-off that most distinguished *Overshoot* and at the same time limited the book's appeal. No other intellectual writing on humankind's perilous future took quite such a steely eyed view of the consequences of overpopulation. His aim, of course, was not to make people despair and turn away from the world's problems but to make them wiser and more humane when things began to crash.

In his later years Bill worked to put across his message wherever he might. He lectured at international conferences on peak oil and climate change. He gave interviews to documentary filmmakers. He facilitated the translation of *Overshoot* into Spanish and Russian. Well into retirement, he self-published one more book, one more warning call for the planet, *Bottleneck: Humanity's Impending Impasse* (2009).

Did Bill Catton's big ideas flow from his World War II experience? I believe they did. In the first place, as a young seaman in the US Navy, he internalized a whirl of world-changing events. He avidly participated in America's mobilization for war. He saw the nation become not just the "Arsenal for Democracy" called forth by FDR but the greatest producer of war materiel the world had ever seen. He went to sea aboard an *Essex*-class aircraft carrier, the most formidable weapon ever made until the appearance of the atomic bomb. In August 1945 Bill lived through the dawn of atomic warfare. He viewed that momentous event from the perspective of a war-weary US serviceman. He felt enormous relief, like so many of his countrymen, that the deployment of the superweapon brought a swift end to the conflict without the horrendous death toll that a land invasion of the Japanese home islands would have entailed. After the Japanese surrender, Bill observed firsthand how American strategic bombing had reduced whole cities to ashes. "Be eternally grateful that you were born an American and not a Japanese," he wrote following his shore leave in Yokohama, expressing the same deep empathy for the Other on that day that he had felt to the core of his being half a year earlier when considering the fate of the kamikaze pilot who crash-bombed *Ticonderoga.*

In *Bottleneck* Bill ruminated on the mighty show of naval power he had witnessed in 1945 shortly after the Japanese surrender, when the US Third Fleet assembled off the coast of Japan for a victory photograph. Until the end of the war, his aircraft carrier operated mostly in a task group with one or two other carriers and a dozen or so smaller vessels; that was as many warships as he ever saw together. But now, with the fleet gathered from all over the western Pacific into one place, he was in awe of the fleet's size. A vast multitude of warships floated on the sea all around *Ticonderoga,* their many gray hulls receding into the distance in every direction. "They were so seemingly innumerable that scanning the scene was as humbling yet spine-tingling as counting stars in a clear night sky," he wrote those many years later.[12] Just a nineteen-year-old sailor in 1945, he had stood at the apex of American power. It made him feel tiny and insignificant on one hand, yet a part of greatness on the other. No wonder the historical moment was deeply affecting.

Bill remained proud of his World War II service throughout his life. He felt patriotic pride not only over having done his part for his country but also in the belief that his country had acquitted itself well through the war. After the attack on Pearl Harbor, the United States had shed its former isolationism and gotten "all in." After the Allied powers defeated Nazi Germany and Imperial Japan, the United States had dealt with the vanquished countries magnanimously. In the peace Americans had generally done a good job distinguishing between Nazism and the German people, and they had mostly overcome their racist attitudes toward the Japanese.[13] The many challenges of the postwar period notwithstanding, World War II was still the "good war."

I never knew my father to be a demonstrably patriotic, flag-waving veteran except once. On that lone occasion he chose to act the part in his own idiosyncratic way. The background was the choice he had made in 1974 to trade in the family car, a Plymouth Satellite station wagon, for an economy car of Japanese make, a Datsun B210. Around that time American car companies were responding sluggishly, even peevishly, to the growing consumer demand for smaller, more fuel-efficient cars. Japanese cars, meanwhile, were making big inroads in the American market. Indeed, car manufacturers were on the leading edge of the "Japanese economic miracle"—the term given to Japan's postwar transformation from a shattered nation into an economic powerhouse. Many Americans looked askance at this economic competition and insisted it was patriotic to "buy American" in support of the ailing US car companies. My dad ridiculed that thinking. To the contrary, he believed that car buyers should force US automakers to contribute to energy conservation by producing smaller cars. As a former airplane mechanic and veteran of the Pacific War—and now the new owner of his first Japanese car—he was bemused by his own conversion from American-made to Japanese-made automobiles. To demonstrate his feelings on the matter, he donned his yellow cap and vest from his plane-handling days aboard the *Ticonderoga,* took a small US flag in each hand, and posed for a picture in the driveway in front of his Datsun B210.

The symbolism contained in that photograph was multilayered. On one level, it was simply a sentimental nod to his earlier days as a plane handler: he held the American flags as he had once held signal flags and now posed with his new car as he had once posed for a navy photographer while spotting an airplane. On another level, it was meant to be ironic: dressed in his navy gear in front of his Japanese-made car, the image hearkened to the US–Japanese conflict of thirty years earlier. In his ear-to-ear grin for the camera, he proclaimed healing; he harbored no ill will toward the former enemy. On still another level, the photograph conveyed a serious environmental message: using his moral authority as a World War II vet, he aimed to say that patriotic Americans really ought to adopt more fuel-efficient cars. Through the remainder of his life, Bill did just that, driving two Honda Civics and finally a Toyota Prius.

Americans' preference for big, gas-guzzling automobiles was symptomatic of what Bill called "the Age of Exuberance" in human history. Modern civilization had formed a dependence on fossil-fuel-driven industry without much awareness of the fact that the global supply of fossil fuels would someday run out. Although the world's finiteness had become painfully obvious by the mid-twentieth century, human societies had so far shown little ability to rein in their ravenous resource appetites. The industrial revolution had turned *Homo sapiens* into *Homo colossus,* but societies by and large refused to recognize that the human species had effectively eaten itself out of a home, all but spoiling its chances for salvaging its place on Earth.

I never asked my dad how he felt about the lionizing moniker "the Greatest Generation" when it became popular in the late 1990s.[14] Did he feel that World War II had been an ennobling experience for his generation? Did he think that the war had tempered his generation in a way that made it act with singular greatness in the postwar years? What did the term "Greatest Generation" mean to him? When I reread his last book, *Bottleneck,* after he was gone, I found my answer to those unasked questions.

When Bill viewed his own lifespan as part of the whole run of human experience, and when he considered it from the perspective of human ecology, he was ambivalent about his generation's mark on the world. True, it had won a decisive victory over fascism, for which it could be very proud. Yet, tragically, his generation had done very little to curb population growth, reduce carbon emissions, stem global warming, or do much of anything to head off the incipient calamities resulting from humans living three-, four-, five-, six-, and then seven-billion-strong on a crowded, depleted, overheated planet. His generation had seen the early warning signs, and by and large it had ignored them. The greatest generation? Greatest in the sense of being prodigal. His generation of Americans, he wrote, had lived in the twilight of the American Dream. He for one was "privileged to live through the best years of the reign of *Homo colossus*—a time when the benefits of being colossal were maximized, and before we were overtaken by their ecologically disastrous denouement."[15] Regrettably, it remained for a later generation to rise to the ever-greater challenge of creating a sustainable future.

For all his pessimism about our chances of averting catastrophe, my father mostly maintained his cheerful demeanor. By the time my children were young adults, they were sometimes perplexed by how their "Bumpa" could be predicting population collapse in the present century and still maintain such a happy outlook toward his loved ones. How could he be so chillingly certain that famine and pestilence lurked in our future, and yet it did not affect his joy in living plentifully in the present? How were we to reconcile his Cassandra-like warnings of a global die-off with his warm expressions of personal fulfillment at a famiy gathering?

There was a tenacity in him to appreciate the happy things in life. It was the same tenacity that got him through the war. "Somebody asked me once," he wrote in 1945, "how it was possible for me to enjoy Navy life. I told him I enjoyed

Navy life simply because I enjoy life. I explained that as long as I had to be in the Navy I might as well make the best of it."[16]

Bill lived a long, happy, and (yes) ecologically prodigal life (for he left a lot of offspring and burned a lot of fuel in travel). He died at the age of eighty-eight in Dunedin, New Zealand, on his ninth or tenth visit to that verdant land. Writing to his sister, Ruth, soon after his arrival in that country for the last time, he beamed home his satisfaction in the email's subject line: "New Zealand is still lovely." In contrast to his voyages to the western Pacific aboard the *Ticonderoga,* his trips to the British Commonwealth country in the South Pacific were all made by jet airliner. After his last transoceanic flight, he wrote in the email that "the Pacific Ocean seemed wider than ever." The connecting flight onward from North Island to South Island took him "above sunlit clouds over Mt. Egmont and across Cook Strait." (Like the aspiring airman he once was, he still loved being aloft in the clouds.) It is tempting to conclude that his strong affinity for the South Pacific island nation related in some way to his youthful experiences in the western Pacific in World War II. It would be a stretch to say the earlier experience led to the latter one. What can be said is that his time on the *Ticonderoga* in 1944–45 and his time in New Zealand in 1970–72 were perhaps equally formative on his thinking, each one making him reflect upon the American Dream from afar and pushing him toward his big ideas.[17]

In the fall of 1944, when Bill voyaged into the western Pacific for the first time, he read *My Days of Anger* (1943) by James T. Farrell. The book was the fourth in a series of novels about a working-class Irish American youth in Chicago named Danny O'Neill. By the end of this book, Danny is attending classes at the University of Chicago, working night jobs, tasting the seamier side of night life in the city, and writing his first novel. Bill identified with the protagonist as a budding young writer himself. On 7 November 1944, two days after the USS *Ticonderoga* launched its first airstrike and had its first brush with kamikazes, Bill read a line of dialogue in the book—a word of advice addressed to the fictional Danny—that spoke to him sharply in his newfound circumstances as a combatant in World War II. He pondered the line of dialogue in relation to his plans to become a journalist after the war. Then he quoted the line in a letter to his father.[18] He might have taken it as a motto to live by, for indeed he did live by it for the rest of his life. It reads:

"If you want to be a writer you'll have to learn how to observe the lunacy of the human race with equanimity."

APPENDIX

Bill's Friends from Manistee High School in Military Service during World War II

Robert Bailey, Class of '43. Enlisted in the US Marine Corps.

Dewey Bucher, Class of '41. Enlisted in the US Navy; completed officer training and served as a lieutenant j.g. gunnery officer on destroyers; honorably discharged in 1946.

James Gutowski, Class of '42. Enlisted in the US Marine Corps; served in the Pacific theater; wounded during a landing in the Gilbert Islands; awarded the Purple Heart.

Kurt Illig, Class of '42. Enlisted in the US Army; served in the European theater; listed as missing in action in February 1945; freed from a German prisoner-of-war camp in May.

Norval James, Class of '42. Enlisted in the US Army.

Ralph Edward La Valle, Class of '35. Enlisted in the US Army Air Corps; served as a flight officer and glider pilot; killed in southern France, 15 August 1944.

Robert Mauzy, Class of '42. Enlisted in the US Navy; completed officer training and served as an ensign training officer at Naval Training Station, Hollywood, Florida.

Richard Mitchell, Class of '42. Enlisted in the US Navy; served in the North Atlantic and Mediterranean theaters; wounded; received medical discharge.

Donald Norton, Class of '44. Enlisted in the US Navy; served as a pharmacist's mate (PhM3/c) at the navy hospital at Pearl Harbor.

William Nungesser, Class of '41. Enlisted in the US Army.

John Peterson, Class of '41. Enlisted in the US Army Air Corps; completed officer training and served as a training officer and hospital registrar at Shepherd Field, Wichita, Texas.

Joseph Rumbel, Class of '44. Enlisted in the US Navy.

Harry R. Sheridan, Class of '42. Enlisted in the US Army; served in the Pacific theater.

Frank Slaton (Slachik), Class of '42. Enlisted in the US Army Air Corps; served three years in the US Army Air Corps Engineers, two in the China-Burma-India theater.

Warren Thomas Stege, Class of '42. Enlisted in the US Navy; served as an electronics technician (ET1/c) during Okinawa Campaign and as part of occupation forces aboard the high-speed transport USS *Kleinsmith* (APD-134).

William Tennant, Class of '42. Enlisted in the US Marine Corps; served as a second lieutenant; killed in the crash of a Helldiver airplane in 1944.

Alex "Hook" Topping, Class of '42. Enlisted in the US Army Air Corps; served as a second lieutenant and bombardier in a B-29 crew in the Pacific theater; awarded Distinguished Flying Cross.

Notes

Introduction

1. "U.S.S. *Ticonderoga* CV-14 Action Report 3 January thru 21 January 1945," Box 1475, USS *Ticonderoga,* Entry A1 351, Series: Action Reports, Record Group (RG) 38, National Archives, Washington, DC; Bill Catton reminiscence, 2 Apr. 1997.

2. Bill Catton to Helen and Robert Catton, 15 Nov. 1945. For other anecdotes about this beloved ship captain as told by one of *Ticonderoga*'s airmen, see Samuel Van Pelt, "'Lum's Boy': The World War II Recollections of John R. 'Dugie' Doyle," ed. James E. Potter, *Nebraska History* 95 (2014): 198–215. Doyle was shot down on 24 November 1944 and survived to tell the tale.

3. These details about the tagging of fragments for gathering intelligence come from J. Bryan III, *Aircraft Carrier* (New York: Ballantine Books, 1954), 8. Bryan, who was assigned to the USS *Yorktown* (CV-10), inspected the damage on USS *Ticonderoga* when it was anchored at Ulithi. The details corroborate Bill's memory (and confirm my own memory of what he related to me in 1982). Incidentally, *Ticonderoga*'s action report identified the first kamikaze plane as a "Zeke 52," better known as a "Zero." The second plane crashed through a section of the bridge and went into the sea, so the plane type was not identified.

4. Colin Hitzemann to Ted Catton, 30 June 2017, re: Veteran's Name: Catton, William Robert, with enclosures.

5. Bill Catton to Helen Catton, 19 Nov. 1944.

6. Bill's surviving letters from January 1943 through August 1945 number 358. In those letters—all addressed to his mom, dad, sister, or brother—Bill frequently mentions his other correspondence, including letters to and from grandparents, aunts, uncles, and cousins; friends from home; new friends made in the navy; columnists; and politicians.

7. Bill Catton to Robert Catton, 20 Mar. 1945.

8. Bill Catton to Helen Catton, 15 July 1945. "Butch" was Bill's nickname for his brother Edward. Uncle Dayton was W. Dayton Willard (1901–84), brother of Helen Willard Catton (1895–1982).

9. Bill Catton to Helen Catton, 19 Sept. 1944.

10. Bill Catton to Helen Catton, 25 Sept. 1944.

11. Bill Catton to Helen Catton, 17 Nov. 1944.

12. Bill Catton to Helen Catton, 8 Nov. 1943.
13. Bill Catton to Helen Catton, 7 Oct. 1944.
14. Bill Catton to Robert Catton, 2 Dec. 1944.
15. Ellis K. Kerr, "William Gleason Willard," *Proceedings of the Institute of Medicine of Chicago* 19, no. 10 (1953): 238–39.
16. Bruce Catton, *Waiting for the Morning Train: An American Boyhood* (1972; repr., Detroit: Wayne State Univ. Press, 1987), 128–50.
17. Manistee High School Yearbooks for 1940, 1941, and 1942, accessed online at www.classmates.com.
18. Bill Catton to Helen Catton, 5 Dec. 1942.
19. Bill Catton to Helen Catton, 12 Aug. 1942; Bill Catton to Robert Catton, 22 June 1943.
20. Bill Catton to Helen Catton, 29 Aug. 1944.
21. Bill Catton to Helen Catton, 6 Oct. 1942.
22. Bill Catton to Helen Catton, 25 Nov., 19 Dec. 1942.
23. Bill Catton to Helen Catton, n.d.

1. Naval Training Station, Great Lakes, Illinois

1. The vaccination shots were notorious. As the vaccines usually produced short-term ill effects, they were not administered until a few days into the induction process after the new recruits had passed their physical and psychiatric examinations. Lee Kennett, *G. I.: The American Soldier in World War II* (New York: Charles Scribner's Sons, 1987), 34.
2. Bill's remark about beans was a tease; beans were a cheap staple, hardly his sister's favorite food. Behind the teasing was a serious observation that his meals in boot camp were more plentiful than the family's rather humble fare at home. Not only were civilians eating humbly in 1943 because of wartime restrictions on food consumption, but most Americans had been eating humbly for many years due to the Great Depression.
3. The little newspaper clipping enclosed with Grandma Catton's letter reads as follows: "I watched two fine, upstanding 17-year-olds take their final oath of office. Right hands raised, eyes ahead, minds alert, fully cognizant of their new responsibilities. You could almost see them change from bubbling, energetic youths into manhood. I've seen fraternity and lodge initiations, wedding ceremonies, oaths of office administered. None of them surpassed in depth of emotion what these young men were experiencing."
4. Uncle Tubby was Thurber Catton (1904–2000), the brother of William Robert Catton Sr. (1895–1972).
5. The postcard message from Uncle Tubby reads: "Dear Bill, Well, I guess this war's as good as won, what with both of us in. Congratulations on finally getting into the Navy! Let me hear from you again when (& if) you get more time to write. Good luck—Uncle Tubby."
6. A wordplay on the French *au revoir,* this signoff was typical of the family's inside humor.
7. *The Bluejacket's Manual* is the basic handbook on naval procedures issued to all new US Navy recruits. First issued in 1902 and periodically updated, Bill's copy was the eleventh edition, published in 1943.
8. "Butch" was Bill's nickname for his brother Edward.
9. Bill's emphasis of the word "naturally" was a tongue-in-cheek allusion to his family's disdain of the *Chicago Tribune* and the paper's arch-conservative owner and publisher, Col. Robert McCormick. The *Tribune* was strongly isolationist, anti-British, anti–New Deal, and anti-Roosevelt.
10. US Naval Training Station, Great Lakes was commissioned in 1911 and trained some 45,000 seamen for service in World War I. Reduced to almost nothing during the interwar

years, it underwent a huge expansion in 1940 and became the navy's largest training center. More than a million sailors, nearly a third of all men in the wartime US Navy, went through boot camp there. The name was changed to Great Lakes Naval Training Center in September 1944.

11. Richard Holzaepfel coached football and gymnastics at Manistee High School from 1937 to 1942. He joined the navy in 1943.

12. Preston Slosson (1892–1984), professor of history at the University of Michigan, and Malcolm W. Bingay (1884–1953), editorialist for the *Detroit Free Press*, exchanged opinion letters in the *Detroit Free Press* in late 1942.

13. This refers to the various martial arts that are generally associated with Japanese and other East Asian cultures. Here Bill uses the word "Jap" in place of the adjective "Japanese," as in "Japanese culture." Elsewhere in his letters Bill uses the word "Jap" as a noun to refer to persons of Japanese nationality or heritage. In the context of World War II, most Americans, Bill included, used the word uncritically despite its obvious derogatory overtones. The term is now considered inappropriate.

14. "Puddle Mush" was Bill's nickname for his sister, Ruth. "Shrimpy" was another nickname (along with Butch) for his brother Edward. Ruth was thirteen years old and Edward was seven.

15. Burton K. Wheeler (1882–1975) was a U.S. senator from Montana and a staunch isolationist before the war. The article discussed the proposal to form the United Nations.

16. There was no formal anti-Japanese alliance between Britain and the United States prior to the declarations of war against Japan made by each nation on December 8, 1941. But the Lend-Lease Act of March 1941 practically made Britain and the United States allies against Germany despite a US pretense of neutrality, and a joint military plan secretly adopted by the two countries that same month, called the ABC-1 Agreement, forged a UK-US military strategy in the event of war. ABC-1 laid out principles of grand strategy, including that if Japan went to war with the United States and Britain, the American war aim would be to defeat Germany first, then Japan. Robert A. Divine, *The Reluctant Belligerent: American Entry into World War II*, 2nd ed. (New York: Alfred A. Knopf, 1979), 112, 119–20.

17. On 21 March 1943 Prime Minister Winston Churchill gave a speech on his vision of a postwar world order.

18. Walter Lippmann (1889–1974) was a journalist, writer, and political commentator.

19. Fred Lewis Crawford (1888–1957), Republican congressman from Michigan, had just voted against a bill to extend the Lend-Lease Act for another year. The House passed the bill by a vote of 407 to 6.

20. The editorial was C. P. Trussell, "Senate Gives Attention to Post-war 'Blueprints,'" *New York Times*, 28 Mar. 1943. It discussed the Ball-Burton-Hatch-Hill resolution, which proposed that the United States take the lead in forming the United Nations immediately in 1943 rather than waiting until victory was at hand. The idea was to jumpstart a new world order by combining prosecution of the war with postwar planning.

21. Raymond Gram Swing (1887–1968) was a journalist, lecturer, and popular radio commentator in the 1930s and 1940s.

22. The navy's service schools were located within the naval training stations and were designed to train enlisted men for an occupational specialty, or "rating," such as aviation machinist's mate, radar man, signalman, and so on.

23. Henry Morgenthau Jr. (1891–1967) was secretary of the Treasury in the Roosevelt administration. In April 1943 Morgenthau laid out his proposal to establish an international-stabilization fund under UN auspices, which would look to the stabilization of national currencies when the war ended. The proposal was further developed at the Bretton Woods Conference in July 1944 and culminated with the establishment of the International Monetary Fund on 27 December 1945.

24. Submarine duty was one of the most dangerous jobs in the war. One-sixth of US submarines in service during World War II were sunk by enemy action.

25. Here, Bill refers to college credits he had earned at Central Michigan College during the 1942 summer session.

26. V-12 was the navy's college-based officer-training program. Through V-12, the navy partnered with 131 colleges and universities to augment the overburdened US Naval Academy and Naval Reserve Officer Training Corps programs. From 1 July 1943 through the end of the war, V-12 enrolled 125,000 participants and produced more than 60,000 offices for the US Navy and the US Marine Corps. Henry C. Herge, *Navy V-12* (Paducah, KY: Turner Publishing, 1996), 22–24.

27. V-5 was the navy's program for training naval-aviation cadets. The V-5 program was shortly afterward merged into the V-12 program. Bill was invited to apply for V-5 not long before he was invited to apply for V-12 while the system was in flux.

28. The service-school training for enlisted men lasted six months, whereas officer training stretched for more than two years, which presented Bill with a dilemma since he was so anxious to get into action, as he says here and reiterates in the next few letters.

29. Toward the end of basic training, navy recruits were divided into "general detail" and "service school" groups. Recruits in the "general detail" group were immediately assigned to ships or stations as seamen, second class. Recruits in the "service school" group continued with basic training for one more week and then went on to further training at one of the service schools to give them an occupational specialty, or "rating." Bill would go on to Aviation Machinist's Mate School and earn the rating of aviation machinist's mate (AMM). Navy men with ratings were "petty officers" (the equivalent of noncommissioned officers in the army.) The navy's rating system had evolved from the nineteenth century and included about one hundred different ratings by World War II. By tradition, the general-detail men (also called nonrated men) could subsequently "strike" for a rating aboard ship—learning specialized skills through on-the-job training—though their chances for advancement would be limited.

30. *Chetniks! The Fighting Guerillas* was a film made by Twentieth Century–Fox about Yugoslav partisans who fought the Germans after Hitler's forces invaded Yugoslavia in 1941. Dragoljub Mihailović (1893–1946) was a Serbian Yugoslav Royalist. Initially, he allied with Josip Broz Tito and his Soviet-backed partisans, but late in the war he collaborated with the Axis Powers against the communists. After the war he was tried for treason and executed.

31. The Tokyo raiders referenced here were American airmen who took part in the Doolittle Raid on 18 April 1942. This US mission involved the launch of sixteen US Army B-25 Mitchell medium bombers from the aircraft carrier USS *Hornet* (CV-8) to make a retaliatory raid on Japan and demonstrate its vulnerability as soon after Pearl Harbor as possible. While the planes were specially modified for take-off from a carrier, landing them on a carrier was not possible. Operating at the extreme limit of their range, the raiders dropped their payloads and flew on toward China, where all but one crash-landed, mostly in Japanese-occupied territory. (One B-25 managed to land in Vladivostok, USSR.) Among the eighty airmen on the raid, sixty-nine survived the mission and evaded capture. Three were killed in crash-landings, while eight were captured. The US public learned in April 1943 that the captured Americans had been tried and sentenced to death, though for an undisclosed number the death sentence was commuted to life imprisonment. Not until after the war was it known that three of these men had been executed, one had died in prison, and four others survived. John W. Dower, *War without Mercy: Race and Power in the Pacific War* (New York: Pantheon Books, 1986), 48–50.

32. Although Bill's view of the enemy could be regarded as enlightened, it was hardly the norm. US official propaganda worked to foment hatred and racism toward the Japanese, and a few high-ranking navy commanders provided some of the most hateful invective against the Japanese of all. Dower, *War without Mercy,* 15–23, 79–87.

33. Satisfied with his service-school assignment, Bill now put aside his application for V-12 officer training as he was intent on getting into action sooner rather than later. Accordingly, his commanding officer informed him two months later that his application was incomplete and no longer under consideration. Commanding Officer to Catton, William Robert, 312–94–59, AS, V-6, USNR, Co. 262, 12 June 1943, National Personnel Records Center, St. Louis, MO.

34. By this, the chaplain meant that Christian principles, while severely *challenged* in a world at war, were not being *destroyed* by the war.

2. Naval Air Technical Training Center, Navy Pier, Chicago

1. Chicago Field Museum of Natural History.

2. The *New York Times* reported on 31 May 1943 that a village in southwest England had been bombed, demolishing a church and killing twenty-one children inside. The Germans conducted bombing attacks against English villages in retaliation for British bombing of industrial plants in the Ruhr Valley.

3. Robert R. McCormick (1880–1955) was a member of the McCormick family of Chicago and owner of the *Chicago Tribune.* A conservative Republican, he opposed the expansion of federal government in the New Deal and supported an "America First" noninterventionism in World War II. Bill's scorn of McCormick and the *Tribune* seems to have been shared by his parents.

4. Telenews Theaters was a syndicated chain of cinemas that specialized in showing newsreels. The first Telenews location opened in San Francisco in 1939. Telenews Theaters closed or converted to regular movie houses with the advent of television in the late 1940s. Chicago's Telenews theater became the Loop Theater.

5. Bob Bailey was a high school classmate of Bill's. Lester C. Bendle was the principal of Manistee High School.

6. The Detroit riot began on a sweltering hot day, 20 June 1943, and continued for four days. The worst race riot during the war, it took the lives of twenty-five African Americans and nine whites. Close observers of the rising racial tension in that city were not surprised by the outbreak of violence and pointed to many underlying causes. Thousands of African Americans and southern whites had moved to Detroit in the preceding two years to work in the city's factories, putting a strain on the city's housing stock and public facilities and spurring racial resentments. Municipal officials had been derelict in addressing the problems, while the city's law enforcement had failed to protect blacks from the rising animosity of hate groups, including the Ku Klux Klan. Andrew E. Kersten, "Jobs and Justice: Detroit, Fair Employment, and Federal Activism during the Second World War," *Michigan Historical Review* 25, no. 1 (Spring 1999): 92–93.

7. The rioting in Los Angeles occurred a couple of weeks before the trouble in Detroit. Over five days in early June 1943, sailors from the Los Angeles naval base formed into small mobs and assaulted "zooters" on the streets of the city while military and city police looked the other way. The "zooters" were boys and young men who wore the so-called zoot suit of baggy, high-waisted pants; long coat; and wide-brimmed flat hat. Most zooters in Los Angeles were Latinos, several of whom belonged to gangs, although not all the gangs were malicious. Many Anglos in Los Angeles disparaged the zooters, believing that the Latino community was riven with criminal gang activity. John Morton Blum, *V Was for Victory: Politics and American Culture during World War II* (New York: Harcourt Brace Jovanovich, 1976), 205.

8. Martin Dies (1900–1972) was a Democratic congressman from Texas. Starting in 1938, he chaired the Special Committee to Investigate Un-American Activities (the Dies Committee), which increasingly centered its investigations on communists.

9. Charles Coughlin (1891–1971) was a Roman Catholic priest and radio broadcaster. His weekly radio broadcasts in the 1930s turned increasingly anti-Roosevelt, anti-Semitic, and pro-Fascist. His radio program was forced off the air in 1939.

10. Tom Stege, Bill's best friend in high school, joined the navy around the same time as Bill. Bill met him at the train station as Stege arrived in Chicago to enroll in school under the navy's V-12 college-training program.

11. Charles Lindbergh (1902–74) was a famous aviator. As an American icon, he was a prominent isolationist in his support of the America First Committee, which opposed aiding Britain in its war against Germany.

12. Gen. Dwight D. Eisenhower (1890–1969) was Supreme Commander, Allied Expeditionary Force in 1943. The invasion of Sicily from North Africa in July marked the beginning of the Allied advance into Europe, with the invasion of the Italian peninsula soon to follow. Gen. Douglas MacArthur (1880–1964) was Supreme Commander, Southwest Pacific Area. In July 1943, American forces were on the move in the Solomon Islands and New Guinea.

13. Field Marshal Erwin Rommel (1891–1944) was commander of the German Afrika Korps, while Gen. Bernard Montgomery (1887–1976) was commander of the British Eighth Army. *Five Graves to Cairo* (1943) featured the British battlefield victory at El Alamein in North Africa.

14. Crystal Lake is in northern Michigan. Bill's mother, sister, and brother spent summers at his maternal grandparents' home in Benzonia, where swimming in nearby Crystal Lake was a perennial favorite attraction.

15. The family's home was still in St. Johns, Michigan, but Bill's mother, sister, and brother spent the summer in Benzonia.

16. This picture, released in May 1943, follows six bombardier candidates through training as the men and their officers test the efficacy of night bombing versus high-altitude precision bombing, first in training, then over Japan. Mostly filmed at Kirtland Army Airfield in New Mexico, the picture was nominated for an Academy Award for special effects.

17. By this date, Allied forces were completing their conquest of Sicily. On 25 July 1943 the Italian dictator Benito Mussolini was deposed and taken into custody by the Italian government. Six weeks later he would be rescued from captivity by the Germans and installed at the head of a puppet regime in northern Italy.

18. The army and navy virtually took over many small colleges during World War II as student enrollment, academic curricula, and even faculties were put under contract to provide officer training. Without these military programs, many small colleges would have had to close their doors, their enrollments having fallen sharply as many young people put off higher education for military service or lucrative work in the war industries. Even the larger colleges and universities were pressed into cutting liberal arts programs and providing more instruction in science and engineering. Geoffrey Perrett, *Days of Sadness, Years of Triumph: The American People, 1939–1945* (New York: Coward, McCann, and Geoghegan, 1973), 371–75.

19. William Robert Catton Sr. had completed the training course for navy chaplains in Williamsburg, Virginia, and was home on leave awaiting assignment to another naval station or ship to commence duty. The eight-week course of indoctrination at the Naval Chaplains School included instruction in naval etiquette, naval correspondence, clerical procedures, choir organization and rehearsal procedures (many navy chaplains had a background in music instruction as well as the ministry), navy relief, military weddings and funerals, and some practical application in shorthand and typing. Bill's reference to his father going to boot camp was meant in humor, for Robert would likely be assigned to a naval training station where he would be ministering to young recruits who were in boot camp.

20. Harold Marsh, formerly of Manistee, had employed both Bill and Stege in his photo-studio business when they were students at Manistee High School.

21. In January 1942 three navy airmen on a long-range patrol from the USS *Enterprise* (CV-6) ran out of fuel and had to ditch their Douglas TBD Devastator at sea. All survived the water landing without injury, but the plane sank so quickly the men were set adrift on a small inflatable life raft with only a pistol, a knife, and a small navigating wheel. They survived at sea for thirty-four days on the flesh of two fish and rainwater wrung from their clothing. The men drifted 1,000 miles before making landfall in the Cook Islands. After their rescue in February 1942, their amazing survival story buoyed the nation's spirit. Their experience was dramatized in the film *Against the Sun* (2014).

22. Along with its sister ship USS *Sable* (IX-81), USS *Wolverine* (IX-64) was a converted Great Lakes steamer that was used on Lake Michigan for training navy pilots how to take off and land on the deck of an aircraft carrier.

23. US Naval Training Center, Bainbridge was located in Port Deposit, Maryland, on the Susquehanna River, northeast of Baltimore. The center was activated on 1 October 1942 as a boot camp for training navy recruits. The government took over the 330-acre campus and buildings of the Tome School for boys, then purchased an additional 1,132 acres and built more than 500 buildings for the 244,277 recruits who went through training there during World War II. Robert Catton was stationed there from the summer of 1943 through the spring of 1944.

24. Comiskey Park, originally called White Sox Park, in southwest Chicago was home to the Chicago White Sox of the American League from 1910 through 1990. On 15 August 1943 the White Sox played two games against the New York Yankees, losing the first game 2 to 7 and winning the second game 4 to 3.

25. The Republic P-47 Thunderbolt was a fighter plane used by the Army Air Force. The Consolidated B-24 Liberator was a four-engine heavy bomber. The Martin B-26 Marauder was a twin-engine medium bomber. The Douglas C-54 Skymaster was a four-engine transport aircraft.

26. Bill's family was moving from one house to another within St. Johns, Michigan. With Robert's departure to the navy, the family had to vacate the parsonage owned by the First Congregational Church. Their new residence was on Oak Street a half mile away. Over the years the family lived in several parsonages and moved many times.

27. Lee T. Redman owned Personality Portraits in Detroit and employed Bill there in the fall of 1942.

28. Aunt Bobbie was Catherine Oskamp (1896–1972), Helen Catton's younger sister.

29. Italy capitulated on 9 September 1943, the same day that Allied forces landed at Salerno on the country's mainland. Although one of the three major Axis Powers was now vanquished, the German army was prepared for it and occupied the Italian peninsula well in advance of Italy's surrender. Douglas Porch, *The Path to Victory: The Mediterranean Theater in World War II* (New York: Farrar, Straus, and Giroux, 2004), 462–76.

30. A. S. "Pete" Oskamp (1895–1989) was married to Aunt Bobbie, and they lived in Glen Ellyn, a Chicago suburb. Uncle Pete met Bill's family at the train station. Ruth did not recognize her uncle and was surprised when he walked up and kissed her mother. Bill's reference to "Fields" is short for Marshall Field's, a famous department store in Chicago, where the purchase of a mop of all things probably seemed amusing as it smacked of the austere times.

31. The Douglas SBD Dauntless was a scout plane and dive bomber. The Grumman F4F Wildcat was a fighter plane used by the US Navy. The Grumman TBF Avenger was the navy's frontline torpedo bomber after the summer of 1942. The Vought F4U Corsair was a fighter plane designed for carrier-based deployment by the navy, though it saw more use in land-based

deployment by the US Marines (some marine units eventually flew off carriers later in the war). The SNJ was the navy variant of the North American AT-6 Texan trainer aircraft.

32. Manitowoc, Wisconsin, was home to the Manitowoc Shipbuilding Company from 1902 to 1968. Before World War II its shipyards built steel ferries and ore haulers. During the war, Manitowoc built submarines primarily.

33. Clarence Streit (1896–1986) was an American journalist. In the 1920s and 1930s, he covered the League of Nations for the *New York Times,* which gave him a front-row seat to the rise of fascism in Europe. He wrote *Union Now: A Proposal for a Federal Union of the Democracies of the North Atlantic* (1939) to plead for a world federation of the democracies against totalitarianism. With his French wife, Jeanne Defrance, he self-published the work to get it before the public without delay. It became a bestseller in the United States as Hitler plunged Europe into war. After Hitler conquered France and the Low Countries in 1940, he wrote another book, *Union Now with Britain* (1941).

34. Wendell Willkie (1892–1944) was the Republican candidate for president in 1940. A lawyer from Indiana, he first gained public stature as a sharp critic of FDR's Tennessee Valley Authority and as an articulate foe of the whole New Deal economic policy. A Democrat by background, Willkie joined the Republican Party in 1939. In the presidential election campaign of 1940, he emerged as the compromise candidate over the three leading contenders: Sen. Robert A. Taft of Ohio, Sen. Arthur H. Vandenberg of Michigan, and Gov. Thomas E. Dewey of New York. Willkie's economic thinking won the support of eastern establishment Republicans, while his credentials as a political outsider offered a way out of the impasse between the isolationist and internationalist wings of the party. Following his election defeat in 1940, Willkie persuaded FDR to send him abroad to meet with world leaders and demonstrate American unity at home. His book about this experience, *One World* (1943), caught fire in the United States, setting up his second run for president in 1943–44. He lost to Dewey in the Republican primaries, however, and died of a heart attack in October 1944. John W. Jeffries, *A Third Term for FDR: The Election of 1940* (Lawrence: Univ. Press of Kansas, 2017), 39–77; Blum, *V Was for Victory,* 262–79.

35. Jackson Park, a 500-acre expanse located in South Chicago, is a legacy of the World's Columbian Exposition held in 1893. After fire destroyed much of the fairgrounds in 1894, the Palace of Fine Arts, the only major building to survive, was converted into the Museum of Science and Industry. The museum was thoroughly renovated in the early 1930s.

36. In Memphis Bill would attend a two-week course in airborne-radar operation.

37. The Vought O3u-1 Corsair was a scout biplane built for the US Navy in 1930. It was a two-seater with forward- and rear-mounted machine guns. A Pratt & Whitney Wasp or Hornet radial engine, generating approximately 570 horsepower, powered the aircraft. The F4F Wildcats built in 1943 had a Pratt & Whitney R-1830–90 radial engine with approximately 1,200 horsepower.

38. The US Navy's system of rates was distinct from the US Army's. In the navy only the officers held ranks, while enlisted men held "rates." Rates were not to be confused with ratings. A navy man's *rate* determined his level of command authority in the organization and his paygrade, whereas his *rating* defined his occupational specialty. Navy enlisted men all started at the rate of apprentice seaman (AS) at the lowest paygrade of $50 per month, designated as seventh grade. General-detail seamen might advance to second-class or first-class seaman and to sixth or fifth grade, respectively, on the enlisted men's pay scale. Meanwhile, those who earned a rating began at third class within their rating and jumped ahead to fourth grade on the pay scale. The rated navy enlisted man might then advance to second class, first class, and chief, advancing on the pay scale to third, second, and first grade, respectively. Bill entered service school at the Navy Pier with the rate of seaman second class (S2c) and graduated with

the rate of aviation machinist's mate third class (AMM3c). That meant he was earning $54 per month when he went in and $78 per month when he came out.

3. *Naval Air Gunners School, Hollywood, Florida*

1. The academy was one of many facilities in Miami taken over by the military for training during World War II. In addition, over 300 hotels were turned into quarters for military personnel as "Camp Miami" became a huge military-training center for the US Army Air Corps, the US Navy, and the US Coast Guard, with 60,000 men and women housed there at once; a quarter of all Army Air Corps officers received their training in Miami. D. Colt Denfeld, "'Camp Miami': The 'Palm Playground' Turns Serious during World War II," *Journal of America's Military Past* 33, no. 2 (Fall 2007): 72.

2. Berlin was being heavily bombed during December 1943. The British and American bomber offensive against Germany had begun in 1942 and reached a crescendo with the raids on the capital city over the winter of 1943–44. Nearly a third of the population evacuated as Berlin underwent relentless attack. John Keegan, *The Second World War* (New York: Viking, 1989), 425–29.

3. This Hollywood picture portrayed the rise of militarism in Japan and its effects on that society through the experience of a young, American-educated Japanese man. Produced and directed by Edward Dmytryk and distributed by RKO Pictures, it was a big hit with American audiences in 1943–44. The only wartime Hollywood film to depict the Japanese home front, it provides a mixed portrayal of the Japanese people, both humanizing and demonizing. Clayton R. Koppes and Gregory D. Black, *Hollywood Goes to War: How Politics, Profits, and Propaganda Shaped World War II Movies* (New York: Free Press, 1987), 271–75.

4. "Crow" is navy slang for the eagle insignia on a petty officer's uniform. The number of chevrons below the eagle indicates a first-, second-, or third-class petty officer.

5. Sir Stafford Cripps (1889–1952) was a British Labour politician, ambassador to the Soviet Union from 1940 to 1942, and minister of aircraft production in Churchill's War Cabinet in 1943.

6. US Coast Guard (Women's Reserve), known as the SPARS, was established by legislation in November 1942 for the purpose of bringing women into the military service branch for duty at shore stations, releasing the Coast Guard officers and men at those installations for duty at sea. The navy had a similar women's reserve; see chapter 4, note 17.

7. Bill's approach to attractive young women bears comment. He was not interested in casual dating or "hooking up," unlike so many of his fellow sailors. His choice to abstain from sex probably centered on his family upbringing; later it would be anchored by the "understanding" he formed with his girlfriend Jane in Michigan. Bill's comments about his car ride with these women and the ribbing he got from his fellow sailors suggests his awareness that many, if not most, sailors took a different view of sex than he. One recent study offers this generalization about sex and the World War II serviceman: "The reality of large numbers of postadolescent men thrown together and segregated from the rest of society created a pent-up sexual desire that was acted on much more often than not." Jane Mersky Leder, *Thanks for the Memories: Love, Sex, and World War II* (Westport, CT: Praeger, 2006), xi. For another serviceman's take on sex during the war, there is this journal entry by Sgt. Henry Giles:

> Drinking & sex & war—they all go together. Doesn't matter if you should or shouldn't, you do. It's got nothing to do with the kind of guy you were back home or want to be when you

> go back. And that's the jinx—you may not go back. Your life expectancy is durned short. What's here & right now is living & all you may have of it. It would shock the hell out of the people in the States if they knew what went on. Everybody's little boy over here is supposed to be as pure as the driven snow. Nuts! Anything that will take the edge off & let you forget for a little while, even an hour or two, there's a war on & tomorrow Graves Registration may be putting a tag on you, is welcome. . . . As for sex—the word we use the most in the army, with practically every breath we draw, is the word most of us saw first scribbled on privy walls & the bigger boys at school snickeringly told us what it meant. War and sex and drinking—they go together like ham, eggs and coffee.

Janice Holt Giles, comp. and ed., *The G.I. Journals of Sergeant Giles* (Boston: Houghton Mifflin, 1965), 72–73.

8. These were people Bill knew from Manistee, Michigan. Kay Barnes was MHS class of 1939. William Schnorbach was MHS class of 1933. Schnorbach's wife was Jane Hardy of Manistee.

9. Pfc. Norval James was a high school classmate of Bill's, MHS class of 1942.

10. Naval Air Station, Miami consisted of three separate airfields and a training base.

11. Lt. Col. Evans Fordyce Carlson (1896–1947) led the 2nd Marine Raider Battalion in a raid on Makin Island on 17–18 August 1942. The raiders employed submarines and inflatable rubber boats to operate deep within Japanese-held territory. The 1st and 2nd Marine Raider Battalions were the first US special-forces units formed during World War II. After this strike the raider battalions were merged with the rest of the Marine Corps, due to the nature of the war in the Pacific having changed to the island-hopping strategy of large-scale amphibious assaults against certain well-defended enemy strongholds.

12. Alex "Hook" Topping, James "Ace" Gutowski, and Frank Slachik were all high school classmates of Bill's.

13. Lucy Von Hagen (1877–1968) was a family friend and the mother of Bill's favorite teacher in Montrose, Colorado—Otto Von Hagen—as well as a warm personal friend to Bill despite their forty-eight-year age difference.

14. Uncle Bruce was Bruce Catton (1899–1978), the younger brother of William Robert Catton Sr. Bruce Catton, the future Civil War historian, started out as a newspaperman for the *Cleveland News, Boston American,* and *Cleveland Plain Dealer.* During World War II, he was director of information for the War Production Board, a job that led to his first book, *The War Lords of Washington* (1948), a critical exposé on war profiteering by big businesses and what he called "government by public relations." Bill visited his uncle and his family several times in the spring and summer of 1943. If Bruce Catton let on to his growing disillusionment with the War Production Board during this period, there is no indication of it in Bill's letters. Lee Mordecai, "Origins of the Epithet 'Government by Public Relations': Revisiting Bruce Catton's *War Lords of Washington,* 1948," *Public Relations Review* 35, no. 4 (Nov. 2009): 388–94.

15. Bill Bruce was Bill's cousin and the son and only child of Bruce and Hazel Cherry Catton (1901–69). Since the cousins shared the same first name, they were known within the extended family as Bill Bruce and Bill Bob. The two were the same age and emotionally close. It is notable that Bill Bruce was talking about submarine duty and V-12. Bruce Catton, like Robert Catton, served in the navy during World War I, and Bill Bruce wanted to serve as his father had. William Bruce Catton (1926–2018) went into the US Army in 1945. After his military service he became a historian and taught at Middlebury College. He coauthored two books with his father and coauthored a two-volume survey of America in the twentieth century with Arthur S. Link.

16. In January 1944 the US Navy had seven fleet carriers in operation and many more under construction. Four others had been lost in combat during 1942: USS *Lexington* (CV-2), sunk during the Battle of the Coral Sea, 8 May 1942; USS *Yorktown* (CV-5), sunk during the Battle of Midway on 7 June 1942; USS *Wasp* (CV-7), sunk on 15 September 1942 during the Guadalcanal Campaign; and USS *Hornet*, sunk during the Battle of Santa Cruz Islands, 26 October 1942. Another ship, the navy's oldest carrier, USS *Langley* (CV-1), was scrapped in 1942. In addition to these first twelve fleet carriers, the navy had at this time nine light aircraft carriers, all of which were commissioned during 1943, and over two dozen escort aircraft carriers (known as "jeep carriers"). The thirteenth and fourteenth fleet carriers, USS *Franklin* (CV-13) and USS *Ticonderoga*, were commissioned during the first five months of 1944. By war's end, the US Navy would have eight new *Essex*-class aircraft carriers (similar to the *Franklin* and *Ticonderoga*) and several dozen additional escort carriers in action, with still more in production.

17. The B-25 Mitchell was a twin-engine medium bomber.

18. Bill refers to the Doolittle Raid of early 1942. See chapter 1, note 31.

19. The Pan American Airways System (PAA) had a civilian school in Coral Gables, Florida, for training navigational techniques to pilots who flew long distances over water. During the war, the Army Air Corps contracted with PAA to train pilots in those techniques. W. F. Craven and J. L. Cate, *The Army Air Forces in World War II*, vol. 6, *Men and Planes* (Chicago: Univ. of Chicago Press, 1955), 470.

20. Bill was very supportive of the government's war-bond drives despite his concerns about war propaganda and biased news reporting. Government propaganda for these efforts used highly emotional imagery of Japanese and German bogeymen and innocent war victims to arouse fear and insecurity and inspire support for the war effort. The idea of framing war-bond drives in such propagandistic terms came from Secretary of the Treasury Morgenthau, who persuaded FDR that these campaigns could be a valuable tool for selling the war to the American public. US leaders justified the vicious propaganda effort in the knowledge that the United States, practically alone among the belligerents in World War II, faced no immediate threat of war in the homeland; the battlefronts were all overseas. Therefore, they reasoned, the American public had to be manipulated by propaganda to be fully awakened to the great perils facing the world and the United States. Blum, *V Was for Victory*, 16–17.

21. Bill's letters from 19 January to 8 February leave no doubt that he was left in the dark while the navy arranged for his transfer to a ground crew. The one-page form in his medical history states: "17 January 1944. Examined this date and found to be—*NOT* physically qualified for duty involving work as Aircrewman. EFFECTS NOTED: Systolic murmur apex and pulmonic area. Circulatory insufficiency." Medical data are listed followed by the note: "Conclusion: Tachycardia. No evidence of myocardial involvement." The form bears the signatures of C. G. DeFoney, captain, Medical Corps, and R. C. Hovde, lieutenant, Medical Corps. The separate one-page transfer order reads: "19 January 1944: Dropped from Aircrewman training for failure to meet physical standard set for Aircrewmen. [Signed] F. X. Carmody, By direction C.O." Below that it continues: "9 February 1944: Transferred this date to Carrier Aircraft Service Unit TWENTY-ONE, Naval Air Station, Norfolk, Virginia, for duty. AUTH: ComAirForAtlFlt ltr. FF13–2/P16–3/MM Ser. No. (1083) of 2 Feb 1944 and BuPers ltr. Pers-632-aet-5 of 28 Jan 1944." National Personnel Records Center, St. Louis, MO. Bill alluded to this episode in a letter on 19 November 1944, recalling his "bitter disappointment of being physically disqualified." He believed the doctor's diagnosis of tachycardia was either made in error or bogus, and no other medical examination ever gave any indication of it.

4. Naval Air Station, Norfolk, Virginia

1. Although Bill used the now-discredited term "colored" to refer to people of African descent, he was not racially prejudiced, as this comment and others attest.

2. Ione Catton (1888–1974) was Robert's older half sister.

3. Directed by Lloyd Bacon and distributed by Twentieth Century–Fox, *The Sullivans* tells the true story of five Irish American brothers who grew up in Iowa during the Great Depression, joined the navy together, and served aboard the same ship, the light cruiser USS *Juneau* (CL-52). The *Juneau* was sunk by a torpedo during the Naval Battle of Guadalcanal, taking the lives of all five brothers.

4. The term "baby flat-top" refers to an escort carrier, which was about half the size and one-third the displacement of a fleet carrier. See chapter 1, note 22, for the USS *Wolverine* and the USS *Sable,* which were at Navy Pier when Bill was there.

5. Bill's father was assigned to the repair ship USS *Oahu* (ARG-5).

6. H. G. Wells (1866–1946), English writer and social critic, published his best-selling *Outline of History* in 1920. The work encompasses the whole history of humankind, from evolutionary origins through the rise of civilizations, concluding with World War I.

7. Gluyas Williams (1888–1982) was an American cartoonist known for his contributions to *The New Yorker* and other major magazines.

8. Here, "draft" refers not to the national draft of the civilian male population for compulsory military service but rather to drafts of navy personnel for a change of assignment or transfer to another command. Bill implies that the drafts he mentions were aimed primarily at filling crews for new ships as they put to sea.

9. Enlisted men were encouraged to draw only a portion of their pay each month since the navy furnished them with room and board, a clothing allowance, and free medical care. They were permitted, with the approval of their captain, to make an allotment of part of their pay to their dependents or to a savings account. Bill arranged for sending part of his monthly allotment home to his mother, then arranged with his parents for that money to be used to buy war bonds, US Treasury savings bonds that would mature in ten years. Thus, Bill was returning most of his salary to the US government in the form of a loan to help finance the war effort while also building a personal savings account for his return to civilian life after the war.

10. American sailors and soldiers ate very well. The typical meal for a US military serviceman in World War II contained a whopping 4,300 calories, one-third from fat. The military diet included copious amounts of meat and sugar as well, both of which were regarded as "high-status" foods in the 1940s. The military diet emphasized meat and sugar both to provide energy and to build morale. US citizens at home endured food rationing so that military personnel would be so well fed. Sailors and soldiers received a daily allowance of about one pound of meat per day, which was two and a half times what civilians could typically obtain. Amy Bentley, *Eating for Victory: Food Rationing and the Politics of Domesticity* (Urbana: Univ. of Illinois Press, 1998), 94, 103.

11. The FM-2 Wildcat continued in production by General Motors under license from Grumman after the latter discontinued production of the F4F Wildcat to concentrate on production of the F6F Hellcat. The FM-2 had a more powerful engine than the F4F; its Wright Cyclone R-1820 engine gave it 1350 horsepower.

12. The USS *Oahu,* Robert Catton's duty assignment, had been built as a Liberty ship in the summer of 1943. The US Navy bought it in September 1943 and converted it to a repair ship. *Oahu* entered service on 4 April 1944.

13. Formed in April 1942, the US Armed Forces Institute (USAFI) provided education opportunities to service members in the United States and abroad.

14. Long-distance telephone service was severely strained during World War II. Family members became separated by distance in unprecedented numbers as they moved to take jobs or joined the military. Masses of new circuitry had to be built to serve new military camps in isolated places. Copper for wiring was in short supply. All these factors stretched a switchboard operator system and infrastructure that was already challenged by burgeoning private telephone use in the preceding decade. "World War II and the Telephone," AT&T Archives, CarrierBid Communications, https://www.carrierbid.com/world-war-ii-and-the-telephone/ (accessed 13 July 2019). See also *AT&T Archives: War and the Telephone,* AT&T Tech Channel, published 11 Nov. 2011, YouTube, https://www.youtube.com/watch?time_continue=15&v=0TtBgbQQjEA.

15. The British baby flattop was the HMS *Speaker.* The escort carrier was on its second aircraft ferry run across the Atlantic, taking US-manufactured aircraft to Britain. These warships were too slow to accompany battle fleets and carried lighter antiaircraft armaments, so they were used instead for convoy escort, aircraft ferrying, and flight training. *Speaker* was one of more than two dozen US escort carriers transferred to the Royal Navy under the Lend-Lease program.

16. These were John and William Millman of St. Johns, Michigan. One year apart in age, the two brothers were both in the US Army.

17. Women Accepted for Volunteer Emergency Service was the Women's Reserve of the US Naval Reserve. Established on 30 June 1942, the organization and the women who enlisted were known as "WAVES" (or "Waves"). The recruits were a highly select and volunteer group. These women were trained on college campuses, housed in separate barracks on naval bases, and fed in separate mess halls from their male colleagues (as Bill's letter indicates). The main purpose of the organization was to release navy men for duty at sea. Waves were generally assigned to traditionally female tasks such as clerical work. They also specialized in public relations and personnel functions while also helping run and staff the Navy Mail Service. Susan H. Godson, "The Waves in World War II," *Proceedings of the United States Naval Institute* 107, no. 12 (1981): 46–51.

18. 4-F was a classification for men who registered for the draft only to be rejected for military service due to physical or mental defects, though it was widely applied for a broad range of conditions. Unfortunately, individuals so classified were stigmatized, and "4-Fer" became a term of disparagement.

19. In 1944 many liberal Protestant churches rallied their congregations in support of creating a world organization or government to maintain international peace after the war. The Congregational Church, for its part, adopted the World Order Compact, which was modeled on the Mayflower Compact of 1620. Andrew Preston, *Sword of the Spirit, Shield of Faith: Religion in American War and Diplomacy* (New York: Alfred A. Knopf, 2012).

20. Bill refers to the 6 June D-Day landings in Normandy as part of Operation Overlord—the Allied invasion of northern Europe.

21. Lt. Gen. Omar Bradley directed his troops during the Normandy invasion from the heavy cruiser USS *Augusta* (CA-31) until his headquarters was moved ashore on 10 June 1944.

22. Bill had studied and taken exams in hopes of a promotion to aviation machinist's mate second class, with an accompanying pay raise from $78 to $96 per month.

23. Bill's cousin (Bill Bruce) had just graduated from Woodrow Wilson High School in northwest Washington, DC.

24. With the capture of Saipan in the Marianas Islands earlier that month, the United States initiated bombing raids against Tokyo using long-range B-29 Superfortress heavy bombers.

25. A V-mail was an ordinary letter written on standardized stationery that folded up to form its own envelope. At a processing center the V-mail was reduced to microfilm for ease

of shipment. At the other end of its journey, the V-mail was turned into a 4½-by-5½-inch photo print on a strip of photographic paper; then cut, folded, and inserted into a small envelope by machine; and finally delivered to the recipient as a facsimile about one-quarter the size of the original stationery. Introduced in 1942, V-mail saved valuable shipping space for other essentials. Hundreds of letters could be put on a single roll of microfilm, and one ton of paper mail could be reduced to about thirty-six pounds of film. Smithsonian Institution, "Victory Mail Online Exhibit," National Postal Museum, https://postalmuseum.si.edu/victorymail/ (accessed 5 Mar. 2019).

26. The Republican National Convention took place in Chicago from 21 June to 25 June 1944. The Republican nominee for president was Governor Dewey of New York. The Democratic National Convention took place in Chicago four weeks later. The Democrats nominated FDR to run for an unprecedented fourth term.

27. Coupons were issued by the federal government for gas rationing. Bill's pleasure driving with Jane blew out his family's gas ration for July. Although the outright ban on pleasure driving was lifted in 1943, gas rationing grew more stringent in the spring of 1944. That summer the standard "A" coupons issued to Bill's family were able to purchase just two gallons of gas apiece. A book of seven "A" coupons was intended to last about a month and a half. The goal of the gas-rationing regime at that time was to limit driving to 120 miles per month per household (thereby reducing consumption of rubber tires; rubber was then the item in critical short supply). A typical car of the 1940s got about 12 miles to the gallon, so Bill probably drove about 276 miles, running through a ten-week supply of coupons during his sixteen-day leave. James A. Maxwell and Margaret N. Balcom, "Gasoline Rationing in the United States," *Quarterly Journal of Economics* 60 (1946): 561–87.

28. Ella Belle (Patten) Brown, a younger sister of his Grandmother Catton, was Bill's great aunt. She lived on Elmhurst Street in Highland Park, a Detroit suburb. After visiting his great aunt, Bill rode the train from Detroit to Norfolk, Virginia.

29. USS *Ticonderoga* was one of twenty-four *Essex*-class aircraft carriers built during the war. It was 888 feet long. These fleet carriers were designed for maximum airstrike capability, with larger hangar decks and flight decks than the aircraft carriers of other navies in World War II. Two inboard elevators and one portside deck-edge elevator allowed rapid transfer of aircraft between decks. Each ship carried 90–110 aircraft and had a crew of over 3,000 men. American shipyards built two dozen *Essex*-class carriers during the war—more than any other class of capital ship.

30. This momentous occasion for Bill became one of the stock stories he told about his navy experience. In 1997 he put it in writing:

> I had just returned from being home on leave in Michigan, and was in the barracks at Fentress Field when the word came over the squawk box, "Any Aviation Machinist's Mate 3rd class interested in sea duty, report to the Officer of the Day immediately." I and another AMM3c arrived at the OD's office almost simultaneously. The young Ensign on duty was unsure how to decide between us. He was probably astonished at the eagerness of both of us for sea duty assignment, since Fentress Field seemed like a neat place to serve for "the duration"—it was not surrounded by any fence, and had an unusually relaxed, almost non-military, atmosphere, seeming almost like a boys summer camp, with a fascinating little general store just across the road from the main entrance. He took out a dime to flip and told me to call it. "Heads," I said as the coin was in the air. It came up heads—and the rest is, as they say, history.

Bill Catton reminiscence, 2 Apr. 1997.

31. Equivalent to year-round daylight savings time, eastern war time (EWT) was put in place by the War Time Act of 1942.

32. Eleanor Richardson was a family friend.

33. Ray Richardson was the husband of Eleanor Richardson.

34. Thomas E. Dewey (1902–71) was governor of New York and the Republican candidate for president in 1944.

35. An effort arose during World War II to lower the voting age from twenty-one to eighteen to match the minimum age of the military draft, which was lowered from twenty to eighteen in November 1942. The slogan "old enough to fight, old enough to vote" animated the movement, and Eleanor Roosevelt got behind it as well as the National Education Association. Georgia lowered its voting age to eighteen during the war, and other states followed in the postwar era. Yet not until the Vietnam War—in 1971—was the voting age lowered to eighteen throughout the United States.

36. Paul Brown was a first cousin of Helen Catton, or a first cousin once removed to Bill.

5. USS Ticonderoga, *the First Voyage*

1. Orders directed the crew to darken the ship at night for protection against the danger of submarine attack. German U-boats prowled the Atlantic coast of the United States looking for American ships that showed their running lights or revealed their silhouettes against the glow of city lights on shore. To counter this danger, coastal blackouts were a well-known feature of the home front along the Atlantic Seaboard.

2. Aircraft carriers were the new decisive weapon in the Pacific War, a fact made plain by the attack on Pearl Harbor and the Battle of Midway in June 1942, which demonstrated the essential role of aircraft both for finding the enemy fleet and for dive bombing and torpedoing enemy ships. Carriers were crucial to facilitating the role of aircraft. Carrier-based planes could deliver the first punch before fleets came within firing range of one another. Adm. William F. Halsey described the carriers' fighting qualities this way:

> These huge, swift ships, capable of great speed and sea-keeping qualities in the heaviest weather, stab deep into the no man's land toward the enemy with full loads of the heaviest bombs and torpedoes. They strike swiftly—and repeatedly if need be—carrying out the age-old rule, "The first blow is half the battle." The most sluggish imagination must stir to the picture of these splendid ships steaming silently and completely darkened at express-train speed throughout the night, to rain trip-hammer blows again and again on enemy ships or coasts a half-thousand miles or more from their starting point of the night before. This is the destiny of our carriers.

Adm. William F. Halsey, USN, "The Carrier," in *The Navy Reader*, ed. William Harrison Fettridge (1943; repr., Freeport, NY: Books for Libraries Press, 1971), 70.

3. The US Navy had its own mail service. Every ship and base had a navy post office. The navy cooperated with the US Post Office in the delivery of mail, with the former accomplishing most of the work offshore. *Ticonderoga* would often come alongside other ships for mail transfers. The navy took great care with mail, recognizing its importance for morale. Letters from home were said to be like a five-minute home leave, vital and restorative. The task of delivering the mail was colossal. In 1944 alone, navy servicemen received more than 310 million items of mail. Meanwhile, the US Post Office, serving the whole nation, handled more than 100 times that volume. With the adoption of V-mail in 1942, the bulk was reduced, but

the quantity remained overwhelming, with more than a billion V-mails delivered during the war. Thomas Wildenberg, "You've Got V-Mail," *Naval History* 19, no. 3 (June 2005): 23–25.

4. FPO stands for Fleet Post Office. During World War II, the FPO system was operated with just two gateways: New York and San Francisco. Writing on the day after *Ticonderoga* passed through the Panama Canal and entered the Pacific Ocean, Bill tried to signal past the censors that his ship had just transferred from the Atlantic to the Pacific Fleet. Given the need for secrecy as to the ship's location, he could not describe his time in Panama. He did describe the experience in his 1997 reminiscence:

> In Panama, half the crew had liberty one evening in Colon, at the Atlantic end of the canal, and I was in the other half who had liberty at the Pacific end the next evening in Panama City. It was my first real foreign country experience (apart from not-noticeably-foreign Canada). I found it fascinating to walk up and down the main street in the evening, looking in shops for souvenirs, and being surrounded by Spanish language. I bought a Walt Disney Big Little Book (in Spanish) to send home to my little brother.

Bill Catton reminiscence, 2 Apr. 1997.

5. The political conventions were past, leaving the choice of major-party candidates now between FDR and Dewey. Later, Bill would imply that he supported FDR, if somewhat reservedly.

6. Twentieth Century–Fox's *Wing and a Prayer* opened in theaters in August 1944. By this point in the war, Hollywood was producing war films that were unabashedly propagandistic. Often they glorified one service branch or another and ended on a note that would inspire people to enlist. In exchange for the film's propaganda value, the service branch helped in making the film. For *Wing and a Prayer*, the navy allowed some filming to be done aboard the newly commissioned carrier *Yorktown* and made available some frontline aircraft: Hellcats (fighters), Helldivers (dive bombers), and Avengers (torpedo bombers). Further authenticity was achieved by the studio through the construction of a replica of an aircraft carrier and the fabrication of a 400-foot-long segment of flight deck for exterior scenes. Set designer Lew Greber supervised the construction of thirty-six separate sets, including a replica of a pilot's ready room, the captain's bridge, and the crew's quarters, with furnishings requisitioned from the Oakland Naval Supply Depot. Harvey Beigel, *The Fleet's In: Hollywood Presents the U.S. Navy in World War II* (Missoula, MT: Pictorial Histories, 1994), 38.

7. *Ticonderoga* was in port at San Diego, loading provisions, fuel, aviation gas, and additional aircraft to be ferried to Hawaii.

8. Bill later recalled this visit:

> San Diego was a larger city than Norfolk, but was reputed to be "the Norfolk of the West Coast," and among Navy personnel that reputation was tantamount to implying that civilians in the area mainly had little respect for sailors and wished there were some other place they could be. I had liberty while the ship was there. It was my first exposure to southern California. I enjoyed a visit to the San Diego zoo, and thought this was a fascinating city, with friendly people. I came away feeling the negative reputation was quite erroneous. But I was excited at the prospect of heading out across the Pacific, too.

Catton reminiscence, 2 Apr. 1997.

9. This was the US gunboat sunk during the Japanese bombing of Nanking, China, in 1937.

10. Bill's father, together with millions of other personnel serving far away from home, cast his vote by absentee ballot weeks before election day. Though Robert Catton was a longtime

supporter of Socialist Party candidate Norman Thomas, he voted for Roosevelt in the 1944 election. He replied to Bill (17 October): "I think Thomas and the socialists see a lot of our economic problems more clearly than any of the leaders of the other parties, but I feel Thomas was and is all wrong on the war." Thomas had opposed US intervention in World War II during the 1940 presidential campaign and argued against Lend-Lease in 1941. After the attack on Pearl Harbor, he reluctantly supported US involvement in the war but was critical of how the administration mobilized the nation for the fight. Thomas spoke out against the administration's internment of Japanese Americans, being one of the few public figures to do so.

11. The Great Atlantic hurricane of 1944 lashed the coasts of North Carolina, Virginia, and New Jersey with 90-mile-per-hour winds and caused 28 deaths in New England from flooding. It also sank the destroyer USS *Warrington* (DD-383), with the loss of 248 men.

12. Angus Fraser MacKinnon (1924–2014) of St. Johns, Michigan, was serving in the navy aboard the destroyer escort USS *Swenning* (DE-394).

13. Bill's reminiscence from 1997 contains these remarks about Honolulu:

> Even though Honolulu was a thoroughly American city, with everyone speaking English, Hawaii was still a Territory, not a state, and (largely due to our preconceptions about it) seemed almost as exotic to some of us who went on liberty in Honolulu as Panama had seemed. The trip into town from Pearl Harbor was by train—a narrow gauge steam train, which for me, at age 18, was marvelously reminiscent of boyhood years in Montrose, Colorado.

14. LST was the navy abbreviation for Landing Ship–Tank. These were vessels built specifically for making amphibious landings, with bow doors that split open and dropped a drawbridge-like ramp so that tanks and other cargo could be quickly disembarked. The LCT (Landing Craft–Tank) was a much smaller amphibious personnel carrier. An LST could carry several LCTs.

15. The master-at-arms force was responsible for law enforcement and disciplinary matters.

16. Here is what Bill wrote about this incident fifty-two years later:

> Suddenly one day aboard ship . . . I was threatened with being transferred to the naval station at Kaneohe Bay, as the *Ticonderoga* seemed somehow to have found itself one or two extra mechanics in its hangar deck division. I didn't want to spend the rest of the war on land, even in Hawaii, and found that as a 3rd class petty officer I could avoid this transfer and stay aboard if I volunteered for duty as a mess deck "Master at Arms"—sort of a "foreman" supervising a number of seamen working in the scullery and cleaning mess tables, etc. Being able to head west with the ship when she sailed seemed to make it worth this slightly ignominious change of role.

Catton reminiscence, 2 Apr. 1997.

17. Bill routinely mentions church service aboard ship in his letters home in part to reassure his mother that church service was available and that he was attending. The US Navy went to great lengths to assign a naval chaplain to each ship, to provide regular church services aboard ship, and to encourage personnel to attend. One anxious mother asked her son, "Can you lead a Christian life in the United States Navy?" The sailor responded to her, "I never saw so much religion harbored in one spot in all my life." Quoted in Clifford Merrill Drury, US Navy, Bureau of Personnel, Chaplain's Division, *The History of the Chaplain Corps, United States Navy,* vol. 2, *1939–1949* (Washington, DC: Government Printing Office, 1984), 210.

18. Stephen Leacock (1869–1944) was a Canadian teacher, writer, political scientist, and humorist.

19. The World Series in 1944 matched the St. Louis Browns against the St. Louis Cardinals—the third and last time in World Series history that the opposing teams shared the same home field (in this instance, Sportsman's Park).

20. Rules of censorship did not allow Bill to relate the rest of the story. Later in his life this was the navy story he most liked to tell:

> Eniwetok Atoll was where my Dad's ship, the ARG-5 was anchored for the duration. He was its chaplain, and his ship, called U.S.S. *Oahu,* was filled with machine shops, equipped to make repairs on destroyers, and similar combat ships. *Ticonderoga* stopped at Eniwetok around noon and stayed overnight. Not surprisingly, my Dad was able to come over from his ship to mine, via motor whaleboat, for an afternoon visit. It was fun getting together out there in mid-ocean, surrounded by various other navy vessels and a ring of low coral islands with palm trees on them. I proudly showed him around areas of the *Ticonderoga* with which I was familiar, including a tour of the hangar deck and flight deck, the mess hall where I "worked," the ship's library, my berthing compartment and out onto the fantail just beyond it (where I spent many subsequent evenings reading mail from home by moonlight). Toward the end of the afternoon, as we were saying farewell near the gangway, and Dad was about to descend to his motor whaleboat, Capt. Kiefer strolled up, noticing this officer with chaplain's insignia who was not a member of ship's company, and introduced himself. Dad explained why he was visiting, and introduced me to my skipper. Capt. Kiefer said to me, "Why don't you go with your Dad and spend the night aboard his ship?" I saluted and thanked him, and said I'd have to go down to let the mess deck Chief Petty Officer know I'd be gone. In a few minutes, aboard the motor whale boat, we were skimming along over to the U.S.S. *Oahu,* where my Dad, being a two-stripe Lieutenant by rank, got a cot brought into his stateroom for me to sleep on.
>
> In the wee hours of the morning, a signalman brought a message to the stateroom and Dad woke me up to say he had to get me back to the Big-T right away. Her orders had been changed, and she was sailing on westward immediately. So we got into the motor whaleboat again, scooted across the lagoon to the *Ticonderoga,* which had already weighed anchor, I gave a goodbye salute to my Dad, scrambled up the gangway, which they hoisted behind me as I ritually saluted the quarterdeck and hastened aboard, and we were underway!

Catton reminiscence, 2 Apr. 1997.

Bill's unusual last-minute boarding briefly lifted him from anonymity among the ship's massive crew of 3,000 men in the Big T's deck log:

> 0455 Lighted fires under boilers #1 and 6. 0545 Cut boiler #6 in on the main steam line. 0553 Cut boiler #3 in on the main steam line. 0600 Set special sea detail and energized degaussing coils. 0605 Tested main engines and completed test at 0609. 0615 CATTON, W. R., AMM3c, returned aboard from visiting a relative on another vessel. 0635 Underway in accordance with dispatch orders of ComAirPac, in company with Task Unit.

USS *Ticonderoga,* 26 Oct. 1944, Box 9629, Entry P 118-A1, Series: Deck Logs, RG 24, National Archives.

21. Usually Task Force 38 was divided into three to five task groups, numbered 38.1 through 38.5. Most of the time *Ticonderoga* was in Task Group 38.3. Each of these included a couple of fast carriers, a couple of light carriers, two or three battleships and heavy cruisers, and a larger number of light cruisers, destroyers, and destroyer escorts. The task groups usually operated in concert as one big fleet spread out over hundreds of square miles. The

number "38" and the alternate name "Third Fleet" were used to confuse the enemy; there were no first and second fleets.

22. The memorial service was for two pilots, Ens. David Frank Greenhagen and George Billy Jackson, whose planes had crashed into the sea. USS *Ticonderoga,* 29 Oct. 1944, Box 9629, Entry P 118-A1, Series: Deck Logs, RG 24, National Archives.

23. At the Dumbarton Oaks Conference, held in Washington, DC, representatives of the United States, the Soviet Union, Britain, and China discussed goals and principles for setting up the United Nations.

24. Robert Trumbull, *The Raft* (1942), was an account of three US Navy airmen who survived thirty-four days in a rubber raft in the Pacific.

25. The ship's war diary includes this clinical report of *Ticonderoga*'s first battle action:

> During the day, Air Group Eighty flew 127 target sorties and 50 CAP [combat air patrol] sorties in making two fighter sweeps and four strikes at targets at Zablon, Mandaluyong, and Pasig airfields and shipping in the vicinity of Manila, P.I. The strikes were launched from an area 150 miles northeast of Manila. Damage to the enemy was 6 aircraft shot down; 9 damaged; 1 aircraft destroyed on the ground; 14 damaged; 1 DD [destroyer] probably sunk; and 1 CL [light cruiser], 2 DD, and 2 AK [cargo ships] damaged. Own material losses were 4 VF [fighters] and 1 VT [torpedo bomber] in combat. Personnel losses were 5 pilots and 4 crewmen in combat and 1 crewman wounded in combat. At 1335 the ship went to general quarters stations on report that enemy bogies were over the formation. The formation commenced emergency evasive maneuvers. At 1347 two enemy aircraft commenced suicide dives on the LEXINGTON; one was shot down and the other crashed into the starboard island structure. A third plane, single engine VF type, started a dive out of low cumulus clouds on the port quarter of this ship. The ship was in an emergency left turn. The plane strafed the ship, hitting and wounding two met at the No. 6 40mm mount and two men on the flight deck. Fire was returned by the AA [antiaircraft] machine gun battery. The plane was hit and that, plus the left turn, caused the plane to pass from the port quarter low across the bridge and crash off the starboard bow. A fourth suicide plane was shot down by own CAP. Bogies were reported at various other times during the remainder of the day and early evening but at no time did they close sufficiently to be brought under gunfire by this ship. 2105 An officer fell overboard and his approximate location was reported to the screen but due to conditions of darken ship he was not located.

USS *Ticonderoga,* 5 Nov. 1944, Box 1518, Entry A1 353, Series: War Diaries, RG 38, National Archives.

At this time Bill's battle station was below waterline down in the 5-inch magazine, where rounds for the ship's 5-inch multipurpose guns were stored. During General Quarters, Bill's job was to send rounds as needed up to the 5-inch gun turrets on a dumbwaiter device. Of the action on this day, he later wrote:

> I remember coming up when the battle was over and hearing shipmates who'd been on the hangar deck and flight deck and could see the action tell about what they'd seen. There was a real sense of astonished shock regarding the [new] kamikaze tactic. "Goddam Japs are crazy!" one of my buddies kept exclaiming, after seeing one of the suicide dives into the *Lexington.*

Catton reminiscence, 2 Apr. 1997.

26. Aunt Nellie was Nellie Catton (1883–1964), Robert's older half sister.

27. When the United States entered World War II, African Americans composed just 2.4 percent of naval personnel, and all African American seamen were restricted to serving in the Steward's Branch. During the war, blacks demanded racial desegregation in all the military services, and they made considerable gains, but found the navy more resistant to change than the army. Full desegregation of all armed services would not become federal policy until 1948. Although general service in the navy opened to African Americans in June 1942, and although the navy officer ranks began to include more black commissioned officers in 1943, still the navy command sought to provide opportunities for African Americans without integrating ship crews. The navy even took the step of manning one warship, the destroyer escort USS *Mason* (DE-529), with an almost entirely African American crew. In 1944 most if not all black seamen aboard *Ticonderoga* were still confined to the ship's mess crew. Bill knew some of these men in his role as master-at-arms in the mess as well as through his battle station. Rawn James Jr., *The Double V: How Wars, Protest, and Harry Truman Desegregated America's Military* (New York: Bloomsbury, 2013), 144, 167–86.

28. Chinese immigration was cut off by the Chinese Exclusion Act of 1882. The act was repealed by the Magnuson Act on 17 December 1943, but Chinese immigration remained severely limited until passage of the Immigration and Nationality Act of 1952, which abolished direct racial barriers, and the Immigration and Nationality Act of 1965, which ended the immigration quota system implemented in the 1920s.

29. The author was Catherine Drinker Bowen (1897–1973), a prizewinning American writer and biographer, and the book was *Yankee from Olympus: Justice Holmes and His Family* (1944). Bill Catton to Helen Catton, 4 Dec. 1944.

30. "Airedale" was navy slang for a plane handler on the flight deck or the hangar deck of an aircraft carrier.

31. V-2 was a division within the aircraft carrier's aviation department.

32. "Jimmy-legs" was navy slang for a master-at-arms.

33. As much as Bill disliked the policing role of master-at-arms, it gave him the supervisory experience to "strike" for a new rating, aviation boatswain' mate (ABM), and head a crew of plane handlers. Thus, he was promoted to a second-class petty officer, with a new rating of ABM2c. Here, Bill uses the word "topside" to refer to the decks above the waterline—the hangar deck as well as the flight deck—as opposed to "below decks," where the mess was located.

34. This was an understatement. On 17 December *Ticonderoga* went alongside the oiler USS *Marias* (AO-57) to refuel, but after two hours of effort, the operation had to be abandoned after it became too hazardous and the fuel hose kept breaking due to weather. Altogether, the warships in Task Group 38 attempted to rendezvous for refueling four times over the course of two days, but refueling proved impossible in the heavy seas. When it was over, the fleet was scattered over a breadth of fifty to sixty miles. Total aircraft losses from planes blown overboard amounted to 146, though the smaller carriers lost most and *Ticonderoga* lost none. After riding out the typhoon, the Big T had to retire to Ulithi with the rest of Task Force 38 for repairs. Samuel Eliot Morison, *The Liberation of the Philippines: Luzon, Mindanao, the Visayas, 1944–1945*, vol. 13 of *History of United States Naval Operations in World War II* (Boston: Little, Brown, 1959), 59–87.

35. The radio reports probably referred to the massacre of about seventy-five American prisoners of war near Malmedy, Belgium, on 17 December 1944 during the Battle of the Bulge. The perpetrators of the massacre were soldiers of the Waffen SS, the Nazi arm of the German army. As reports of that and other German atrocities spread, some in the US military believed SS prisoners should be shot in reprisal. The killing of German POWs by US troops is known to have occurred, though such incidents were not reported in the US media nor ever officially confirmed.

36. Bill wrote fifty-two years later:

> I remember going up on the flight deck after dark on Christmas eve and looking around at the many other ships in harbor at Ulithi. By this point in the war, Ulithi was considered a secure enough area so the ships anchoring there no longer had to darken ship at night. The lights all around us resembled city lights.

Catton reminiscence, 2 Apr. 1997.

37. "From the Captain: At this Christmas time when we are so far from home, you can rest assured that those we love are thinking of us. Many of you straight out of civilian life are making a big sacrifice for your country, but you will have something to be proud of for the rest of your life. My thanks and appreciation for your loyalty during the past year, and the best wishes for the coming year.—Dixie Kiefer, Capt. U.S.N."

38. "Ticonderoga IV (CV-14)," *Dictionary of American Fighting Naval Ships*, vol. 7, *Historical Sketches: Letters T through V*, ed. James L. Mooney (Washington, DC: Navy Department, Office of the Chief of Naval Operations, Naval History Division, 1981), 182–87; Morison, *Liberation of the Philippines*, 182–83.

39. Bill Catton to Helen Catton, 10 Jan. 1945.

40. "U.S.S. *Ticonderoga* CV-14 Action Report 3 January thru 21 January 1945," Box 1475, USS *Ticonderoga*, Entry A1 351, Series: Action Reports, RG 38, National Archives.

41. Catton reminiscence, 2 Apr. 1997.

42. Sumner Welles (1892–1961), American diplomat and foreign-policy advisor to FDR, wrote *A Time for Decision* to urge support for a new postwar order founded on international cooperation. It was a Book-of-the-Month Club selection for August 1944 and sold almost a half-million copies. James MacGregor Burns, *Roosevelt: The Soldier of Freedom* (New York: Harcourt Brace Jovanovich, 1970), 515.

43. Blue Star Mothers of America, Inc., is a nonprofit mutual-aid society for mothers of military-service personnel. The first chapter of the organization was formed in Michigan in 1942 and additional chapters quickly opened in other states.

44. Here, Bill probably is referring to news about the progress of the war in Europe. The German Ardennes offensive in November and December 1944 took Americans by surprise and checked people's hopes that the fighting in Europe was nearly over. By the second half of January 1945, however, the outlook was improving again. The Battle of the Bulge was over—the bulge in the western front had flattened—and Allied forces were preparing to make their final push across the Rhine and into Germany. On 15 January Soviet forces launched their winter offensive across the Oder River; the collapse of Hitler's Germany was finally in sight. In the Pacific War, meanwhile, General MacArthur was driving on Manila in his campaign to liberate the Philippines.

45. Referring to the Pacific War, not the war in Europe.

46. Probably Bill made this remark with heavy thoughts about his many shipmates lost in the kamikaze attack on 21 January. There was more to this than he could disclose under the military censorship rules. Bill had disparaged the men in his plane-handling crew in an uncharacteristically shrill and venting letter to his father. Bill Catton to Robert Catton, 10 Jan. 1945. Eleven days later two of those men lost their lives in the kamikaze attack. Catton reminiscence, 2 Apr. 1997. Unable to write about this attack or his crewmembers killed in action, Bill wrote obliquely to his father on 24 January: "That pessimistic letter I wrote you last week about how juvenile I thought the average human mind was, I hereby retract. I have changed my mind completely. Someday I shall tell you why." It seems that his earlier disparagement of fellow sailors still weighed on him.

47. Catton reminiscence, 2 Apr. 1997.

48. Herbert Agar (1897–1980) was an American historian and journalist.

49. Ernest Taylor Pyle (1900–1945) was an American journalist and war correspondent. He accompanied US troops during the North African and Italian Campaigns, the invasion of Normandy, and finally the Pacific War, where he was killed by enemy fire in April 1945. Pyle reported on the war from the viewpoint of the GI. His syndicated column was carried by 400 daily and 300 weekly newspapers across the nation. Pyle won the Pulitzer Prize for his war correspondence in 1944.

50. Adm. Chester W. Nimitz (1885–1966) was commander in chief of the US Pacific Fleet.

51. American forces invaded the volcanic island of Iwo Jima on 19 February 1945, and the resulting battle lasted five weeks. While US forces were in control of the air and sea, assuring ultimate victory, Japanese ground forces were dug in, well supplied, and under orders not to surrender. As a result, the fighting was fierce and prolonged, with both sides suffering heavy casualties.

52. Ulithi Atoll consists of a ring of islets, of which one is called Mog Mog. In the last year of the war, the US Navy developed the atoll into a major naval base. Repair ships, oilers, and floating dry docks were moored in the lagoon at its center. Mog Mog was turned into a fleet recreation center capable of accommodating up to 9,000 officers and men daily.

53. Bill remarked in 1997 on the changes in the crew at this point:

> Of course, we also had replacements aboard for all the personnel who had died or left the ship badly wounded from our kamikaze encounter. These replacements included a new skipper, a Capt. [William] Sinton. I guess he was no less competent, but did not have the personality and popularity of Dixie Kiefer. But he must have been a reasonable man, as there was one occasion when I got infuriated with one of my hangar deck buddies and was just calling him a very derogatory name when my eyes happened to look past him and straight into the eyes of Capt. Sinton who just happened to be walking past us at the exact moment of my utterance. From the look on his face I inferred that he must have thought, "Surely the kid couldn't have meant me!" and perhaps he gave a little shrug as he continued walking away!
>
> Many of the new guys were newly recruited seamen, fresh out of boot camp. Naturally we "old salts" regaled them with hair raising tales of combat.

Catton reminiscence, 2 Apr. 1997.

6. USS Ticonderoga, *the Second Voyage*

1. On this day San Francisco began hosting a conference of forty-six nations that were allied against Germany and Japan to discuss the formation of the United Nations. The conference ran from 25 April to 26 June 1945.

2. The "news" refers to the defeat of Italy and Germany, with the defeat of Japan still to be achieved. On 2 May 1945 the Russians announced the fall of Berlin and Allied commanders announced the surrender of German forces in Italy and Austria. The unconditional surrender of Nazi Germany followed on 8 May.

3. Eleanor Richardson was a family friend.

4. The official notice of promotion in Bill's service record listed his new rate as ABM(PH)2c. The "ABM" part of the designation was not a new rate. The "PH" stood for "plane handler" and may have been the "new rate" Bill refers to. The "2c" indicated petty officer second class.

5. In other words, he was promoted from petty officer third class to petty officer second class. The promotion raised his pay grade from $78 to $96 per month.

6. "U.S.S. *Ticonderoga,* CV-14 Action Report 24 May through 13 June 1945," Box 1475, USS *Ticonderoga,* Entry A1 351, Series: Action Reports, RG 38, National Archives.

7. Samuel Eliot Morison, *Victory in the Pacific, 1945,* vol. 14 of *History of United States Naval Operations in World War II* (Boston: Little, Brown, 1960), 298–309.

8. United Services Organization (USO) was a nonprofit charitable organization founded during World War II to provide live entertainment and other morale-boosting services (such as tours) for US military-service personnel.

9. *Black Boy,* by Richard Wright, is a memoir of growing up in the Jim Crow South. Published in 1945, it was a Book-of-the-Month Club selection.

10. Edward Stettinius Jr. (1900–1949) was secretary of state in 1944–45 and led the US delegation at the San Francisco Conference.

11. "Ticonderoga IV (CV-14)," *Dictionary of American Fighting Naval Ships,* 7:182–87.

12. This was the US Treasury's seventh and final war-bond drive, and it ran up the biggest total of them all: $26.3 billion. One more bond drive, called the Victory Loan, followed in the fall. James J. Kimble, *Mobilizing the Home Front: War Bonds and Domestic Propaganda* (College Station: Texas A&M Univ. Press, 2006), 101–2.

13. "U.S.S. *Ticonderoga,* CV-14 Action Report 1 July through 15 August, 1945," Box 1476, USS *Ticonderoga,* Entry A1 351, Series: Action Reports, RG 38, National Archives. The Japanese still had about 5,000 planes left, but these were being saved for the American invasion of the home islands. Gerhard L. Weinberg, *A World at Arms: A Global History of World War II* (New York: Cambridge Univ. Press, 1994), 877.

14. Edna S. (Willard) Case (1899–1972) was Helen Catton's sister.

15. Robert Catton had been notified that he would be reassigned but did not yet know where.

16. The film *Wilson* was released by Twentieth Century–Fox in August 1944. Although it was critically acclaimed and garnered five academy awards, it flopped at the box office.

17. Bill may have underestimated the strength of public support for internationalism at this time. By the summer of 1944, opinion polls showed that two-thirds of voters favored the creation of a new international organization and American membership in it. One poll found that college students supported the creation of the United Nations by fifty to one. Strong majorities favored giving a world organization military power to stop aggressors. Burns, *Roosevelt,* 515.

18. See Robert Sherrod, "Captain Dixie and the *Ti,*" *Time* 46, no. 4 (23 July 1945): 10–11.

19. Eddie Bracken (1915–2002) and Peggy Ryan (1924–2004) were Hollywood actors. The USO show was in mid-July 1945. On the seventeenth Bill wrote to his mom: "The other night we had a big U.S.O. show aboard, instead of a movie. The master of ceremonies was Eddie Bracken and the star was Peggy Ryan. There were several others of lesser note on the program, too. It was a pretty good evening's entertainment and we all enjoyed it."

20. Adm. William Halsey Jr. (1882–1959) was commander of the Third Fleet.

21. Harold Stassen (1907–2001) was a former Republican governor of Minnesota and at this time a lieutenant commander in the US Navy.

22. The HMS *Indefatigable* was an *Implacable*-class aircraft carrier of the Royal Navy. Its 760-foot-long armored flight deck was 125 feet shorter than the Big T's. Two small hangar compartments plus a permanent deck park on the flight deck accommodated altogether about twenty fewer planes than Bill's carrier. The ship went into service early in 1944, first engaging German forces in Norwegian waters before transferring to the British Pacific Fleet late in the year. In January 1945 the British carrier attacked enemy oil refineries on the island of Sumatra. In May and June it joined US forces for the Okinawa Campaign. In July and August the *Indefatigable* joined in attacks on the Japanese home islands.

23. Bill wrote to his English acquaintance, Edward Flawn, later that month. Flawn, who was an aircraft-maintenance engineer with British Naval Air Squadron 1772, replied to Bill on 8 October from his squadron's temporary base near Sydney, Australia.

24. The Supermarine Seafire was the Royal Navy's carrier-based complement to the RAF's legendary Supermarine Spitfire. An excellent fighter, its narrow landing gear was not well suited for carrier landings. The Fairey Firefly was another British-made carrier-borne fighter.

25. Monty Woolley (1888–1963) was an American actor.

26. At the end of the war, 85 million Americans held war bonds worth a total of $185.7 billion, for an average of $2,185 per person. The maximum any individual could purchase was $10,000.

27. Rear Adm. Thomas L. Sprague (1894–1972) was commander of Task Group 38.1 during the final stages of the war.

28. Robert Catton's furlough ended in September 1945. But when he reported back to receive his new assignment, the navy gave him a thirty-day notice of separation and terminal leave. He remained active in a reserve for several years, though, attending naval-reserve meetings and doing two weeks of duty each summer.

29. Zigzagging was a way to protect the ship against submarine torpedo attack.

30. The GI Bill of Rights was enacted in 1944 to provide federal aid to returning World War II veterans. Qualifying veterans of all military-service branches could obtain financial aid for a college education or a loan for a startup business. Eric F. Goldman, *The Crucial Decade—and After: America, 1945–1960* (New York: Vintage Books, 1960), 13.

31. Rear Adm. Clifton Sprague (1896–1955) was commander of Carrier Division 2. *Ticonderoga* was his flagship.

32. The Cliff House remains a popular restaurant that sits precariously on a sea cliff just north of Ocean Beach in San Francisco. It has been extensively renovated five times since its establishment in 1858.

33. The twin-engine navy plane carrying six passengers, including Commodore Kiefer, got lost in a rainstorm on a short flight from Caldwell, New Jersey, to Quonset, Rhode Island, and slammed into a mountainside near Beacon, New York. There were no survivors. Rescuers found the wreckage spread over a large area. Kiefer's body was identified by the cast that he had worn on one arm since the attack on the *Ticonderoga* ten months earlier.

34. Bill was transferred from the ship to the hospital on the evening of 11 December as recorded in the *Ticonderoga*'s deck log: "Dec 11. 16 to 20 [1600 hours to 2000 hours]: 1730 received injury report on CATTON, W.R., Jr. (ABM2c), 312 94 59) USNR, who received simple and multiple fracture of the pelvis; and WATSON, K. E., (Slc), (631 34 10), USNR, who received scalp lacerations and contusions when #1 elevator descended unexpectedly at 1555 this date causing a motor vehicle to fall onto elevator. 1830 pursuant to orders of Commanding Officer, Catton, W. R., Jr., (ABM2c, (312 94 59) USNR and LEIBERSPERGER, R. C., (Flc), (922 11 01), USNR were transferred to the U.S. Naval Hospital, Alameda, California for treatment." USS *Ticonderoga*, 11 Dec. 1945, Box 9630, Entry P 118-A1, Series: Deck Logs, RG 24, National Archives.

Epilogue

1. William R. Catton Jr., "It Did Happen Here," review of *Americans Betrayed: Politics and the Japanese Evacuation*, by Morton Grodzins, *ETC: A Review of General Semantics* 8, no. 2 (Winter 1951): 145. On his appreciation over the GI Bill, see William R. Catton Jr., *Bottleneck: Humanity's Impending Impasse* ([US]: Xlibris, 2009), 26.

2. Catton, *Bottleneck*, 13.

3. The US Census Bureau officially designates the postwar baby boom as US births from 1946 to 1964. The sustained rise in the birth rate after the war was attributed to general economic prosperity and a culture of domesticity prevailing through the period, not to mention the more immediate factor that the war had put so many young people's lives on hold for a time.

4. David M. Kennedy, *Freedom from Fear: The American People in Depression and War, 1929–1945* (New York: Oxford Univ. Press, 2005), 747–48.

5. Bill Catton reminiscence, 2 Apr. 1997.

6. William R. Catton Jr., *From Animistic to Naturalistic Sociology* (New York: McGraw Hill, 1966), vii–viii.

7. William R. Catton Jr., "The Recreational Visitor: Motivation, Behavior, Impact," in *Recreational Use of Wild Lands*, by C. Frank Brockman and Lawrence C. Merriam Jr., 2nd ed. (New York: McGraw Hill, 1973), 71–93; Catton, "Destructive Momentum: Could an Enlightened Environmental Movement Overcome It?" in *Life on the Brink: Environmentalists Confront Overpopulation*, ed. Philip Cafaro and Eileen Crist (Athens: Univ. of Georgia Press, 2012), 16–28.

8. William R. Catton Jr., "A Retrospective View of My Development as an Environmental Sociologist," *Organization & Environment* 21, no. 4 (Dec. 2008): 471–77.

9. Don Duncan, "He's Had It! U. of W. Prof Will Move to New Zealand," *Seattle Times*, 3 Nov. 1969.

10. William R. Catton Jr., *Overshoot: The Ecological Basis of Revolutionary Change* (Urbana: Univ. of Illinois Press, 1980), vii.

11. See collected book reviews and tributes to the author in Michael Dowd and Connie Barlow, "Tribute to William R. Catton, Jr., a Leader in Environmental Sociology (1926–2015)," on the Web at thegreatstory.org/william-catton.html (accessed 29 Apr. 2019).

12. Catton, *Bottleneck*, 216.

13. Catton, *Overshoot*, 221–22.

14. No one did more to popularize the phrase than the journalist and news anchor Tom Brokaw with his bestseller *The Greatest Generation* (New York: Random House, 1998). For a more critical view of the generation and its legacy, see Kenneth D. Rose, *Myth and the Greatest Generation: A Social History of Americans in World War II* (London: Routledge, 2008).

15. Catton, *Bottleneck*, 217.

16. Bill Catton to Helen Catton, 19 Aug. 1945.

17. Several of Bill's letters contain evidence that the *Ticonderoga* experience was formative in his intellectual development, but see especially his letter of 23 September 1945 from the sixth paragraph onward. On the formative influence of New Zealand on his thinking, see William R. Catton Jr., "Sociology in the 1970s," *Australian and New Zealand Journal of Sociology* 7 (Oct. 1971): 89–90; and Catton, *Overshoot*, 199–201.

18. Bill Catton to Robert Catton, 7 Nov. 1944.

Index

Note:
Ti stands for *Ticonderoga*
MHS stands for Manistee High School
WRC stands for William R. Catton Jr.